EVIDENCE AND COMMENTARY

Historical Source Books

SERIES EDITORS:
C. M. D. Crowder, M.A., D.Phil.
L. Kochan, M.A., Ph.D.

LUTHER

Luther

EDITED BY

IAN D. KINGSTON SIGGINS
Yale University

BARNES & NOBLE BOOKS · NEW YORK
(a division of Harper and Row Publishers, Inc.)

Published in the U.S.A. 1972 by
HARPER & ROW PUBLISHERS, INC.
Barnes & Noble Import Division

Published 1972 by
OLIVER & BOYD
Tweeddale Court,
14 High Street,
Edinburgh, EH1 1YL
A division of Longman Group Limited

ISBN   06 496247 4 (Paperback)
       06 496246 6 (Hardback)

Printed in Great Britain by
Cox & Wyman Ltd, London, Fakenham and Reading

CONTENTS

GENERAL EDITORS' PREFACE

HISTORICAL WRITING IS based on the control of evidence and commentary. Everything that has happened in the past is potentially historical evidence, and it therefore follows that the historian must apply rigorous selection if his story is to have intelligible form. The inroads of time and common sense greatly reduce the quantity of evidence that is effectively available; but what is left still demands discernment, if its presentation is not to be self-defeating in volume and variety. Even the residue left from this process of irrational and rational refinement does not tell its own story. Documents may speak for themselves, but they say different things to different listeners. The historian's second task is commentary, by means of which he completes the interpretation of the evidence which he has previously selected. Here he makes explicit the insights which have guided his choice of what to include and what to omit. Here he may go beyond what have hitherto been accepted as the common-sense limits of historical territory; the history of public events is extended to the history of private thoughts and beyond this to the historical analysis of instinctive, unreasoned attitudes, and to the gradations of man's experience between these extremes. By this extension of its range, history as a discipline has moved some way to meet sociology, borrowing some of the sociologist's methods to do so.

As a result of the processes by which the historian has become increasingly self-conscious and self-critical, students are introduced nowadays not only to the conclusions drawn from new historical exploration, but to the foundations on which these conclusions rest. This has led in turn to the proliferation of collections of historical evidence for senior students, mainly documentary evidence of a familiar kind rather than the visual and aural records which are made available to younger age-groups.

The question has already been asked whether any further series of this kind is needed. The volumes to be included in this series will effectively prompt an affirmative answer by their choice of significant subjects which, as they accumulate, will provide the basis for comparative study. Each title will authoritatively present sufficient material to excite but not exhaust the curiosity of the serious student. The passages chosen for inclusion must often abbreviate the original documents; but the aim has been to avoid a collection of unconnected snippets. The necessary framework of interpretation is provided, but the student still has the opportunity to form his own judgements and pursue his own insights. A modest critical apparatus and bibliography and an editorial conclusion will, we hope, direct readers beyond these selections to seek further evidence for use in constructing their own commentary.

CHRISTOPHER CROWDER
LIONEL KOCHAN

ABBREVIATIONS

Book of Concord *Concordia or Book of Concord: The Symbols of the Evangelical Lutheran Church.* St Louis 1957.

Br *Luthers Werke, Briefwechsel.* Luther's letters in the Weimar Edition. 11 vols. Weimar 1930–48.

CR *Corpus Reformatorum.* Braunschweig 1834 ff.

DB *Luthers Werke, Deutsche Bibel.* Luther's German Bible in the Weimar Edition. Weimar 1906 ff.

LCC *The Library of Christian Classics.* London 1953 ff.

Lenker *Standard Edition of Luther's Works.* Ed. J. N. LENKER, 11 vols. Minneapolis 1903–09.

LW *Luther's Works* (American Edition). Ed. HELMUT LEHMANN and JAROSLAV PELIKAN. St Louis and Philadelphia 1955 ff.

MPL *Patrologiae Cursus Completus, Series Latina.* Ed. J. P. MIGNE. 217 vols. 1844–55.

PE *Works of Martin Luther* (Philadelphia Edition). 6 vols. Philadelphia 1943.

Smith I & II *Luther's Correspondence and Other Contemporary Letters.* Vol. I. Ed. PRESERVED SMITH, Philadelphia 1913. Vol. II. Ed. PRESERVED SMITH and CHARLES M. JACOBS. Philadelphia 1918.

Smith, *Martin Luther* PRESERVED SMITH. *The Life and Letters of Martin Luther.* Boston and New York 1911.

St L *Dr Martin Luthers sämtliche Schriften.* Ed. JOH. GEORG WALCH. 23 vols in 25. St Louis 1880–1910.

SW *Selected Writings of Martin Luther.* Ed. THEODORE G. TAPPERT. 4 vols. Philadelphia 1967.

Three Treatises MARTIN LUTHER. *Three Treatises. Philadelphia* 1943.

Tr *Luthers Werke, Tischreden.* Luther's Table Talk in the Weimar Edition. 6 vols. Weimar 1912–21.

WA *Luthers Werke, Kritische Gesamtausgabe.* The Weimar Edition of Luther's Works. Weimar 1883 ff.

Wace and Buchheim *First Principles of the Reformation or the Ninety-Five Theses and the Three Primary Works of Martin Luther*. Ed. HENRY WACE and C. A. BUCHHEIM. London 1883.

Woolf *Reformation Writings of Martin Luther*. Ed. BERTRAM LEE WOOLF. 2 vols. New York 1953–56.

Note: Biblical references are given to the Authorised Version (A.V.) only, except in the case of the Book of Psalms where the Vulgate (Vulg.) reference is also given.

INTRODUCTION

MARTIN LUTHER WAS a prodigious man in a prodigious age, a hero in a time of heroes. His life spanned those crowded decades in which (it may be said without too much exaggeration) Europe began an all-encompassing inward and outward transformation which placed her, for the first time, in unrivalled ascendancy. These were seminal years of cultural rebirth, social ferment, economic and political transformations, and undreamt of discovery, years in which not only the fabric of society but literally the shape of the world changed for western man. Nor did the monolithic structure of western Christendom escape the upheaval.

Even a glance at the events that fell in Luther's lifetime, and the people who flourished then, displays the stature of the age. It was an age of unprecedented discovery and conquest. When Luther was a child of five, Bartolomeu Dias reached the Cape of Good Hope. Columbus set foot in the New World just before Luther's ninth birthday. During his fourteenth and fifteenth years, John Cabot reached Newfoundland, and Vasco da Gama rounded the Cape and reached India by sea. Luther was approaching thirty and taking up his duties as a professor of the Bible when Ponce de Leon landed in Florida and Balboa crossed Central America to the Pacific. Six years later, at the height of the indulgence controversy, Cortez brutally subdued Mexico for Spain, and Magellan undertook Portugal's voyage of world circumnavigation. In the balance of his lifetime, the colonies and trading posts of Spain and Portugal spread over Latin America in the West, and in the East to India, the China coast, Japan, and the Philippines.

At home, too, this was a time of the making and breaking of dynasties. In 1485, before Luther was two years old, the English house of Tudor came to power with Richard III's defeat at Bosworth. The Catholic rulers of Aragon extended their power into southern Spain: in 1492 the last Moors were expelled from Europe, and in the following decade Spain wrested North African domains from Moorish hands. In France, the house of Valois, under Charles VIII, Louis XII and Francis I, chaotically pursued the fruitless goal of annexing Italy, and posed a constant problem to the Holy Roman Emperor Maximilian I, and to his grandson Emperor Charles V (who was to play so dramatic a role in Luther's own story). An even greater threat was posed from the

east, where a renewed Turkish drive to the west endangered the survival
of Europe. In 1499 the Turkish cavalry penetrated deep into Italy;
again in 1529 a new offensive resulted in a prolonged siege of Vienna;
and the possibility of Turkish invasion remained real to the end of
Luther's lifetime. In the years before Luther's break from Rome, the
papacy and its territorial wealth were in the hands of the families of
Borgia and Medici; Julius II, the most powerful pope for three centuries, won more renown for his military than for his spiritual prowess.

This age of prodigious vitality and ferment produced a staggering
wealth of creative talent. Botticelli, Leonardo da Vinci, Dürer, Cranach,
Giorgione, Titian all flourished in his time. Michelangelo, greatest of
them all, was eight years Luther's senior; Raphael and Correggio were
almost exact contemporaries. The greatest composers of his day were
(his own favourite) Josquin des Prés, forty years his senior, and
Palestrina, forty years his junior. Many famous books besides his own
were first published in his lifetime: Sebastian Brandt's *The Ship of
Fools* in 1494, Erasmus's *The Praise of Folly* in 1508, Machiavelli's
The Prince in 1513, Thomas More's *Utopia*, Erasmus's *Greek New
Testament* and Ariosto's *Orlando furioso* in 1516, Rabelais's *Pantagruel*
in 1533 and *Gargantua* in 1535, Copernicus's *De revolutionibus orbium
coelestium* (with Luther's hearty disapproval) in 1543.

Even so superficial a sampling of the towering figures and world-
shaping events of Luther's sixty-four years must give some flavour of
this seminal age; and it is the measure of Luther's stature that from
that day to this he has stood out as one of its giants. Like our own day,
it was an age of one breath-taking discovery upon another; unlike our
own, it was an age when religious commitment loomed very large among
the vital issues of public policy, and when men of all persuasions saw
fervent justice in imprisoning, and even slaying, those who opposed the
faith as they saw it. Yet these decisive events, and the debilitating
hundred years of religious war they introduced, finally issued in that
flowering of intellectual toleration and freedom of conscious the modern
world has prized so dearly. Luther's Reformation, and the other huge
events that surrounded it, stood on the threshold of an expansion of
human horizons whose outcome is still unimaginable. It was one of the
seismic movements which gave birth to the modern age.

The Reformation was demanded by the state of the Church. Some
elements of the Church's condition were of very long standing, and some
relatively recent.

The western Church, as western Europe in general, had been in a
desperately parlous state during the Dark Ages. As Europe began its
long, gradual struggle out of the darkness in the tenth and eleventh
centuries, the vitality of the monastic movement, especially the Cluniac

movement, was an extremely important element in a resurgence on political, economic, cultural and military fronts. As the West grew strong, and began to expand again towards the East, the Church also grew greatly in strength. The Roman Church in particular managed to gain an hegemony over western Christendom it had never really held before. But in order to gain this ascendancy, and to set its own house in order, the Church under the Hildebrandine reformers sought to set free the hierarchy from lay control, and to place oversight of the Church's affairs solely in the hands of the clergy. Hence during the 'twelfth century renaissance' the papacy emerged as not only a great spiritual force but a very great temporal force. By the end of the twelfth century the Pope vied in power and influence with any of the crowned heads of Europe, and exercised his power with international authority.

Yet even when the image of a united Christendom was most strongly projected—its spiritual sword wielded by the pope and its temporal sword by the Emperor—concerned and faithful men knew that all was not well. Peter Damian and Bernard of Clairvaux had already warned popes of the dangers of seeking spiritual ends by political means. Innocent III's great Fourth Lateran Council in 1215, perhaps the most triumphal of all papal councils, itself set before the Church the goal of thorough-going internal reform; and throughout the Middle Ages there were recurrent calls to restore the Church to apostolic purity. Some of these calls seemed so radical to the Church that it suppressed them. (One of the early signs that the twelfth-century resurgence of European culture was to turn inwards instead of expanding was that the crusading zeal which had been directed against infidels in the east was turned by the papacy to suppressing such calls for purification.) Other such calls were domesticated, as in the case of the Franciscan and Dominican orders, which started as calls for reform of the religious life and return to evangelical poverty, but by being domesticated actually became most effective arms of the papal power.

The resurgence of western vitality and its crusading drive to the east were relatively short-lived. From the thirteenth century, Europe went into another period of semi-decline; and similarly, the real power of the papacy never regained the pinnacle it achieved under Innocent III, although its pretensions became even more inflated. During the troubled fourteenth century, when the papal curia was rather ignominiously removed from Rome to Avignon, disquiet at the papal claims grew in intensity.

During the two hundred years before the papacy removed to Avignon, the local situation in Rome itself had been in such turmoil, and the struggle of the papacy to retain a hold on its estates within Italy had been so bitter, that the papal court had actually been in Rome for less than half that time. Thus the removal to Avignon was not a tremendous

change in the situation of the curia, which had been on the move constantly because of its local military and political position even in the
midst of its greatest ecumenical ascendancy. The idea that the papacy
while it was in Avignon was in a state of 'Babylonian captivity' to the
king of France is somewhat exaggerated. It is true that being across the
Rhône from French territory the protection of the French king was
essential to the papacy; moreover, the possibility of sustaining the
greatly increased costs of the curia required the compliance of the
French court in elaborating the system of papal taxes. It is also true that
every one of the popes during these years was French by birth and
culture. In that sense, it was indeed a period of French captivity for the
papacy. Yet, in another sense, the situation of the curia was not altogether different from what it had been: it was in an ideal location on
the key southernmost route across the Rhône; and it successfully evolved
an extraordinary system of garnering benefices and collecting their
income so that the wealth accruing to the Church from its prodigious
holdings in landed estates all over Europe flowed in increasing proportion to its centre. The burgeoning curial bureaucracy and its diplomatic
service financed itself by an elaborate taxation system which grew
steadily in both complexity and revenue.[1]

In this period of cultural decline and population loss, however, a new
national consciousness was arising, in northern Europe especially: the
concept of the autonomous nation state, and of the political realm as
quite separate from the spiritual realm. As a result of the growing
national cohesiveness of some of these states, the secular authorities
were able to take some steps against the depredations of national
wealth by the papal tax system. Both France and England attempted
during the fourteenth and fifteenth centuries to stop too much property
or money finding its way into the hands of the Church. In the case of
Germany, however, where the Empire was more loosely composed of
semi-autonomous states—ducal, electoral, and episcopal principalities
and free cities—there was not enough national cohesion or unity to
withstand the inroads of papal financing. In fact, Germany suffered
because of the very success of some other areas in limiting funds to the
papacy, since it came to bear a disproportionate load.

This was a period of great internal tensions for the Church, tensions
which gave rise to radical questioning of ecclesiastical authority by some
of the outstanding intellectuals of the age, like Marsiglio of Padua and
the English Franciscan, William of Ockham. The issue of authority was
forced to the surface at the end of the fourteenth century when, owing
to a dispute between the pope and the cardinals, the papacy was split
between a Roman pope with a Roman college of cardinals and an

[1] For details, consult Guy Mollat, *The Popes at Avignon 1305–1378*, Edinburgh 1963, pp. 319 ff.

Avignon pope with an Avignon college of cardinals. This scandalous situation persisted for thirty years, and when the cardinals took counsel at Pisa in 1409 to put an end to the 'Great Schism', the effect was an even more anomalous situation for five years when there were three popes and three papal bureaucracies. Because of the ludicrous character of the schism and the inability of the popes themselves to solve it, their subordinates simply took the matter into their own hands. National rulers and their hierarchies forced the pope with the largest obedience to call the Council of Constance (1414–18). It was decided *de facto* that primacy in the Church was to be exercised by the Church meeting in council rather than by pope and curia acting alone. The Council of Constance's representatives were present by national delegations. They purposed to set the Church in order, and to chart a conciliarist pattern for the administration of the Church thereafter. But the Council established insufficient machinery and continuity to keep the government of the Church in conciliar hands, whereas the wealth and existing bureaucracy of the reunited curia soon allowed the fifteenth-century popes to regain practical primacy and to achieve what Hubert Jedin calls 'the triumph of the papacy over the reform councils'.[2] By the time of the lingering collapse of the Council of Basle, the popes were clearly back in the saddle.

During the closing decades of the fifteenth century, a new resurgence in European life took place—a resurgence which in this case was to be permanent in that it led to the evolution of the modern world as we know it. The renewed power and immense wealth which accrued to the papacy led to a degree of secularisation which the Church both before and since would have regarded as quite unchristian. These were the years in which the Borgias and the Medicis took control of the papacy. The ambitions and personalities and manner of life of the renaissance popes were in a sense quite appropriate to an institution wholly committed to a system of military and diplomatic alliances and adventures, and to an immense bureaucracy which involved distressing corruption, nepotism, graft, and an extraordinary entanglement (both on the curial and the local levels) of the powerful and wealthy figures of the Church with the great new financial houses of Europe. These bankers often financed the transactions which led to the mutual advantage of powerful local prelates and of the papacy itself. It was just such an arrangement between Albecht of Brandenburg and Pope Leo X, funded by the Augsburg banking house of the Fuggers, which provided the immediate occasion for Luther's first protest against the Church.

The situation was not uniformly bad. Indeed, by the outbreak of the

[2] Hubert Jedin, *A History of the Council of Trent* Vol. I, translated by Dom Ernest Graf, O.S.B., Edinburgh 1957, p. 5.

Reformation, the worst might be said to have passed. Continuing pressure to reform had remained alive in the Church. There were lay movements like the Brethren of the Common Life, which had sprung up in the Netherlands in the late fourteenth century, and had had much success in spreading the simple christocentric piety exemplified by *The Imitation of Christ* and in establishing schools to teach such uncomplicated piety to laymen. Within the orders, there was a growing movement towards self-reform, and at the beginning of the sixteenth century many of the orders were divided into those who observed the rule of their order strictly and those who observed the rule laxly. Savonarola had made his brief, obsessive outcry against the degradations of Florentine life. In a far more sweeping and lasting way, Cardinal Ximenes had instituted a pervasive renewal of Spanish church life; and the Christian humanists of northern Europe were appealing fervently for a similar renewal of the Church in head and members. Indeed, despite the reputation which late medieval scholasticism (not undeservedly) attained during the Reformation itself and later, the situation in theology was not uniformly dark. It is true that the sort of theology taught in the schools was a theology which both by Catholic and Protestant standards is less than adequate; yet the tradition represented by the disciples of Gabriel Biel does demonstrate a sort of vitality which, if it did not prepare the way for Luther's Reformation, at least provided many of its seminal questions. Even if the reformers regarded scholastic theology's answers about the knowledge of God, the freedom of the human will, the action of grace, the efficacy of faith, and the possibility of merit as anti-Christian, nevertheless they regarded them as answers to the right questions—the same questions that Reformation theology attempted to answer. It is also clear that the answers the scholastics gave were intended to have pastoral application—it was not an entirely academic and detached pursuit, but one which the preaching orders felt they could translate, albeit in simplified and banal forms, for lay consumption.

For all that, one is bound to say that the religious state of Europe on the eve of the Reformation was anything but healthy. As far as the pastoral structures of the Church are concerned, absenteeism and pluralism among the higher clergy and an abysmally ill-educated lower clergy were the rule rather than the exception. The level of educational and spiritual attainment in most monasteries was shockingly low. Clerical concubinage had been winked at (and even made a source of revenue in the cradle tax) for generations; and Pope Alexander even publicly acknowledged his own bastards. The forms of popular piety had a huge admixture of superstition in them: the veneration of relics, pilgrimages, the elaboration of the cult of the saints had reached a point higher than at any previous period in Christian history. Even though theological theory protected the Church against the accusation, it really was the case that the message reaching the laity was that they could buy their salvation.

Both positively and negatively, then, the Church was ripe for reformation. The intellectual climate for reform had been prepared in part by the growth of humanism, in both the broader and the narrower senses of that term. In its broader sense, humanism was a fresh, impassioned, spontaneous movement animated by intense and confident interest in man, his world, his pursuits, and his potentialities. The object of the humanist's admiration was not his medieval forbear subordinating worldly activity to eternal ends and human accomplishment to the glory of God; but the civilised, fully-rounded, self-confidently poised man of classical antiquity seeking fame and attainment and delighting in his own accomplishment and style for their own sake. Humanism found its stimulus and model in the literature, philosophy, and art of the Greeks and Romans. Religiously, it was not anti-Christian. Many of its exponents retained a profound commitment to expressing their faith by their creativity; many prominent churchmen were its chief patrons. The Florentine school of Marsilio Ficino and Pico della Mirandola saw pagan philosophy and neo-Platonist mysticism not as a threat to Christian belief but as a noble enrichment of it. Yet in practice it generated an outlook radically alternative to the ideal of medieval catholicism and highly critical of its scholastic expressions.

More specifically, the humanist intellectual movement took the form of a literary fashion, a controversial but widespread desire to reform human studies according to classical literary models. This New Learning took a distinctively northern shape in the Christian humanism of Colet, Erasmus, More, and the scores of writers and teachers in England, France, Holland, the Rhineland and Germany who laboured with them. Their efforts prepared the way for the Reformation in several important respects. First, it focused intense reflection on the question of interpretation, the relations of grammar and meaning and text. The humanists' passionate desire to return scholarship to the examination of classical sources had created in poetry and rhetoric and literature a concentrated revival of philological studies; and naturally, this revival was bearing rich fruit for biblical studies as well. The New Learning encouraged the study of biblical languages, and several monuments to the humanists' interest in biblical studies appeared on the eve of the Reformation. The French humanist Lefèvre d'Etaples published a critical exposition of the text of the Psalms and a commentary on the Pauline epistles; in 1516 the first edition of Erasmus's Greek New Testament was published; Cardinal Ximenes in Spain had a team of scholars producing the Complutensian Polyglot Bible; and Rhineland scholars were embarked on an ambitious programme of critical editions of patristic

B

writings. The minor fracas concerning the scholar Johann Reuchlin and whether or not it was anti-Christian to study and teach Hebrew created a stir in the German universities during the decade in which the Reformation broke out. (In this dispute, the characteristic satiric sharpness of some highborn northern humanists was displayed in *The Letters of Obscure Men,* which pilloried Reuchlin's opponents.) Thus Luther, when he himself became engaged in teaching the Bible, had a body of scholarship at his disposal which gave him guidelines and ideas and philological tools, and provoked him to think very carefully about the nature of interpretation. By the time he began to lecture, he had already undertaken his own intensive examination of the Bible independently of the overlay of subsequent commentary. He tried to acquire as much of the biblical languages as he could then attain, and as more philological tools became available to him in the course of those early years, he made ready use of them.

At the same time, the New Learning helped to create a ferment in the universities about what the content of a sound university curriculum should be. In particular, the humanist critique of scholasticism had found a ready target in theology: well before Luther's time humanists were already sharply satirising the turgidity of late scholastic dogmatising. The Erasmians were suggesting very pointedly that such logic-chopping actually came between the believer and the simple, practical, peace-loving Christian philosophy which was the essence of the gospel. These intellectual movements not only created an atmosphere in which some of Luther's ideas could be heard, but quite specifically gave him insights which he immediately incorporated into his own lectures. He became the leader in the Wittenberg faculty of a sustained effort to obtain a revision of their curriculum in a humanistic direction, to abandon the Aristotelian scholastic studies which had been the staple of the new university's philosophical curriculum up to that point. And during the critical months of the indulgence controversy itself, he was active in formulating a curricular reform which was formally implemented in 1519. Moreover, the critique which northern humanist scholars were levelling against much that was going on in the theological and ecclesiastical realm gave Luther's initial public utterances a very ready audience, an audience which in some cases discovered only later that Luther's critique of the Church was pointed in a very different direction from the one their humanism had already encouraged them to take.

In this connection, it would be hard to overestimate the importance of the recent invention of the printing press for the success of the Reformation. From the moment when versions of the 95 Theses were distributed in unauthorised broadsides far more widely than Luther ever expected, everything that he wrote received a prodigious circulation.

The printers were always avid for copy, and the new cultural tool available to educated people made them equally avid to consume everything the printers turned out. About 2,000 editions of the relatively few things Luther wrote before Worms (totalling perhaps 300,000 separate copies) were circulating throughout Europe. It was already becoming important to academics to publish their scholarly materials in order to gain a wider audience and a substantial reputation. And as soon as it became clear that the breach from Rome was irreparable, Luther made very direct, deliberate, and constant use of the presses to let Europe know what was happening at the seat of the Reformation, to publish biblical commentaries, to give ethical advice, and to prosecute polemics; and himself undertook a major publishing venture in producing a careful and scholarly German vernacular translation of the whole Bible.

On a broad scale, the immediate occasion of the Reformation is relatively minor among the causes of the Reformation. It is true that some of the economic and political aspects of the indulgence traffic were responsible for creating a climate in Germany receptive to the revolt against Rome. Germany, by virtue of its lack of national cohesiveness, had come to bear a disproportionate burden of papal taxation; and the estates of the German nation were at this very period complaining more and more vociferously about the injustice of these impositions. As a result, when a dispute arose having an immediate economic occasion, many members of the German nobility were swift to respond.

On the other hand, it is quite clear that Luther's reasons for objecting to the indulgence traffic had nothing to do with the economics of it, because as he himself said later, he did not know, when he began the indulgence dispute, where the money was going. In fact, it was going in equal amounts to Albrecht of Brandenburg and to Rome for the rebuilding of St Peter's. Albrecht, seven years Luther's junior, already controlled two bishoprics and had negotiated for a third, namely the archbishopric of Mainz, the primatial see of Germany; but in so doing he incurred a very large debt to the papacy for the customary annates due to Rome. Albrecht had raised a loan from the Augsburg banking house of the Fuggers, and the Pope issued to Albrecht a licence to distribute a plenary indulgence on the understanding that half the proceeds would go to St Peter's and half to Albrecht to repay the Fuggers. Luther's objection, however, was to the faulty theology and particularly the disastrous pastoral consequences of the preaching of this particular indulgence by the expert Dominican salesman, Johann Tetzel. Friar Tetzel had indeed been prevented from selling the indulgence within Electoral Saxony but had come as close as he could to its borders, so that Luther came in direct pastoral contact with parishioners of his own who believed they had bought full salvation by buying this indulgence.

In the preceding eighteen months, he had already expressed grave mis-givings about the idea that salvation could be had for a price, or for any work of merit which supplanted true repentance. He had directed criticism even against his own patron's extraordinary relic collection in the Castle church at Wittenberg itself. The theses concerning indulg-ences, therefore, were simply a set of tentative propositions concerning the theology and pastoral effect of indulgences, offered out of deep personal and local concern, and intended to call in question what Tetzel was preaching. It was certainly not his intention at this juncture to revolt from the Church, an intention which did not really occur to him for many, many months after the indulgence controversy began. Indeed, it can even be said that he was not yet a Protestant theologian when he began that controversy. His theology had reached a point of refined Augustinianism in the homely style of German mystical piety; his biblical lectures were already a breath of fresh air in the stale corri-dors of medieval exegesis; but he had not yet departed in any essential from a Catholic theological position. In this sense, then, the indulgence controversy was certainly the occasion, but paradoxically only an in-cidental cause, of the Reformation.

Yet no account of the origins of the Reformation can even pretend to be complete without attention to the personality of Martin Luther him-self. It is with this subject above all that the following selections are concerned. If it had not been for Luther—his theological genius, his courage, his blunt and desperate honesty, his verbal brilliance—the Reformation simply would not have happened as it did. Certainly, a reformation of some sort must eventually have occurred: whilst the so-called Counter-Reformation was catalysed by the Protestant schism, the movement towards internal Catholic reform was also real and growing independently. But until the student of history has given account of the towering Luther himself, his Reformation story still lacks its central chapter and its formative personality.

It is not the purpose of this introduction to deal at length with the lively problems of studying Luther. Rather, the documents which form the core of the book invite the reader to address these problems himself, if possible to pursue them further on his own, and to seek an informed and independent judgement upon them. In a short closing essay, I shall express some of my own judgements on several of these issues; here let me simply outline the chief areas of scholarly interest in Luther's career and thought. Very broadly, there are five such areas (and the materials in this book are arranged accordingly).

First, in trying to explain Luther's stamp upon the Reformation, scholarship has turned increasingly in this century to the formation of his personality in childhood, adolescence, and young manhood. Funda-mental investigations have been carried out in this area by Otto Scheel and Heinrich Böhmer, and the most thorough review of the results in English is Böhmer's *Martin Luther: Road to Reformation*.[3] These researches are also thoroughly reflected in the standard modern biographies (of which two may be singled out for special mention: Roland H. Bainton's delightful *Here I Stand*, and Ernest G. Schwiebert's massive *Luther and His Times*).[4] These biographies and others address the all-important questions: What influences from his home and his schooling made Luther so anxious to seek all the churchly means of grace? What were the psychological ingredients of his scrupulous anguish in the monastery? Who helped him find escape from his scruples? How much did his own youthful experience of bondage and release dictate the shape of his Reformation doctrine. Although Luther's youth has attracted so much careful attention in recent years, the reader should be aware of the extremely sketchy character of the primary sources for this period of his life, and should assess how much explanatory weight they may be asked to bear. The nature of these sources is a particularly pressing issue in light of Erik Erikson's controvsial *Young Man Luther: A Study in Psychoanalysis and History*.[5] In considering this extremely stimulating and thought-provoking book, the student should be alert to two sorts of problem: the theoretical issue of how validly and how accurately psychodynamic explanations can be given of historical personalities; and the practical issue of whether Erikson has handled the Luther materials in an acceptable fashion or not.

The second area, which is currently receiving the lion's share of scholarly attention, is Luther's early theological development—the sources of his doctrinal instruction, the character of the theology he learnt and its continuing influence upon him, the development of his own theories of biblical interpretation, and his earliest halting formulations of the doctrine of justification. Luther's radical break from medieval dogma has been a familiar theme for generations; only in very recent years have the elements of continuity between the late medieval theologians and Luther come in for the intensive scrutiny they deserve. An illuminating account of some of these developments forms the central section of Professor Gordon Rupp's *The Righteousness of God*, and some essential primary sources are gathered in Heiko Oberman's

[3] Otto Scheel, *Martin Luther. Vom Katholizismus zur Reformation*, 2 vols., Tübingen 1917; Heinrich Böhmer, *Martin Luther: Road to Reformation*, translated by John W. Doberstein and Theodore G. Tappert, Philadelphia 1946, from *Der Junge Luther*, Gotha 1925.

[4] Roland H. Bainton, *Here I stand: A Life of Martin Luther*, Nashville 1950; Ernest G. Schwiebert, *Luther and His Times: The Reformation from a New Perspective*, St Louis 1950.

[5] Erik H. Erikson, *Young Man Luther: A Study in Psychoanalysis and History*, London 1959.

Forerunners of the Reformation.[6] The constant new light being thrown on Luther's theological progress has paradoxically only intensified the sharpest controversy in modern Luther studies, a dispute over the chronology of certain decisive shifts in his theological outlook. His development was a drawn-out process, punctuated by shafts of sudden insight.

Deep controversy continues to rage over when these insights may be said to have taken Luther beyond a Catholic position to an identifiably Protestant position; or when those insights which are distinctively the marks of mature Lutheran theology first appear. In order to reach his own judgement on this subject, the reader would have to consume many more materials than can be included in this selection, of course. However, an attempt has been made to give the reader at least a flavour of the issues. The fascination of the debate lies in the contention of some scholars that some essential developments did not take place until well after the Church struggle had begun in the furor over indulgences.

The details of Luther's fate in the Church struggle itself are sufficiently well-established to be beyond controversy (although the German scholar Erwin Iserloh has recently questioned whether the 95 Theses were indeed ever nailed to the church door at Wittenberg).[7] An admirable account of these tumultuous events is Professor Rupp's *Luther's Progress to the Diet of Worms*;[8] and again the standard biographies contain detailed narratives of the break from Rome. All too often, however, this dramatic rush of events—the issuing of the Theses, the Heidelberg assembly, confrontation with Cajetan, the Leipzig debate, burning the Bull, and the breath-taking speech at Worms—is allowed to be the end of the story. Naturally, a few later events are mentioned: the peasants' revolt, Luther's debate with Erasmus, his marriage, and the sacramental controversy with Zwingli; but for many a student, Luther's accomplishment ends with the bold creation of the schism. Yet Luther was anything but idle during his remaining quarter-century. His relationship to the national affairs of Germany in these years offers another area of great interest. Some nationalistic historians have accused him of betraying Germany, on the grounds that he could have grasped national leadership, yet refused the opportunity. Marxist historians (beginning with Engels) have also regarded Luther as a defender of the established order, and have preferred his radical rival, Thomas Müntzer, as hero of the Reformation because he championed the revolutionary cause of an

[6] E. Gordon Rupp, *The Righteousness of God: Luther Studies*, London 1953; Heiko A. Oberman, ed., *Forerunners of the Reformation: The Shape of Late Medieval Thought Illustrated by Key Documents*, translations by Paul L. Nyhus, New York 1966.

[7] Erwin Iserloh, *Luthers Thesenanschlag, Tatsache oder Legende?*, Wiesbaden 1962. The reaction of other scholars has been generally sceptical.

[8] E. Gordon Rupp, *Luther's Progress to the Diet of Worms*, Chicago 1951.

oppressed peasantry. How far are such partisan views just, and how far romantic? Is there any underlying consistency to be found in Luther's attitude when he insists on a stringent separation of the temporal and spiritual realms, yet appeals to nobles and princes to accept Christian leadership in reforming the Church? (*Luther's View of Church History*, by John Headley, sheds informative light on Luther's belief that the gospel had brought an historical crisis upon Germany.)[9]

Luther's influence on the social structure of his followers' lives was unquestionably great. As Jaroslav Pelikan has pointed out in *Spirit versus Structure*,[10] the schism immediately confronted the leaders of the Reformation with an urgent need to decide how the Church was to be governed, its clergy appointed, and its worship conducted; how revenues formerly owing to the Church and to monasteries were to be disposed; how moral regulation was to be maintained in the absence of canon law; and how monastic services to welfare and education were to be replaced. It is a fascinating (if somewhat academic) question to ask what elements of a medieval outlook and what elements of modernity appear in Luther's extensive writings on these subjects.

Finally, the years of Luther's advanced maturity have been most adequately treated in one aspect, and virtually ignored in another. A prodigious literature has appeared on Luther's Reformation theology, an unending torrent of monographs on every aspect of his doctrine. Few other Christian theologians (perhaps Augustine, Aquinas, Calvin) have attracted such constant and intensive study, and keeping abreast of the literature could almost be a full-time occupation. (Still the most comprehensive summary of Luther's theology in English is Philip Watson's *Let God be God!* A more general introduction may be found in Heinrich Bornkamm's *Luther's World of Thought*.)[11] The great themes of justification by faith, the uniqueness of Christ, the freedom of the Christian, the dialectic of law and gospel, the clarity of Scripture—these and many others continue to receive exhaustive attention. Biographically, however, the opposite is the case. Luther's senior years have received the scantiest attention from his modern biographers, though they are not lacking in real narrative interest. The selections in this book try, even in brief compass, to redress the balance a little by devoting a considerable part of their length to Luther's later career.

It is a well recognised fallacy (the Greeks had a word for it) to sup-

[9] John M. Headley, *Luther's View of Church History*, Yale Publications in Religion, 6, New Haven and London 1963.

[10] Jaroslav J. Pelikan, *Spirit versus Structure: Luther and the Institutions of the Church*, New York 1968.

[11] Philip S. Watson, *Let God be God! An Interpretation of the Theology of Luther*, reprinted London 1958; Heinrich Bornkamm, *Luther's World of Thought*, translated by Martin H. Bertram, St Louis 1958, from *Luthers geistige Welt*, Gütersloh 1947.

pose that explaining the origins of an event is to have explained the event. The error of this assumption is nowhere more clearly illustrated than by Reformation history. When the student has examined the long-standing causes of unrest in the Church and the short-term occasions of the schism, and has understood the personality and accomplishment of Martin Luther, his account of the Reformation is anything but complete. Criticisms like Luther's had been made before—in some cases (Erasmus's for one) criticisms far more sweeping and pointed than Luther's first outcry: yet a reforming revolution had not followed. On the other hand, earlier instances of recalcitrance and rebellion had been swiftly crushed. Luther early compared himself with the Bohemian churchman, Jan Hus, who had been burnt at the stake during the Council of Constance for relatively minor departures from the Catholic consensus. One is bound to ask, therefore, why on the one hand Luther provoked such a disproportionately fierce reaction from Rome; but on the other, why this reaction did not succeed in silencing Luther as it had silenced others. Why did a minor pastoral dispute involving an obscure young Saxon theologian become the occasion for the disruption of western Christendom?

The factors which allowed Luther's protest to survive and become a movement, the tidal wave of the Reformation, have in some cases surprisingly little to do with the underlying issues. On the contrary, a series of entirely fortuitous events conspired to allow first Luther's own survival, and then time and opportunity for the incipient movement to take root and burgeon.

Certainly without foreseeing the sequel to his actions, the key figure in these events was the Elector Frederick the Wise of Saxony. In the first place, he was extremely proud of his young university at Wittenberg. The maintenance of an eminent school not only helped his administration with advice and consultation, but also greatly enhanced his own political standing in the Empire. He had reason to be well pleased with the men that served him in its faculties. To Martin Luther, his professor of the Bible, he had granted life tenure on the warm recommendation of Johann von Staupitz, superior of the Augustinians in Germany. He knew that Luther had already attained a fine reputation as a leader in both theology and pastoral administration within his order. His own contacts with Luther were mediated through his chaplain-secretary, Georg Spalatin, whose admiration for Luther bordered on veneration. So when the curia first summoned Luther to Rome in 1518 to answer charges of heresy and insubordination, Frederick gave his spontaneous undertaking to Luther that he would not have to go to Rome. Hence adjudication was committed instead to the papal legate in Germany, Cardinal Cajetan. When Luther's confrontation with Cajetan at Augsburg aggravated rather than resolved the issues, a moratorium on further proceedings against Luther was effected by the death in January, 1519, of the Holy Roman Emperor Maximilian I.

As a real power, the Holy Roman Empire retained only a shadow of its former might; yet it kept a significant symbolic and federal role in the balance of European power. Frederick the Wise was one of the seven electors who should choose a new emperor from the princes of all Europe. The electors knew that the real power in Europe rested in the hands of the kingdoms of France and of Spain, yet they wished for a native German Emperor. The Pope, too, wished for a German Emperor in order to strengthen his own position in his power struggles with France and Spain. The result was that for six months in 1519 Frederick of Saxony, Luther's protector, was widely regarded as a possible successor to Maximilian. He was the Pope's own preference, and in an effort to persuade Frederick to accept the candidacy the Pope not only sent Count Carl von Miltitz to Frederick with the accolade of the Golden Rose, but even found it expedient to adopt a conciliatory tone regarding Luther. The bumbling Miltitz further complicated the issue by representing Luther to Rome as far more compliant than by this stage he had become. In June, 1519, Frederick the Wise, recognising that no German prince had enough power either to compete with the western powers or to withstand the Turkish threat from the east, settled the issue himself by voting for the young Hapsburg, Charles of Spain.

Meanwhile, however, vital months had expired in which Luther's tracts were read far and wide, his views reported throughout Europe, and, perhaps most importantly, his own theology was growing much more radical (so that at the Leipzig debate in July, 1519, Johann Eck of Ingolstadt was able to draw from Luther a challenge to ecclesiastical power far more damaging than he had ever expressed before). All the while, Luther's public stature was growing; he was becoming a folk-hero to his dissident countrymen, the 'Saxon Hus' to liberal and reform-minded churchmen, and to the *literati* the 'German Hercules' who would cleanse the Augean stables of the Church. So long as the Elector Frederick refused to hand over his protégé, and so long as the emperor-elect was wholly occupied with internal matters in his own Spanish domain (as he was for a year and a half), the curia could do nothing to halt the growing fame of the Saxon reformer or to stem the groundswell of adherence to his views.

Luther's 1520 writings joined issue with the whole ecclesiastical system and theology with such boldness, skill, and eloquence that the papal forbearance was exhausted. Luther was excommunicated and his errors anathematised in the bull *Exsurge, Domine*: 'Arise, Lord, and judge your cause!' Luther threw the bull to the flames.

When finally Charles assumed his imperial duties and summoned Luther to the Diet of Worms, his attempt to execute the papal decree by adding outlawry to excommunication also failed in its turn. It was Frederick the Wise, again, who frustrated the fatal plans of Pope and Emperor by spiriting Luther away as he rode from the Diet to hiding and disguise at Wartburg Castle. From that day on, Luther lived always under the ban, and his life was forfeit to anyone who would execute the imperial decree. Yet he remained inviolate while his doctrines gave birth to a whole new family of churches and schools, of outlooks and aspirations.

Again, coincidental factors played an all-important role. Whilst it is true that the spiritual dynamic of the Reformation faith spoke very deeply to the needs and sensibilities of thousands and thousands of men and women, and the renewal of the Church was accepted with gladness and relief by large numbers of churchmen, yet it is doubtful whether Luther's Reformation could have evolved into Protestantism in less propitious circumstances. Throughout the 1520s the Emperor Charles was far too preoccupied with the concerns of his western domains and with his own intermittent power struggles with the Pope to take a hand directly in the execution of his decree or in the religious alliances which formed within the German territories.

The example of the highly honoured Elector Frederick the Wise in defying the bull *Exsurge* and the Edict of Worms was soon followed by the secular authorities in Germany in their demand for independent self-determination. In his fragmentary 1522 pontificate, Pope Adrian VI admitted that the curia and hierarchy bore a large measure of responsibility for the current troubles. Before his election he had advocated council and reform; but in his brief incumbency he did nothing to execute this purpose. Accordingly the Diet of the German Estates and Free Cities at Nürnberg in 1522 demanded 'a free Christian council in a city on the German border, such as Strasbourg, Mainz, Cologne, or Metz'. At the same time the Diet submitted a list of one hundred grievances (*Gravamina*) on behalf of the German nation.

Campeggio, who was sent by the new pope, Clement VII, to deal with the German situation, found that there was still a Catholic majority at Nürnberg; yet even among the princes of the ecclesiastical Estates national feeling was so strong that his appeal for execution of the Edict of Worms was met by a counter-appeal for a national council. The strong intervention of the Emperor put an end to the plan of the Estates for a free national council at Speyer in 1524; but Charles's absence from Germany considerably reduced his later control over the course of events. Campeggio met the resulting deadlock by organising a papal party, the League of Regensburg (Ratisbon), among the Catholic Estates, on the basis of a plan for conservative reform and opposition to heresy. Its effect was to begin the disruption of the united nationalist sentiment evident at Nürnberg.

However, the deadlock also gave opportunity for those Estates and cities which were sympathetic to the evangelical movement to adopt the reform openly. The work of reform had been started in Zürich by Ulrich Zwingli in 1518; in Augsburg by Johann Oecolampadius in 1519, and Urbanus Rhegius in 1520; in Erfurt by Luther's old friend, Johann Lang, in 1521; in Nürnberg by Andreas Osiander, 1522; in Bremen by Henry of Zütphen, 1522; in Altenburg by Wenceslas Link, 1522; in Constance by Ambrose Blaurer, 1522; in Schwäbisch Hall by Johann Brenz, 1522; in Basle by Oecolampadius, 1522. After the decree of the Diet of Nürnberg that 'nothing but the true, pure, genuine and holy gospel' should be taught, the work of these men obtained open reception. In 1523 the townsmen of Frankfurt-am-Main, Schwäbisch Hall and Magdeburg adopted the reformed religion; the next year Ulm, Strasbourg, Bremen, Nürnberg, and Zürich followed suit.

It must be noted that the princes, and the councillors of the Free Cities, took their responsibility to the Church with the greatest seriousness and with no intention to disrupt Christendom's unity. But the absence of effective papal action and the persistent deferment of conciliar action forced the management of the religious revolution into the hands of secular authorities for whom political considerations had inevitably to weigh very heavily beside religious motives.

The papalist South German League of Regensburg in 1524 was emulated by a similar northern alliance of papal loyalists the following year at Dessau. The League of Dessau pledged to extirpate what they considered the root of social disruption, the Lutheran sect. The Emperor shortly gave assurances of his support to the League. Its formation in turn provoked a defensive alliance among the Lutheran princes, the League of Gotha and Torgau.

On the day when Magdeburg was admitted to complete this Lutheran alliance, the Imperial Diet of Speyer met under the presidency of the Emperor's brother, Ferdinand. The princes produced a programme of national reforms which might have led to united action, had not Ferdinand presented blunt orders from Charles in Spain forbidding innovations, and demanding execution of the Edict of Worms. The failure of the common programme of reform meant the final division of authorities into opposed religious parties; but the Turkish threat and the Emperor's involvement in hostilities with the Pope (which led in 1527 to the Sack of Rome) gave the Free Cities a chance to declare the Emperor's wishes impossible.[12] It was feasible neither to repeal the Edict in the Catholic Estates, nor to carry out its requirements in the Lutheran Estates. The Diet therefore simply fell back on the principle

[12] On the effect of the Turkish offensive on the course of the Reformation, see Stephen A. Fischer-Galati, *Ottoman Imperialism and German Protestantism 1521–1555*, Harvard Historical Monographs XLIII, Cambridge, Mass. 1959.

cuius regio, eius religio: each authority was to act according to conscience in his own territory.

This alignment of religiously hostile groups had its counterpart in Switzerland. In the middle years of the decade, the conservative cantons centring on Lucerne began their resistance to the course of reform spreading from Zürich. As more cantons were won for the reformed doctrine, the animosity of the Catholic cantons grew. The religious cleavage was rapidly translated into political division: the resulting split in the Swiss Federation threatened the hard-won independence of the whole of Switzerland from the Hapsburgs.

It was Philip of Hesse who saw the vast political potential of an alliance of all the adherents of the evangelical cause in both Germany and Switzerland. In 1524, as a young man of twenty, Philip had espoused the cause of the Reformation when he made profession of sincere evangelical faith. In his own territories he had carefully followed Luther's prescriptions for dissolving the monasteries and reforming the churches. His support, however vital, was at times an embarrassment to Luther: in the early years because of his impetuosity, in later life because of his promiscuity. With the political situation in Germany becoming increasingly grave, Philip was alarmed beyond measure by the outbreak of a bitter, intractable public dispute between the German and Swiss reformers about the nature of the Eucharist.[13] If the dispute persisted, prospects for a united evangelical front were doomed. The Strasbourg reformer Martin Bucer, who had a passion for conciliation, convinced Philip that concord was possible; and the Strasbourg leaders and Zwingli were one with him in believing it was politically vital. From 1527 Philip was determined to achieve agreement by means of colloquy.

Luther refused Philip's first request for a conference. For Luther, the concept of political alliance to defend the gospel was abhorrent, a disastrous confusion of the two kingdoms. It was the Word, and the Word alone, which must conquer in the spiritual warfare. But Philip persisted in his desire for a colloquy as the need for alliance became ever more urgent. In 1528 religious war was barely averted in Germany, and seemed inevitable in Switzerland when the Emperor's younger brother, Ferdinand, made an accord with the Catholic cantons. The Emperor had healed his breach with the Pope, had been victorious over Francis I, and was shortly expected to enter the German situation in person. The evangelical cause was strained when the adventurer, Otto von Pack, persuaded Philip by means of forgeries that an armed attack by Catholic opponents was imminent, and provoked him to violence against some neighbouring bishoprics. In light of the drastic political disruption of the Empire, the reformed Estates and cities had to face a

[13] See Hermann Sasse, *This Is My Body: Luther's Contention for the Real Presence in the Sacrament of the Altar*, Minneapolis 1959.

truculent and determined Catholic opposition at the Second Diet of Speyer, summoned by Charles at the Pope's urgent request on October 28, 1528. By an overwhelming majority, the Diet revoked the 'Recess' containing the resolutions of 1526, reaffirmed the Edict of Worms, and forbade further innovations or alienation of Church property in those territories which had ignored the Edict.

Immediately six princes and fourteen cities prepared the famous 'Protest' which was to give Protestantism its name. They claimed that the Diet's rejection of the Recess was not binding and they asserted their religious liberty. Philip saw not only the urgent necessity but also the ideal opportunity for alliance, and while the minority resolution was still in preparation at Speyer he was extending his secret alliances and renewing efforts to bring Luther and Zwingli together. When in spite of Luther's continued reluctance the Swiss and German theologians met at Marburg in October, 1529, the outcome was inconclusive: some misunderstandings were temporarily relieved, but the sacramental issue remained an apple of discord. However, by now it was clear that events were to take their course in virtual independence of such theological colloquy: the disposition of the Reformation's destiny on the political level rested in the princes' hands. For while the Marburg Colloquy was actually in progress, Elector John of Saxony, Margrave George of Brandenburg-Ansbach, councillors from Hesse and representatives of the south-western cities met at Schleiz to discuss again the confessional basis of their future alliance. So it was that in the crucial year of 1530, when the Diet of Augsburg met to deal with the religious turmoil of Germany under the Emperor's own chairmanship, the state of the evangelical representation was determined, not by the Reformers, but by an independent conference of secular powers.

Charles V had returned to Germany in person after nine years. His earlier promises to effect a settlement of Germany's religious disputes by means of a Church council he had rejected in favour of an Imperial Diet. This rejection was prompted by the opposition of both the Pope and Francis I to a conciliar solution, and by the Emperor's urgent need of financial and military support against the renewed threat of Ottoman aggression on the eastern frontier. Furthermore, in his absence Charles had formed the erroneous impression that Lutheranism was not yet firmly entrenched in Germany, and that minor concession would lead to swift compliance by the Lutheran princes. At the Diet of 1530, he discovered that his hopes of a simple solution to the religious problem were entirely misplaced. The evangelical groups were uncompromising in maintaining their theological positions. The Lutheran confederacy presented the Augsburg Confession, anxiously prepared by Melanchthon from materials drawn up beforehand by Luther. (Luther himself, who in law was still under the imperial ban, could not safely go to

Augsburg, but waited in the Coburg Castle on the borders of Saxony.)
Melanchthon himself was greatly concerned to maintain as many points
of contact with Catholic theologians as he could; the Augsburg Confession therefore tended to emphasise rather than minimise those
features of Lutheran doctrine which the Swiss rejected. It remains a
definitive statement of Lutheran faith to this day. When Luther saw it,
he commented: 'It pleases me very much, and I do not know what I
could change or improve in it.' Protestant disarray was dramatised by
the presentation two weeks later of Zwingli's *Fidei Ratio Confessio*
on behalf of the Swiss, and three days later still, Bucer's *Confessio
Tetrapolitana* on behalf of the Upper German cities of Strasbourg,
Constance, Memmingen, and Lindau.

Nevertheless, Bucer privately made strenuous exertions to convince
the wary Melanchthon of his genuine desire for concord in sacramental
doctrine. Bucer travelled to meet Luther at Coburg in order to seek an
agreement. Luther too was suspicious at first; but soon he was persuaded that Bucer's intentions were indeed in earnest. Whilst they did
not reach agreement in that conversation, both men felt at least that
concord was possible. Bucer then travelled to Zürich to seek that concord, but was received coolly, and mutual distrust persisted between
Luther and Zwingli. Yet Bucer's newly encouraged hopes of unity did
have a powerful psychological influence in the political situation, which
was tense in the extreme.

Charles V, having gained what seemed to be a diplomatic victory in
his tactical handling of the Diet, put an end to the Diet by promising
a council and requiring religious conformity until it met. Relying on the
Catholic Estates for practical support, he approved on September 22
the drastic provisions of the Recess of the Diet: the Augsburg Confession was declared refuted; April 15, 1531, was fixed as the dead-
line for conformity by the Lutherans, pending a council; meanwhile, the
Imperial Chamber (or *Kammergericht*) was invested with special
judicial powers to enforce the Recess and have its decisions implemented
by Catholic military action.

The dominance of the Emperor seemed overwhelming, but in fact
the Protestants evolved methods of retaliation. With new hopes of
evangelical concord in the air, even those Lutheran princes who had
previously honoured Luther's teaching on non-resistance to secular
authority twisted Luther's opinions to justify their urgent desire for an
alliance. On February 27, 1531, the Lutheran princes set up the defensive League of Schmalkalden on a basis of mutual protection. At
Speyer in 1531, and again at Regensburg in 1532, Charles V found
himself forced to discuss concessions with the Lutherans. His hand was
weakened by the renewed threat of Turkish invasion provoked by his
brother Ferdinand's military ineptitude. After protracted demands and

counter-demands, threats and concessions on both sides, Charles finally offered the Schmalkaldians the terms which were formalised in the Religious Peace of Nürnberg, July 23, 1532. By this agreement, both parties accepted the territorial *status quo* until the calling of a council; and in return for a cessation of *Kammergericht* action in religious matters, the Protestants promised allegiance to Charles as Emperor and to Ferninand as King of the Romans.

The effect of the Peace of Nürnberg was to allow a period of Lutheran expansion. Pomerania, Mecklenburg, Leignitz Brieg, and other areas adopted the reform, and the Reformation was introduced into Württemberg when collusion between the Schmalkaldians and France forced its return to Duke Ulrich in 1534. The precarious moratorium provided by the Peace allowed the sacramental issue which had divided the Protestants at Augsburg to be raised again as a local issue in region after region. The Schmalkaldic League already numbered among its members signatories to both the Augsburg and Tetrapolitan confessions. From his study in Wittenberg Luther was at first impatient of an issue on which he could admit no compromise. As Bucer appeared to move closer to a Lutheran understanding, however, Luther's suspicions began to wane. When the city of Augsburg, at Bucer's urging, asked Luther in 1535 to appoint a Lutheran preacher to Augsburg, Luther was profoundly moved. He felt that these developments truly afforded new hope of doctrinal harmony.

Early in 1536, Bucer and Capito attended a meeting of Swiss reformers to prepare an official confession for all the reformed cantons. On the basis of this confession, Bucer immoderately gave Luther the impression that the Swiss had now adopted an almost Lutheran position. In April, 1536, Luther invited Bucer to bring representative reformed theologians to a conference at Eisenach. By the date of the projected congress, high hopes had again been dampened. Luther was ill, and the meeting had to be transferred to Wittenberg. Melanchthon was perturbed, fearing a repetition of Marburg. The Swiss, in clarifying their intent, had published Zwingli's *Expositio Fidei* and a collection of letters by Zwingli and Oecolampadius with a foreword by Bucer. These had incensed the ailing Luther. After a day and a half of tense and tentative discussion, Bucer succeeded somewhat in allaying Luther's doubts of the delegates' sincerity. Finally a basis of agreement was reached. It was incorporated in the Wittenberg Concord, which asserted doctrinal agreement between the Lutheran and South German churches, and remained a confessional standard in the South German cities for some years.

However, the appearance of Lutheran solidarity was short-lived. Before these discussions had taken place, Charles V, under further pressure from the Turks and the Schmalkaldians, had accelerated his negotiations with the new pope, Paul III, for a council. Luther himself had been visited in 1535 by the papal nuncio, Pietro Paolo Vergerio, announcing tentative plans for a council. At length the bull *Ad Dominici Gregis Curam* of June 2, 1536, summoned a general council at Mantua on May 23, 1537. The Elector John of Saxony and the Landgrave Philip of Hesse reacted by proposing instead a Protestant council, to be convened by Luther in opposition to the papal council. They proposed that invitations be sent to the English and the French, and that an army of eighteen thousand men be mustered to protect the assembly. Their counter-proposal, however, was roundly condemned by their own theological and legal counsellors, who foresaw in such a course of action an irrevocable commitment to schism and the impossibility of ever achieving *rapprochement* with Catholic Europe. The princes were prepared to ignore this advice; but as events turned out, plans for the papal council proved abortive. Nevertheless, the articles which the Elector had asked Luther and his colleagues to prepare in December, 1536, for use at a council or counter-council gave the Wittenbergers an opportunity to state their position plainly. Luther himself attributed great significance to these Schmalkald Articles, and in 1538 published a carefully re-edited version of them.

Repeatedly, political exigency and theological sophistry combined to produce agreements that were more apparent than real. Protestant churchmen became signatories to statements which avoided rather than resolved their differences. Nevertheless, these temporary accommodations did create an appearance of concerted action among the evangelicals, and strengthened the hand of the Protestant princes in their dealings with the Empire. The breathing-space was to prove short-lived. But in the meantime Protestantism continued to spread, to put down strong roots, and to establish its own church system. That religious war was averted for so long was in no small measure owing to Luther's own wise and statesmanlike counsel to the hotter heads of the Schmalkaldic League that the tolerance extended by the Emperor under the Peace of Nürnberg should be accepted as a privilege and not demanded as a right. The developments of these years left Luther torn between increased hopefulness at the freedom afforded the Word of God by peace and concord, and foreboding that the Church situation was really poised on the brink of doctrinal and moral disaster. While he rejoiced that evangelical preaching and discipline was now available in churches throughout the Lutheran realms, and that sweeping educational reforms had been instituted, he was dismayed by the continued indifference and obtuseness revealed by the Church visitations. Even in the circle of his close associates he discovered the seeds of doctrinal dissension.

The fortunes of the Protestant alliance were indeed extraordinarily chequered. Positively, the Protestant movement was growing in both extent and strength. In the late 1530s there were real fears that the Emperor Charles, if he succeeded in repulsing the Turkish threat, would then divert his armies to attacking the evangelical princes. Luther did not believe that the Turk would be so easily overcome, but argued unequivocally that should religious war break out the princes were perfectly entitled to resist the Emperor. Yet at Frankfurt in 1539 and again at Hagenau in 1540 the Emperor adopted an increasingly conciliatory attitude to the Protestants, and continued to hope that the issue would be settled by a Church council in Germany. At the Diet of Regensburg in April, 1541, the Emperor oversaw a colloquy between the papal legate Cardinal Contarini, von Pflug, Eck and Gropper on the Catholic side, and Melanchthon, Bucer, Calvin and others on the evangelical side. They agreed on formulas which brought the two parties as close as they ever came, and held out genuine promise of a peaceful settlement. Regrettably, the representatives from both sides were more eirenical than those whom they represented. The Regensburg articles were treated with impatience in both Rome and Wittenberg. The Emperor, however, was encouraged to continue pursuing a conciliar solution. Meanwhile, Luther's old arch-enemy, Duke George of Saxony, had died in 1539, and Ducal Saxony passed to his brother Henry, who introduced the Reformation forthwith. Three years later, the reform was imposed upon the territories of Duke Henry of Brunswick by armed force. The Protestant alliance had not only become a major political force in Europe, but there was now a real possibility that the great majority of the German nation would adopt the Lutheran faith. At the Diet of Speyer in 1544, Charles V was more graciously conciliatory than ever before, urging the German Estates to agree on a plan of unity and reform, and pledging, in spite of intense opposition from the hierarchy, to seek a council in Germany.

Yet all was not progress for the Protestant cause. Incident after incident added fuel to the fires of animosity in the Catholic Estates. The respectful reserve which had existed between Luther and the primate, Albrecht of Mainz, had been shattered when Luther justly but violently attacked Albrecht for immoralities climaxing in the judicial murder of his confidential steward, Johann Schönitz. Archbishop Albrecht became an outspoken opponent of conciliation with the Lutherans, and encouraged the curia to repudiate the Emperor's peaceful overtures. Luther did nothing to allay hierarchical opposition with his scathing anti-Catholic polemics, such as his *Preface to the Advice of a Committee of Cardinals* (1538), *Against Jack Sausage* (1541), and *Against the Papacy at Rome, an Institution of the Devil* (1545). The princely leaders of the alliance themselves brought their cause into jeopardy by their own actions. Philip of Hesse acted scandalously by contracting a bigamous marriage in 1540, with the consent of Luther, Melanchthon, and Bucer. Under what they took to be the seal of the confessional, Philip had confessed to them that neither was he able to tolerate relations with the wife of his youth, whom he found repulsive, nor could he remain continent. He was, he claimed, in an agony of conscience. Not without precedent, they reluctantly concluded that bigamy was preferable to either adultery or divorce; but they advised him, if the weakness of his flesh forced him to this expedient, to keep the second marriage secret. They then found themselves deceived when Philip openly took a highborn wife. The result was not only a moral scandal, but the Emperor made political capital from it, agreeing not to prosecute Philip, if Philip in turn would prevent Duke William of Cleves from joining the Schmalkaldic League. Instead of gaining in strength, the concerted action of the League was thus greatly weakened. It was weakened still further by a boundary dispute between two neighbouring Protestant princes, Maurice of Ducal Saxony and John of Electoral Saxony. Military action was narrowly averted by Luther's urgent intervention; but he correctly divined that the powerful and ambitious Duke Maurice would one day prove unreliable to the alliance. In Rome, the conciliatory advice of a group of moderate cardinals was gradually losing ground to hard-line sentiment, and anti-Protestant attitudes were cemented when the Elector John intervened in the appointment of a new Bishop of Naumburg. Against the advice of both Luther and his courtiers, the Elector set aside the candidate selected by the chapter and appointed instead the evangelical theologian, Nicholas von Amsdorf. Luther rightly foresaw that this course would be regarded as extremely objectionable. Nevertheless, he was glad to see his friend Amsdorf in this position, and took an even more controversial step by agreeing to consecrate Amsdorf in concert with several Lutheran superintendents. He justified this novel action by his treatise, *An Example of the Way to Consecrate a True Christian Bishop*.

Despite the greatly enhanced position of the Schmalkaldic League, then, and despite the Emperor's continuing preoccupation with his French and Turkish wars, the religious situation in Germany remained extremely precarious. Repudiating the Emperor's own efforts at conciliation, the Pope rejected out of hand the possibility of a 'free Christian council' in Germany, and decreed instead that the long-awaited council would take place under papal authority in Trent beginning in December, 1545. It was this uncompromising decree which provoked Luther's vitriolic *Against the Papacy at Rome*. The council met a quarter of a century too late, and without Protestant representation, to take in hand the reformation of the Catholic Church. As if to reveal the lateness of the hour, its convening was swiftly followed by two tragic events: Luther's death, and the first outbreak of the long religious wars between Catholic and Protestant Europe.

.   .   .   .   .   .

This collection is offered to two groups of readers. Primarily, it is designed for the use of history students and their teachers; secondly, I hope it will be of value to the general reader who is interested in history or biography, and who enjoys hearing of great men's accomplishments in their own words.

For its student users, this book is clearly not intended to stand alone. On the contrary, many key documents are omitted altogether, or merely represented by short passages, on the understanding that the serious student will want to read them in their entirety, since they are readily available in English. To take the most obvious examples, this is the case with the 95 Theses; the 1520 treatises *The Freedom of the Christian Man*, *Address to the German Nobility*, and *The Babylonian Captivity of the Church*; and Luther's speech before the Diet of Worms, all of which have appeared several times in English translation. At appropriate points, the reader is referred to these editions.

Since one purpose of such a collection is to introduce the budding historian to the nature of documents and the critical use of sources, the book would be self-defeating if it attempted to encompass the whole subject and did not point beyond itself to the materials from which it is garnered. It would also be self-defeating if the extracts were so partial or idiosyncratic that they failed to represent the nature of their wider setting. In this latter danger has lain the chief difficulty of the subject before us: for by no stretch of the imagination could brevity be called a feature of Luther's style. The standard critical edition of Luther's Works, the Weimar Edition begun in 1883, is now approaching conclusion in just under one hundred volumes. Naturally, in our narrow compass no selection can pretend to be truly representative—it is the merest drop in a bucket. Moreover, with the sole exception of some dinner-table anecdotes and an occasional letter to a friend, Luther normally spoke and wrote so lavishly that the inclusion here of whole tracts is quite out of the question. So I have tried to escape the scissors-and-paste devil by forswearing mere snippets, and the monotonous deep blue sea by selecting extracts which are not only narrative but also characteristic of Luther's life and thought.

It would be well in conclusion to say a little more in detail about the nature of the source materials. Luther's own works fall into five major categories: biblical expositions, the translation of the German Bible, treatises, letters, and table talk.

For the most part, the biblical expositions were delivered as lectures or sermons, either extemporaneously or from outlines. They have reached us in the form of listeners' transcripts, or printed editions based on those transcripts, or both. It was the exception rather than the rule for Luther himself to prepare his commentaries for publication, though his colleagues normally submitted their editions to him for approval before publication. Some of the transcribers were faster and more accurate than others. Where the transcript was by Luther's long-time amanuensis, Georg Rörer (deacon of the parish church in Wittenberg), his notes, in a mixture of Latin and German shorthand, have proved extremely reliable, and have allowed scholars to check the accuracy of printed versions. In cases, however, where a printed version exists but the notes are lost, there is no precise way to determine how many liberties Luther's editors have taken. It is clear that in some instances their editions were précis, or paraphrases, or even amplifications of what Luther actually said. In spite of these minor text-critical difficulties, we possess huge quantities of Luther's exegesis—a score of complete commentaries, partial expositions of many books, and well over two thousand biblical sermons, more than enough to establish his unique expository power and to provide a quite reliable guide to his theological thought and terminology. This is far and away the largest part of Luther's output. It reveals that he took seriously the distinction he observed between the Old Testament as scripture, strictly speaking, and the New Testament as a record of preaching, since the majority of his university lectures were on Old Testament books, whilst he usually chose New Testament (and most often gospel) texts for his preaching. Heinrich Bornkamm has accurately observed that Luther's appointment in a modern university would have been to a Chair of Old Testament.

Luther's fine sensitivity to the minutest point of biblical vocabulary revealed in his expositions sprang not only from his constant personal familiarity with the text of Scripture, but gained the firmest possible grounding in the monumental task of translating which he began in 1522, issuing in his masterful German Bible. This translation played an all-important role not only in the establishment of Protestant piety, but in the very evolution of the modern German language. Luther began the work alone in the Wartburg when he was in hiding after the Diet of Worms, and continued it over several years in Wittenberg with the aid of his colleagues. The notes of his translating committees reveal the meticulous care that was applied to the smallest points of philology and doctrine. (This labour of love has been rewarded in kind in the latest volumes of the Weimar Edition's German Bible, where Hans Volz and his colleagues have executed some of the finest editorial work yet devoted to Luther sources.) Moreover, each successive edition of the Bible included Luther's individual prefaces to the books of the Bible, guides which had an incalculable effect on the way Protestantism has read and understood the Scriptures.

The main body of material directly from Luther's own pen are the treatises he wrote on all manner of ethical, doctrinal, polemical and pastoral issues, especially in the early years of the Reformation. Since these treatises attained huge circulations, copies of their early editions are often quite accessible in major libraries. In this case we have few textual problems apart from minor variants amongst editions. We can be sure that we have precisely what Luther wrote, and in some cases the manuscripts themselves are extant. The one caution that needs to be voiced here is that these tracts were often penned at breakneck speed. (It has been said of *The Bondage of the Will*, Luther's polemical response to Erasmus's *The Freedom of the Will*, that it was composed faster than most people can read it!) Both for this reason, and because they are normally directed towards some specific issue, they are inevitably less balanced, and in this sense less typical, than the lectures and sermonic materials.

Far more text-critical problems surround the other major body of materials from Luther's pen, namely his correspondence. This was voluminous, and though naturally only a part of it has survived, we possess nearly 2,600 letters which we can be certain Luther wrote. However, we cannot always be as certain of the details of what he wrote. In most cases, the autograph is not available, and we possess many letters instead in sixteenth-century copies—sometimes conflicting copies of the same letter—and in early printed versions. The texts are sometimes obscure or incomplete, and it is not always clear whether these obscurities go back to Luther's own haste in writing or to errors in transmission. The modern editors of Luther's correspondence (Enders and Kawerau, Otto Clemen) have laboured mightily on these text-critical problems, but have not resolved all the difficulties. They have nevertheless produced versions which inspire confidence and may be relied upon by the student of Luther. It is often the case that nothing so reveals a man's personality as his letters; this is so with Luther. The corpus includes intimate personal letters to friends and family, letters of exhortation and admonition, letters of advice on the reform of the Church, deferential but forthright letters to dignitaries in Church and State, vigorous, unguarded letters to close associates reacting spontaneously to people and events—a correspondence, in short, which reflects every aspect of Luther's multifarious existence. For obvious reasons, there are relatively few extant letters from the period before the Reformation crisis. Luther's friends Johann Lang and Georg Spalatin did, however, preserve a few letters which are highly revealing of Luther's developing identity. For the later period, the letters form an abundant source both of historical information and of biographical insight.

Even more severe critical problems surround the most problematic part of the Luther corpus, the Table Talk—isolated incidents, remarks, anecdotes and reminiscences recorded for their own use by Luther's friends and colleagues largely from mealtime conversation in the

Luther home. Here the problem is not text-critical, but concerns the reliability of the reporters. Fortunately there are often several reports of a single anecdote, providing us some guide to the alertness of each reporter. Such comparisons reveal that inevitably the completeness of the reports varies with the skill and speed of the note-taker, and that what we have cannot be relied upon as a precise verbatim account. But they also make clear the substantial accuracy of some reporters, especially Viet Dietrich and Georg Rörer, and inspire some confidence that the utterly frank self-disclosure, the wisdom, the humour, the tenderness, the bawdy, are authentic testimonies of the man. One note of caution should be added, however: the earliest (and for more than three centuries the only) published edition of the Table Talk was that of Johann Aurifaber in 1566, and it was from this edition that various selections, including Captain Henry Bell's and William Hazlitt's English selections, were derived. Modern comparisons of Aurifaber's work with the manuscripts of Dietrich, Cordatus, Schlaginhaufen, Lauterbach, Mathesius and the rest have revealed that Aurifaber freely paraphrased his sources, changed their context, bowdlerised, added and subtracted material to make theological points of his own, and generally presented a far less authentic portrait of Luther than is available from the reporters upon whom he drew. Their notes, like the lecture transcripts, were taken in a macaronic Latin–German shorthand, partly reflecting the fact that the conversation at Luther's table was freely bilingual, partly also because it was easier to translate some German phrases while recording them in Latin-based abbreviations. Altogether, nearly six thousand separate items have been recorded, and they are a treasure trove of information and insight.

In addition to these major blocks of material there are also sundry notes written in the margins of books and Bibles, prefaces to works by other authors, theses prepared for candidates in academic disputation at university examinations, rough summaries of the discussion at such disputations, and so on, which yield bits and pieces of useful material.

In the selections which follow, the Luther materials have been newly translated from the Weimar Edition text, or, in the case of a few treatises, from first editions available to me. In each instance, the location of the passage in the Weimar Edition is given in the note, together with an indication of where else the same material is available in other English translations. For a more complete account of where these blocks of primary material are available in English editions, the reader should consult the Bibliography. Readers whose knowledge of German and Latin makes the originals accessible to them will discover indispensable guidance in finding their way around the corpus in Kurt Aland's *Hilfsbuch zum Lutherstudium.*[14]

[14] Kurt Aland, *Hilfsbuch zum Lutherstudium*, enlarged 2nd ed., Gütersloh 1957.

I

THE EARLY YEARS

FOR ALL THE intense biographical interest shown in Martin Luther by his contemporaries, let alone since, the piecing together of details from his earliest years is fraught with difficulty. Most of the early information available to his biographers comes from second-hand reports of Luther's dinner-table reminiscences many years later; and although he possessed an unusually frank and retentive memory, the details of his childhood and schooling and especially of his monastic experience are largely introduced as illustrations of some doctrinal or polemical point. These sources are thus few in number, fragmentary, coloured by later reflection, and transmitted by the sometimes faulty recollection of his companions at table. Moreover, his earliest biographers showed scant interest in these formative years, but concentrated instead on the church struggle. For the monastic period, however, there is a small number of extant letters, and the notes of his early labours in academic theology are also available. The character of the material should warn us against reconstructing with too much confidence—we really know very little, and some of the evidence is contradictory. Yet these documents do yield a coherent sketch of the emergence of Martin Luther.

I.1 CHILDHOOD AND SCHOOLING

We first follow Luther from his birth in Eisleben in 1483, through elementary and Latin schools in Mansfeld, his year at a Nullbrüder school at Magdeburg in 1497, and three happy years at school in Eisenach. In 1501, he matriculated at the university of Erfurt, where in 1505 he graduated Master of Arts, ranking second in his class. He began the study of law, but abruptly abandoned his studies to enter the cloister of the Augustinian Eremites at Erfurt.

I.1.A   Even the year of Luther's birth is open to question. Most later historians have agreed with Melanchthon, who on the authority of Luther's family gave November 10, 1483 as the date, and Eisleben as the place. Luther himself, however, had different impressions about both, as his 1540 list of key events reveals. (*Table Talk*, Summer, 1540: Latin text in Tr 5, 76: 5347.)

From the good Doctor's own hand: 'I was born in Mansfeld in 1484—
that is certain. In 1497 I was sent to school in Magdeburg; I was there
a year. In 1501 I went from Eisenach to Erfurt; I had been four years in
Eisenach. In 1505 I became a master at the beginning of the year. At
the end of the same year, 1505, I became a monk. In 1508 I came to
Wittenburg. In 1510 I was in Rome, where the devil has his throne. In
1517 I began to dispute about indulgences. In 1519 the Leipzig debate
took place. In 1525 I took a wife. In 1540 I reached the age of 56.'

I.1.B   Luther enjoyed suggesting that his family background was
        humbler than it really was. Hans Luther rapidly established him-
        self as a prosperous burgher of Mansfeld, and provided solid
        schooling for his son, for whom he cherished high ambitions. For
        schoolboys to beg food was the custom, not a mark of poverty.
        (*Table Talk*, Summer, 1540: Latin text in Tr 5, 95: 5362.)

On Luther's parents and schooling: He came of poor parents. His
father was the son of a farmer in Moehra, a village not far from Eisenach. Then with his wife and first son he moved to Mansfeld, and
became a miner, a quarrier; it was there that Luther was born. He went
to school in Eisenach and begged his bread from door to door; then he
found lodging in the home of Henry [Schalbe], a citizen of Eisenach,
and accompanied his son to school. Later he went to Erfurt and became
a monk against his father's wishes.

I.1.C   Luther's references to childhood discipline are so few that no
        description of his relationship to his parents can safely be based
        on them. But at least one caning left a lasting impression! (*Table
        Talk*, May, 1532: German–Latin text in Tr 2, 134: 1559.)

On cowering in children: Once should not cane children too hard; for
my father once caned me so severely that I ran away from him, and I
was frightened of him until he regained my confidence. And I am quite
reluctant to hit my little Hans very much, lest he become timid and
hostile with me; I know of nothing more disagreeable. This is how God
does it: 'I shall correct you, my children, but through someone else,
through Satan or the world; but if you call upon me and run to me, I
shall rescue you and set you on your feet.' For God has no desire at all
to make us hostile to him.

I.1.D   Hesitant attempts have been made to find sources of his religious
        passion in his parents' piety or his year at the Common Life school
        at Magdeburg; but his intense biblical curiosity apparently did
        begin in childhood. (*Table Talk*, November, 1531: Latin text in
        Tr 1, 44: 116.)

Once as a boy he came across a Bible, and there by chance read the story of Samuel's mother in the Book of Kings. The book pleased him immensely, and he thought he would be happy if he could ever own such a book. A little later he bought a book of gospel sermons; this also pleased him immensely because it contained more gospels than were customarily taught in the course of a year.

When he became a monk he gave up all his books. Only shortly before he had ordered the *Corpus Iuris* and a number of other books. These he returned to the bookseller. He took none with him into the monastery except Plautus and Virgil. There the monks gave him a Bible bound in red leather. He made himself so familiar with it that he knew what was contained on any given page, and when any sentence was adduced he knew at first glance where it was written. 'If I had kept it,' he said, 'I would have been an expert biblical place finder! There was no other study which pleased me so much at that time as Holy Writ. I read physics with great distaste, but my heart used to glow when it could return to the Bible. I used the *glossa ordinaria*, but Lyra I despised, although later I realised that he was valuable for the history.[1] I read the Bible diligently. A single important statement would occupy all my thoughts for a whole day; such sentences were particularly character-istic of the weightier prophets (although I could not follow them fully), and I remember them still, such as the statement in Ezekiel: "I do not desire the death of a sinner", etc. [Ezek. 33 : 11].'

I.1.E   The elderly Luther's own plan to write a memoir was cut short by his death. In 1546, therefore, Melanchthon wrote this first formal biography, which begins with an account of the early years. (*Praefatio Melanchthonis* in *Tomum secundum omnium operum Reverendi Domini Martini Lutheri*. Wittenberg, 1546: Latin text in CR VI, 155–158.)

Philip Melanchthon greets the sincere reader.

Martin Luther, that revered man, had offered us hope that he would relate the course of his own life and the causes of his struggles in the preface to this part of his collected works. He would have done so, had the printers completed this volume before its author was called out of this mortal life to eternal fellowship with God and the Church in heaven. It would have been invaluable if he had written both a first-rate con-sideration of his private life (for it was full of examples which would have served to strengthen piety in godly minds), and an account of its decisive events (which could have forewarned posterity about the issues involved). Secondly, he would also have refuted the calumnies of those who have claimed that he burst the bonds of his monastic service either

[1] Nicolas of Lyra (c. 1270–1340), Franciscan expositor who rejected allegory in favour of an exact historical sense. His *Postilla Litteralis*, the first commentary ever printed, drew heavily on Jewish rabbinic commentaries.

because he was incited to it by prominent men or others in order to
shatter the status of the bishops, or because he himself was inflamed by
private greed. Even if the malicious had made their usual objection: 'He
is blowing his own trumpet!', we know nevertheless that there was so
much seriousness in the man that he would have told his story quite
faithfully. Since he was aware that the course of these events was well
known to many good and wise men who are still alive, it would have
been ridiculous for him to make up another story (as sometimes happens
in poems). But since he died before this volume was issued, we shall tell
the story of the same events, which we have partly heard from him and
partly seen ourselves, with the same faithfulness.

There is an old and widely distributed family of ordinary people,
surnamed Luther, within the jurisdiction of the renowned counts of
Mansfeld. The parents of Martin Luther, however, had their first home
in the town of Eisleben, where Martin Luther was born. Then they
migrated to the town of Mansfeld, where Martin's father, Hans Luther,
became a magistrate and won the utmost respect of all good men for his
integrity. Whilst his mother Margaret, Hans Luther's wife, possessed
all the other virtues which are fitting in an honourable woman, she shone
especially in modesty, fear of God and prayer, and other upright women
used to take her as an example of virtue. On several occasions when I
asked her about the time when her son was born, she answered that she
clearly remembered the day and the hour, but was doubtful about the
year. She affirmed, however, that he was born on November 10, past
eleven o'clock at night, and that the name of Martin had been given to
the infant because the next day, when he was grafted into the Church of
God by baptism, had been designated St Martin's Day. But his brother
Jacob, an honourable and upright man, used to say that the family's
opinion about his brother's age was that he was born in A.D. 1483.

When he was old enough to be taught, his parents accustomed the boy
Martin, by diligent instruction at home, to the knowledge and fear of
God and to the duties of the other virtues; and as is usual with honourable people, they took care that he should learn to read. While he was
still very small he was carried to primary school by the father of Georg
Oehmler, who since he is still alive can bear witness to this account.
Now, at that time there were some mediocre grammar schools in the
cities of Saxony, so when Martin had entered his fourteenth year he was
sent to Magdeburg for a year, together with Johann Reinecke, later an
outstandingly able man who enjoyed in these regions the wide authority
conferred by such ability. Between these two, Luther and Reinecke,
there was always a quite unusual goodwill, either from some harmony of
character or from the characteristic fellowship born of boyhood studies.
Yet Luther did not stay at Magdeburg for more than a year. He next
attended school in Eisenach for four years, where he heard his teacher

present grammar more correctly and skilfully than he had heard it presented elsewhere. I remember hearing Luther praise this man's talent. But the reason that he was sent to Eisenach was that his mother had been born in those parts, of an old and respected family. Here he completed the study of grammar. The force of his intellect was so keen, and above all he was so eloquent, that he rapidly outstripped his peers, and in the richness of his spoken vocabulary and in written prose composition he easily surpassed some boys who had been studying them for a year.

Having thus tasted the delights of literature, and aflame with a natural greed for learning, he aspired to the university as to the fount of all teaching. And such brilliance could well have grasped all the arts in order if only he had found suitable teachers, and perhaps the gentler studies of true philosophy and a concern for polished discourse might have served to relieve the vehemence of his nature. But at Erfurt he came upon the current dialectic, which was thorny enough, but which he absorbed rapidly because his penetrating intellect enabled him to grasp arguments and fundamental precepts better than others. His mind was avid for teaching and kept on demanding more and better things, so on his own he read most of the collections of ancient Latin writers, Cicero, Virgil, Livy and others. He used to read these not like the boys who were merely gathering vocabulary, but for what they could teach him as representations of human life. For this reason he examined the opinions and advice of these writers more closely, and as he had an accurate and retentive memory, most of what he heard read to him remained in his mind and before his eyes. In this way, then, he was outstanding as a youth, and the whole university admired Luther's brilliance. So when he had been invested with the degree of master of philosophy at the age of twenty, acting on the advice of his kinsfolk who believed that cleverness and eloquence as great as his should be brought out into the open and into public affairs, he began the study of law. . . .

I.2 THE MONASTIC YEARS

The spiritual turmoil which first drove Luther into monasticism, and then occupied so much of his energy as a monk, has so much drama in it that it obscures the outward course of the monastic years—a brilliantly successful academic preparation for theological teaching. Luther became a novice at Erfurt in 1505, professed his vows in 1506, was ordained and said his first mass in 1507. Under the direction of his preceptor Nathin, he began theological study, and was encouraged to read the Occamists, especially Gabriel Biel. He taught for a year in Wittenberg in 1508–9, and returned to Erfurt to pass the degrees of *Biblicus, Formatus,* and *Sententiarius* in 1509. In 1510–11 he visited

Rome, and on his return was transferred to Wittenberg, where he was presented for the doctor's degree in 1512.

I.2.A   Melanchthon's biography (continuing here from I.1.E above) next describes Luther's intellectual and spiritual progress during his first decade as a monk. As we shall see, the chronology of this narrative is not entirely accurate. (Latin text in CR VI, 158–160.)

A little later when he was twenty-one years old, against the advice of his parents and friends, he suddenly went to the cloister of the Augustinian monks at Erfurt, and asked to be received. After he was received, he not only studied the doctrine of the Church most zealously, but also subjected himself to the severest discipline, far surpassing everyone in the appointed reading, disputation, fasting, and prayer. And it was his nature to eat and drink with extreme moderation (as often surprised me in one who was physically neither small nor weak: I have seen him eat and drink absolutely nothing for four days on end, when he was in perfectly good health, and on other occasions I have often seen him content to go for many days on a daily scrap of bread and soup).

Now, the reason for his entry upon that way of life, which he believed would be more conducive to godliness and to the study of the doctrine of God, is as follows, as he himself used to relate and as is widely known. On those frequent occasions when he was thinking especially about the wrath of God or about extraordinary instances of retribution, such sudden violent terrors afflicted him that he almost died. I have seen him, distressed by his concentration upon some dispute over doctrine, lie down on a bed in a nearby room and mingle with his prayer this oft-repeated sentence: 'He has concluded all under sin so that he may have mercy upon all.' He felt these terrors for the first time, or at least in their sharpest form, when he lost a close friend who died (of what cause I am not sure). So it was not poverty, but the desire for godliness, which led him into the monastic life. Even though that way of life meant that every day he studied the doctrine which is customary in the schools, and read the commentators on the *Sentences*,[2] and in public disputations admirably and eloquently explained the mazes which others had made inextricable, yet, because what he was seeking in that way of life was not fame for his brilliance but nourishment for his godliness, he treated these things as mere incidentals and easily mastered the scholastic methods. Meanwhile, on his own he avidly read the prophetic

---

[2] The *Four Books of Sentences* of Peter Lombard (c. 1100–1160) became the standard compendium of doctrine in the late middle ages. Scholastic theology was often written in the form of commentaries upon the *Sentences*, amongst others by Thomas Aquinas, Bonaventura, Duns Scotus, William of Ockham, Gabriel Biel, and Guillaume Durand. (See 1.2.1.)

and apostolic writings, the sources of heavenly doctrine, in order to instruct his own mind about the will of God and to nourish his own fear and faith by firm testimonies. As he pursued this study more and more, he was shaken by the grievings and fears he experienced. And he used to relate that he was often strengthened by the discourses of one of the older men in the Augustinian cloister at Erfurt: when he took his anxieties to him, Luther listened to him speak at length about faith, and said that he was led back to the creed where it says: 'I believe in the forgiveness of sins.' The old man had interpreted this article as follows: 'It is not enough to believe in principle that others are forgiven (as even the devils believe), or that David or Peter is forgiven, but the command of God is that every one of us men should believe that our sins are forgiven.' And he related how this interpretation was confirmed by a dictum of Bernard's: a passage in his sermon *On the Annunciation* was pointed out where the words appear: 'But in addition you must also believe that through him *your* sins are forgiven. This is the testimony which the Holy Spirit engenders in your heart when he says: "your sins are forgiven you". For thus the apostle judges that man is justified freely through faith.'[3]

Luther used to say that he was not only strengthened by this instruction, but that he also became aware of the entire purpose of Paul who everywhere drives home the statement: 'We are justified by faith.' After he had read the works of many expositors on this subject, he recognised, both from his conversations with the older men and from his own peace of mind, that the interpretations presently available to him were worthless. Gradually, by reading and gathering the sayings and examples related in the prophets and the apostles and by stirring up his faith in daily prayer, he gained more understanding. And then, too, he began to read the books of Augustine and found both in the exposition of the Psalms and in the book *On the Spirit and the Letter* many clear statements which confirmed this teaching about faith and the consolation which had been kindled in his breast. Yet he did not entirely abandon the commentators on the *Sentences*. He could recite Gabriel [Biel] and the Cardinal of Cambrai [Peter d'Ailly] almost word for word from memory. For a long time he read widely in the works of Occam, whose acumen he preferred to Thomas and Scotus. He also read Gerson diligently. But most often he read all Augustine's works and remembered them best of all. He began this very taxing study at Erfurt, the city where he spent four years in the Augustinian monastery.

At this point that reverend man Staupitz, who had assisted in the foundation of the university of Wittenberg, wanted to enhance the study of theology in the recently founded school. Having assessed Luther's

[3] Bernard of Clairvaux (1090–1153), *In festo annuntiationis Beatae Mariae Virginis Sermo I*, in MPL CLXXXIII, p. 384 A.

brilliance and erudition, he transferred him to Wittenberg in the year 1508, when he was twenty-six years old. Here, gaining daily practice in teaching and lecturing, his brilliance began to shine even more publicly. Learned men, such as Dr Martin Mellerstadt often said that the force of genius was so great in this man that it plainly presaged a complete change in the very character of the doctrine which was then exclusively taught in the schools.

Here he first lectured on the *Dialectics* and on the *Physics* of Aristotle, but he did not abandon his own study of theological writings. Three years later, he travelled to Rome in connection with disputes among the monks. After his return the same year, according to normal academic custom he was employed at the invitation of the Duke of Saxony, the Elector Frederick, and (as the saying is) was invested with a doctor's degree. For the Elector had heard him lecturing, and had been most impressed by the power of his intellect, the vigour of his speech, and the excellence of the content of his lectures. And to show you that the doctor's degree was conferred upon him for his maturity of judgement, you should know that Luther was approaching thirty. He himself used to tell how he was commanded by Staupitz, despite his own reluctance and actual refusal, to allow himself to be elevated to this degree, and Staupitz told him jokingly that there would be much business for God to be done in the Church, and that God would make use of him for these works. But even though this statement was made in jest at the time, the outcome has indicated that many a premonition anticipated future changes.

I.2.B Thirty-four years later, Luther himself gave this dramatic account of his becoming a monk. (*Table Talk*, July, 1939: Latin–German text in Tr 4, 440: 4707.)

On July 16, 1539, St Alexis's Day, Dr Martin Luther said: 'Today is the anniversary of the occasion on which I entered the monastery at Erfurt.' And he began to tell the story of how he had made his vow. Barely a fortnight before, whilst he was travelling, he was so terrified by a storm near Stotternheim, not far from Erfurt, that he had cried out in terror: ' "Help me, St Anna, I will become a monk!" But then God understood my vow in Hebrew—"*Anna*" meaning "under grace, not by the law". Later I regretted that I had made the vow, and many tried to dissuade me. But I persevered, and the day before St Alexis's Day I invited some of my very best friends to a farewell celebration, in the hope that the following day they would escort me into the monastery.' But when his friends tried to hold him back, Luther said to them: ' "You see me today, but never more!" Then with tears they accompanied me. And my father was angry about my vow, but I persisted in my determination. I thought I would never leave the monastery. I was quite

dead to the world until God thought the time was right, and Squire
Tetzel provoked me and Dr Staupitz incited me against the Pope.'

I.2.c   Luther completed his novitiate in 1506 and was ordained in 1507.
        Both the awful trauma and the rude bathos of his first mass (May
        2, 1507) are revealed in this account he gave to Johann Schlagin-
        haufen in 1532. (*Table Talk*, May, 1532: Latin–German text in
        Tr 2, 133: 1558.)

Luther spoke about celebrating masses as a sacrificing priest: 'Christ
must be a more gracious person than Philip or Pomeranus to be able to
forgive us for the fact that we used to sacrifice him as we did,' he said.
After everyone else had left, Luther stood with me in the atrium and
said to me: 'When I was about to hold my first mass, my father sent
ahead twenty gulden for the kitchen, and then came himself with twenty
people, whom he paid for. Someone said to him: "You must have a
very good friend, that you visit him in such style!", and so on. Now
when I came to the altar and was about to consecrate, at the words "to
the eternal, living, and true God" I wanted to rush from the altar, and I
said to my prior: "Lord Prior, I am afraid, I must leave the altar." He
shouted at me: "Keep going! Faster, faster!" Thus I was rescued in
the face of these words. It was a clear indication to me that all was not
right. But God has now finally granted recognition of this fact.'

I.2.d   The breach with his father created by abandoning law for mon-
        asticism was outwardly mended by the time of the first mass; but
        complete reconciliation waited many years until the reformer
        abandoned the monastic way of life. In 1521 he dedicated his
        polemical treatise (*On Monastic Vows* to Hans Luther as public
        testimony to that reconciliation. (Latin text in WA 8, 573–4; also
        translated in full in Smith II, 66 ff.)

My dear father, I want to dedicate this book to you . . . I have spent
almost sixteen years as a monk, a life to which I submitted against your
will and without your knowledge. In your fatherly affection, you were
anxious because of my immaturity. I was only a youth entering my
twenty-second year—to borrow a phrase of Augustine's, 'clothed in
burning youth'[4]—and you had heard of many examples of this sort of
life turning out unhappily for some men, and besides you were determined to contract an honourable and wealthy marriage for me. Your
concern was owing to fear, and for a time you refused to be reconciled
with me, in spite of your friends' vain attempts to persuade you that if
you wished to offer something to God you should offer your dearest and
best. Meanwhile, in your own thoughts, the Lord was shouting (but to
deaf ears) the verse of the Psalm: 'The Lord knows the thoughts of men,

---

[4] Augustine, *Confessions*, Book II, 3: 'inquieta indutum adulescentia'.

that they are vain' [Ps. 94 : 11; Vulg. 93 : 11]. At length you desisted and submitted to God's will, but you never resolved your fears for me. For I remember, all too graphically, that occasion after we had been reconciled when you were talking with me, and I claimed that I had been called by terrors from heaven—for I had not become a monk freely and from choice, much less to gratify my belly; but walled in by the terror and agony of sudden death, I was compelled by need to take my vows. Then you replied: 'Grant that it is not an illusion and deception!' That sentence penetrated and lodged in my inmost being, as if God were speaking through your mouth, but I steeled my heart as much as I could against you and your word. And you added something else: when in filial trust I began to give way to your indignation, you suddenly retorted, and stopped me short so fittingly and aptly that in my whole life I have scarcely heard a single word from anyone which has produced a more powerful or abiding reaction in me. 'And have you also not heard,' you said, 'that parents are to be obeyed?' But I was so secure in my own righteousness that I heard you as just a man and was boldly contemptuous; whereas in my heart I was not able to feel contempt for that word. . . .

However, it was the Lord's wish (as I now see) that I should have experience of the wisdom of the academy and the holiness of the cloister at first-hand—in other words, of many sins and impieties—so that there would be no opportunity for ungodly men to boast against their future opponent that I condemned things of which I was ignorant. And so I lived as a monk, not indeed without sin, but without reproach.

I.2.E   By all accounts, Luther was a devout, energetic, and successful monk. This was not a time of unrelieved wretchedness, though in his later disgust with monasticism he seemed to suggest it was. Here is part of a 1527 lecture on 1 John 2 : 18. (Latin–German text in WA 20, 672, 8–19.)

Monks fight a two-fold battle against the doctrine of the gospel, in that they do not fulfil their proper rôle in the world, yet at the same time each monk thinks he has fulfilled his rôle perfectly. He should pray to God: 'Forgive my sin, that by living in an order I have neglected my neighbour, and I have not preached.' When St Bernard was alive and well he urged men to enter an order, but as he lay dying he confessed: 'I have squandered my days—my only consolation is that Christ has a two-fold claim on heaven'[5] . . . I myself was a monk without any complaint. I kept the three vows devotedly day and night and yet I felt no repose in maintaining my duty so purely, for there was no Word of

[5] This quotation, a favourite of Luther, is from Chapter CXV of the *Legenda Aurea* of Jacobus de Voragine (translated by Granger Ryan and Helmut Rippiger, *The Golden Legend of Jacobus de Voragine* Part II, New York 1941, p. 471).

God in it, but only opinions of the doctors. I squandered my life there, and acted more disgracefully than if I had entered a brothel.

I.2.F   From his fellow monks later came some staunch supporters, but also some bitter enemies—such as Johannes Cochlaeus who forty years later, after Luther's death, included this dubious story of a fit in his scurrilous 1549 *Commentaria*. Even Cochlaeus, however, gave Luther credit for his monastic fervour. (Latin next in Otto Scheel, *Dokumente zu Luthers Entwicklung (bis 1519)*, Tübingen 1911, 201: 533.)

At that point, he was a law student. While he was in the country, however, terror-stricken and laid low by a bolt of lightning (as the common report has it), or else grieving over the death of one of his companions, out of contempt for the world and to many people's amazement he suddenly entered the monastery of the Brethren of St Augustine, commonly called the Eremites. There, after a year of probation, he fulfilled the requirements for profession in that order, and for four years battled strenuously for God in his study and spiritual exercises. Yet he did seem to the brothers to be somewhat unusual, whether because of some occult dealing with a demon or simply from being socially maladroit. There were various indications of this, but especially because one day in the choir, while the gospel about the casting out of the deaf and dumb demon was being read in the mass, he suddenly fell down shouting: 'I am not, I am not!' Many believe, therefore, that he made use of secret familiarity with some demon, especially since he has occasionally written things about himself which can cause the reader to suspect this sort of commerce and evil intercourse.

I.2.G   In 1508 Luther was abruptly transferred for one year to the new university of Wittenberg to teach moral philosophy. In a letter of March 17, 1509, he explained to his old friend Vicar Braun the suddenness of his departure, and the burden of his present duties. (Latin text in Br 1, 16: 5; also translated in full in Smith I, 23.)

Brother Martin Luther sends you his greeting, and wishes you both salvation and the Saviour himself, Jesus Christ.

Master and Father, whom I love more than I revere! Stop, I beg of you, stop wondering (as you have been) that I left you—or would have left you, were we not still so closely bound together—secretly and in silence, as if the force of ingratitude had frozen our love like the north wind and blown the memory of your kindness from my heart. No, no, that is not what I have done, or at least that is not what I meant to do, although I may have been forced to do so against my will and thus given you grounds to think badly of me.

c

I admit that I went away, and yet in another sense I did not—a larger and better part of me remains with you. Your own confidence in me is my only means of convincing you that this is the case. Since that confidence springs only from your own kindness and graciousness, I hope that now, as in the past, you will never allow it to be shattered or reduced unless I deserve it. This way, my departure from you in the body has put me nearer to you in spirit (so long as you agree, which I certainly hope you do).

And if I may come to the point: so that I am no longer forced to suspect that your love is doubtful about my fidelity (and one hopes that the suspicion by its very nature is next door to a lie), see with what violence I have succeeded in snatching this snippet of time from my very many and varied affairs to write this letter to you, especially since the messengers at my disposal are few and far between, and even if they were more readily available they would become scarce because of their ignorance and inefficiency. And what else do you suppose that I intend by this letter if not that by its commendation you will continue to regard me as you have received me in the past, and that you will expect from we whatever you would wish me to expect from you? Although I never could or would equal you in any of your good qualities, yet even if I lack everything else I do have a great feeling for you; if I am not at this moment displaying it to you in person, at least I can say that I have often done so in the past. And I know that there is nothing your generous spirit expects from me except things which are of the spirit, that is, that we share a single discernment in the Lord, and have one heart and one soul, just as we have one faith in the Lord.

But do not be surprised that I left you in such silence. For my departure was so sudden that it almost happened without my colleagues' knowledge. I wanted to write to you, but I could not for lack of time and leisure, but I was able to regret that I had unexpectedly to break away without saying good-bye to you. And so now, by God's command or permission, I am at Wittenberg. If you are interested in knowing how I am getting on, by God's grace I am well, except that the study is very severe, especially philosophy, which from the very beginning I should most gladly have changed for theology—that theology, I mean, which digs out the kernel of the nut and the germ of the grain and the marrow of the bones. But God is God; man often, indeed always, is mistaken in his own judgement. He is our God, he himself will rule us sweetly and for ever.

Please condescend to accept this letter, written hastily and off the cuff, and if you can send any messengers to me, let me have a share of your own letters. In return, I shall try to do the same for you. From first to last, farewell, and believe that I am such as you should hope. Farewell again.   Brother Martin Luther, Augustinian.

I.2.H   Returning to Erfurt to continue his theological studies, Luther's
        displeasure with scholastic philosophy grew apace as he passed
        the successive degrees—*Biblicus, Formatus, Sententiarius.* He
        wrote these marginal notes on Augustine's *de trinitate* and *de
        civitate dei* ca. 1509. (Latin text in WA 9, 23–27.)

Augustine argues better and with greater truth about happiness than
that storyteller Aristotle with his frivolous defenders. Because they do
not read Augustine on this subject, they boldly distinguish different
kinds of happiness for us in this life, and in an utterly discordant and
distorted way make the contradictory Aristotle harmonise with pure
faith. . . .

Today the majority of philosophers are relics of Stoicism. They argue
in meagre novelties and equivocations of terms. . . .

The fanatic philosophers of our day, too, almost all want to harmonise with our Scripture, even though they never agree amongst
themselves! . . . Far more amazing is the error of our contemporaries
who gabble very impudently that Aristotle does not clash with catholic
truth.

I.2.I   Luther became *Sententiarius* in autumn, 1509. His duties were
        to lecture on the *Sentences* of Peter Lombard, the standard
        medieval compendium of doctrine. Luther's overriding concerns
        are already evident in his notes for this course, albeit in a tortuous
        form. (Latin text in WA 9, 71, 5 ff.)

'Thus good will follows upon grace, not grace upon good will': grace
acts as a leader. The free will in evil is to be understood in the same
fashion. For just as the world follows grace as its leader and attractor to
good, so it follows weakness, or the law of the flesh to which it is joined
(like grace in the other instance), as its leader to evil. Thus in both
cases it is free, and in both cases it refuses to act otherwise (I am speaking about grace when it has been brought to perfection, and weakness
when it has not been cured). In faith, however, there is a mixture and
tempering of both extremes, so long as we are dealing with the external
reality.

Hence, just as the will is free in that it can choose amongst many
evils, even though it cannot by itself choose good, by the same token the
will is free when it can choose amongst many goods yet is no longer
able to choose evil. But life-in-between, that is, Christian life, finds
itself as it were in a middle position, tending to both extremes—finding
it difficult to tend to the good, but not impossible (like the first case),
and easy to tend to the evil, but not in necessary bondage (like the second
case). It is not as easy to do the good as for the blessed, nor yet impossible to do good as for the wretched. Nevertheless both extremes, the

one in necessity, the other in impossibility, do exert effort. So does this middle way, but now in ease and difficulty. For the blessed necessarily choose the good, and it is impossible for them to choose the evil. But the wretched find it impossible to choose good and necessarily choose evil. We, however, choose the evil easily and the good with difficulty. Or to express it differently, it is certainly impossible for the wretched to choose the good, just as it is impossible for the blessed to choose the evil, yet perhaps the one does not choose the evil necessarily, nor the other choose the good necessarily, but both choose freely; even though the former are necessarily in bondage to sin and the latter are necessarily in the service of justice, in neither case does their servitude diminish their liberty, but both retain their liberty.

Whether it is expressed one way or the other, it is enough that the reality itself should be clearly understood. For in either case it is true that if it is impossible for a man to lift himself up to good in his own strength, he is necessarily turned towards evil in his own strength (or at least remains under evil if he has not chosen it himself). Nevertheless, God is always at hand, and does not condemn the free will just because it does not or cannot possess grace, but because it does not accept grace offered and displayed, or fails to guard the grace received, and does not follow grace as its leader, but slides back and rebelliously insists upon making its own progress. In this sense, the beatitude of the blessed does not consist simply in having grace, but in accepting it and consenting to have it.

I.2.J   The Augustinian order in Germany was split over the issue of merger between the monasteries which observed the Rule strictly and the laxer houses. Luther was one of two delegates who unsuccessfully appealed the issue at Rome in 1510–11. (*Table Talk*, March–May, 1537: Latin–German text in Tr 3, 431: 3582A.)

I would not take a lot of money in exchange for having been in Rome. I would not have believed it if I had not seen it myself. For the ungodliness and evil there are so huge and shameless that no one pays any regard either to God or to man, either to sin or to shame. All godly men who have been there testify to this, and so do all the ungodly who come back from Italy worse than before! However, my chief object in going to Rome was that I wanted to make a complete confession of everything I had done from my youth up and become holy, even though I had already made such a confession twice at Erfurt. But then in Rome I came upon men who were completely unschooled. Ah, dear Lord God, how could the cardinals, overloaded with so much business and government, be expected to know anything? It is hard enough for us who study every day and practise every hour.

I.2.K   The dominant recollection of these years was the agony of conscience as his scrupulous soul sought a gracious God. So seriously did he take the demand of full confession that constant recourse to penance led him only into deeper despair. (*Table Talk*, November–December 1531: German text in Tr 1, 50: FB 3, 135.)

I often made my confession to Dr Staupitz, not about women, but about the real snags. He replied: 'I don't understand!' In other words, he really consoled me! Later, I went to another confessor, and the same things happened to me. In short, there was not a single father confessor who knew anything about it. So then I thought: 'No one but you undergoes this temptation and trial.' At last I became like a dead body. Finally Dr Staupitz began to speak to me at the table, since I was so deathly despondent, and said: 'Why are you so sad, Brother Martin?' I replied: 'Ah, how can I be otherwise?' He said: 'Oh, you do not realise that such trial is good and necessary for you? Otherwise nothing good would come of you!' He himself did not understand what he had said, for he thought that I was clever and that if I did not experience trials I would become proud and arrogant. But I interpreted the situation according to Paul's remark: 'I was given a thorn in my flesh to keep me from being puffed up by such revelation' [2 Cor. 12 : 7]. And so I received it as the word and voice of the Holy Spirit.

I was very holy under the papacy: I was a monk! And yet I was so sad and depressed that I thought that God was not gracious to me. There I celebrated mass, and I prayed, and I had no wife—you never saw or experienced such a member of an order or monk as I was (so to speak). Nowadays, I must suffer other thoughts from the devil. For he often casts in my teeth: 'Oh, what a huge crowd of people you have led astray with your teaching!' Sometimes in the midst of trial a harsh word comforts me and gives me new heart. On one occasion, my father confessor said to me when I was constantly bringing stupid sins to him: 'You are a fool! God does not rage at you, but you rage at him; God is not angry with you, but you are angry with him!' A precious, mighty, and noble word, even though he said it before the light of the gospel broke!

I.3   PROFESSOR OF THE BIBLE

Luther's superior, Staupitz, personally arranged for the Elector of Saxony to employ Luther for life as professor of the Bible at the university of Wittenberg. The early years of his incumbency were incredibly busy and fruitful years. He found release from inner turmoil, boldly developed both the style and the principles of his theological teaching, and spearheaded a revolution in the university's curriculum. In addition, he shouldered a heavy burden of pastoral and administrative duties. He was clearly a leader of men.

I.3.A   Johann von Staupitz, superior of the order and Luther's confessor, had two motives in ordering Luther to take his doctorate. It would relieve Luther's introspection; and it would groom him to replace Staupitz himself as professor of the Bible at Wittenberg. (*Table Talk*, August–December, 1531: Latin–German text in Tr 2, 379: 2255A.)

One day, Staupitz, my prior, was sitting and thinking under the pear tree which is still standing today in the middle of my grounds, and at length he said to me: 'Lord and master, you should undertake the doctor's degree: that would give you an opportunity to accomplish something!' That came true two years after my doctorate, when the questions about penitence and indulgences became public. He had approached me a second time under the pear tree about the same matter, and I had demurred, pleading many excuses, especially the fact that I had used up all my energies on myself, so much so that I could not possibly have a long life remaining to me. To this Staupitz said: 'Do you not know that our Lord God has very many great things to accomplish? So he needs many clever and wise people to help advise him. So if at some time you should die, you will become his counsellor.' I had no inkling at the time how this prophecy would be fulfilled. But four years later I began to wage war against the pope and all his deeds.

I.3.B   Professor Luther's first extant lectures at Wittenberg were on the Psalms (1513–1515). Luther wrote this record of his introductory address, delivered on August 16, 1513. (Latin text in WA 3, 13, 34 g.)

Fathers and noble sirs, my brothers in this undertaking: I see you have come with grace and a benevolent spirit to honour this renowned prophet, David, whom we address today. Perhaps I too ought not to have failed in this duty of honour, indeed to have led the way before you all, by adorning with some preface of praise this most illustrious prophet, who is certainly very wonderful and excellent in every respect, and truly worthy of praise. But it seemed to me more useful to omit such a preface, lest I should seem to promise some grandiose sequel, and lest anyone should imagine that I possess greater abilities than he sees. I certainly feel the weight on my shoulders of a responsibility which I have long resisted in vain, but to which at last I am forced by order to yield. For I confess frankly that there are many psalms which even today I do not yet understand, and unless the Lord enlightens me by your merits (as I trust), I shall not be able to interpret them.

However, there are some other things to be said which are more essential to our exposition. Clearly, more effort has been devoted to the exposition of the Psalter by a greater number of Greek, Latin, and Hebrew commentators than upon any other book of the divine Scriptures. But so far all this effort has not been productive, with the result that in many places the interpretations seem to need more interpretation than the text itself, and 'night unto night' scarcely 'declares knowledge' [Ps. 19 : 2; Vulg. 18 : 3], let alone transmits it! . . . Since, then, I take up this prophet for interpretation, who am neither a prophet nor the son of a prophet [Amos 7 : 15], I wished (as I said) to leave out the commendatory preface and to display to you David himself, in his comeliness and beauty, as the source of his own praise.

I.3.c   The glosses for the lectures on the Psalms begin with the traditional principles of interpretation. Luther was still an allegorist, but already regarded the christocentric and moral senses as primary. See II.2.B for an extract from these lectures. (Latin text in WA 3, 13, 6 ff.)

Every prophecy and every prophet ought to be understood to be about Christ the Lord, except where it obviously speaks about something else in plain words. For so he says himself: 'Search the Scriptures, for these are they which testify of me' [John 5 : 39]. It is perfectly certain that those who search otherwise will fail in their quest. Accordingly, some commentators expound far too many Psalms not prophetically but historically, following some of the Hebrew rabbis, who are writers of lies and moulders of Jewish vanities. No wonder, since they are alien from Christ (that is, from the truth)! But we have the mind of Christ as the apostle says [1 Cor. 2: :16].

Anything that is said literally about the Lord Jesus Christ in his own person should also be understood allegorically about aid which comes from him, and about the Church conformed to him in every respect. At the same time, it should also be understood tropologically about the spiritual and inner man in contrast to the flesh and outward man. Here is an obvious example: 'Blessed is the man who does not walk,' etc. [Ps. 1 : 1]. Literally, this is the Lord Jesus, in that he did not yield to the desires of the Jews and the depraved and adulterous generation which flourished in his time. Allegorically, it is the Holy Church, in that it has not given way before the evil intentions of persecutors, heretics, and ungodly Christians. Tropologically, it is the spirit of man yielding to the blandishments and pressures of its adversary the flesh and the ungodly motions of the body of sin. Similarly Psalm 2: 'Why do the nations rage,' etc. Literally, this is the jeering of Jews and gentiles against Christ in his passion. Allegorically, it opposes tyrants, heretics, and ungodly princes of the Church. Tropologically, it opposes the tyranny, temptation, and onslaught of the carnal and exterior man buffetting and afflicting the spirit which is the dwelling place of Christ. So Psalm 3: 'Lord, how are they increased who trouble me?' is literally the complaint of Christ against his enemies the Jews. Allegorically, it is the complaint and accusation of the Church about tyrants, heretics, etc. But tropologically, it is the complaint or plea of the devout and afflicted spirit placed in the midst of temptations. Every other case is to be understood in its own way, so that we shall not be burdened by a closed book, and thus fail to benefit.

I.3.D   In addition to his academic duties, Luther was given very exten-
         sive responsibilities as a parish priest and district vicar of the
         Augustinians, as he described in this letter to a former colleague,
         Johann Lang. (Latin text in Br 1, 72: 28; also translated in full in
         LW 48, 27 ff.)

To his friend the Venerable Father Johann Lang, Bachelor, Prior of the Augustinians at Erfurt.

Jesus.
Greetings. I almost need two scribes or secretaries—I do almost nothing all day except write letters; and so I do not know whether I am always writing the same things over and over. You will see! I am lecturer at the convent, reader at meals, I am asked daily to be preacher at the parish church as well, I am the director of studies, I am vicar—in other words, I am prior of eleven convents, I am supervisor of the fish in Leitzkau, mediator in the Hertzbergers' case in Torgau, lecturer on Paul, collector of material on the Psalms, and as I have already said, I occupy the greater part of my time in the business of writing letters. I rarely have any unencumbered time for catching up on my Hours and for celebrating mass, let alone my own trials with the flesh, the world and the devil. See what an idle fellow I am!
I think that my opinion and reply about Brother Johann Metzel has reached you in the meantime; nevertheless I will see what I can do. How do you suppose that I can place your Sardanapales and Sybarites?[6] If you have trained them poorly, poorly trained you must keep them. There are enough useless friars for me elsewhere. Yet perhaps to a long-suffering soul none of them is useless: I have persuaded myself that the useless are more useful than the most useful! So for the time being keep them.
I think (but I am not sure) that I wrote to you recently about the friars you had sent to me. I have sent the novice with the younger friar

[6] That is, friars who preferred a life of ease. 'Sardanapales' were followers of King Sardanapalus, or Asshurbanipal, of Assyria (c. 660 B.C.); 'Sybarites' were citizens of Sybaris, an ancient Greek settlement in southern Italy. Both had a reputation for love of luxury.

to Master Spengenberg's place because they asked not to stay in this climate, which is unhealthy for them. I have kept two of the others, and the two from Cologne, because I felt such compassion for their aptitude that in spite of the obvious damage I should prefer to keep them than to send them back. Twenty-two priests, twelve novices, and altogether forty-one people are living on our more than utterly meagre provisions; but the Lord will provide.

You write that yesterday you began to lecture on the *Sentences*; and tomorrow I shall begin the *Epistle to the Galatians,* though I feel that the current plague may not permit this beginning to have a sequel. The plague is taking at most two or three among us (though not yet every day); the son of the craftsman who is our neighbour opposite was healthy yesterday but was buried today, and a second son is down with the infection. What can I say? It is here, and it attacks quite cruelly and suddenly, especially among the younger generation. But both you and Master Bartholomew urge me to flee. Where should I flee? I hope that the world will not crumble when Friar Martin is laid low. Indeed, if the plague continues I shall disperse the friars throughout the country, but I am firmly fixed here through my obedience—it would be wrong for me to flee until the obedience which has enjoined me to leave enjoins me a second time. Not that I do not fear death (for I am not the Apostle Paul, but only a lecturer on the Apostle Paul), but I hope that the Lord will rescue me from my fear.

The Reverend Father Dr Johann Huisden, the prior of Cologne, has written to me that Master Spangenberg was received with great glory and charity by the citizens of Dordrecht, and that in a very short time their convents will be more distinguished than the rest. The prior there is Lector Heinrich, at one time (so they say) a fellow student of ours; previously he was second-in-charge at Cologne. Lector Fug writes that Reuchlin's case is going favourably, and he is feeling remarkably cheerful. Concerning the *Order or Permission*: I ask that you also send a seer at the same time—I cannot read what those sheets contain! Greet all those who ought to be greeted, and since I am unable to write to my fathers, the Masters, just now, I shall write at another time; read them this letter if you wish.

Master Wenceslas has been released and is a lecturer at Munich, and Bachelor Fladenstein has been released at Colmbach. In Neustadt, Friar Michael has been released, and Heinrich Zwetzen is prior; but I took this action because I was hoping that I myself would be in control there by the middle of the year. That place desperately needs a head. The Reverend Father Vicar wrote to me again on October 8 from Alberkirchen at the home of Pfeffinger, who with his Sara is now 'fattening a Bavarian pig'. He writes that he will enjoy himself quietly in Munich for the winter. Farewell in haste, and remember us in this day of the visitation of the Lord, to whom be glory, Amen. October 26, 1516.

                                                    Friar Martin, Augustinian vicar.

I.3.E During the same period, Luther gradually won more and more
       support from his colleagues for reform of the curriculum away
       from scholasticism towards biblical humanism. (Latin text in
       Br 1, 88: 34; also translated in full in LW 48, 36 ff.)

To the venerable Father Johann Lang, Bachelor of Theology, Prior of the Erfurt Eremites, his beloved in the Lord.

Jesus.

Greetings. I am sending this letter, my father, to my distinguished teacher Jodocus [Trutvetter] of Eisenach, full of questions against logic, philosophy, and theology—that is, full of blasphemies and cursings against Aristotle, Porphyry, commentators on the *Sentences*, in short against the ruinous studies of our age. At least, this is how they will be interpreted by those for whom it is decreed that not just for five years with the Pythagoreans but perpetually and eternally with the dead one is to remain silent, believe everything, always comply, and not ever skirmish or mutter against Aristotle and the *Sentences* by even so much as a mild preface. What will they not believe who have accepted as true those things which Aristotle, that most calumnious calumniator, inflicts and imposes upon others, things so absurd that a donkey or a stone could not keep quiet about them?

So please make sure that you forward this letter to that excellent man, and then kindly take care to scent out what judgement he and all the others make of me on this issue, and let me know. My soul has no more ardent desire than to unveil publicly that actor who has so effectively deluded the church with his Greek mask, and to show everyone his ignominy, if I had the chance. I have in hand some short comments on the first book of the Physics, with which I have decided to re-enact the story of Aristaeus against this Protheus of mine, the craftiest conjurer of brilliant people, so much so that if Aristotle had not been flesh I should not have hesitated to assert that he was really the devil. Part of my cross—its greatest part—is that I am forced to watch friars with an excellent innate capacity for good studies passing their lives and wasting their efforts in these charades, whilst the universities do not stop burning and condemning good books, but publish (or rather dream up) bad ones instead!

I could wish that both Master Usingen and the gentleman from Eisenach might refrain from, and indeed eventually repress, such labours. All my files are full of things against their editions, which I regard as entirely useless; and everyone else could see this too if they were not bound (as I said) by the perpetual rule of silence. Farewell, and pray for me. From Wittenberg, February 8, 1516.

Friar Martin Luther, Augustinian.

I.3.F   The patron of the university, Elector Frederick, appointed a commission to review the school's progress. But even before curricular reform was officially instituted, Luther and his like-minded colleagues gained enthusiastic support from the students for their reaction against scholastic theology. (Latin text in Br 1, 99: 41; also translated in full in LW 48, 41.)

To Father Johann Lang, Prior of the Augustinian Eremites at Erfurt.

Jesus.

Greetings. I have no other reason for writing to you except that it seemed wrong to be sending a monk to you without sending a letter and greetings. By God's grace, I am relieved that Brother Johann Guman has come home safe. The Reverend Father Vicar writes that he will be coming to us quite soon.

Our theology and St Augustine are forging ahead prosperously, and by God's operation they reign in our university. Little by little, Aristotle is going down to a doom everlasting and near at hand. It is extraordinary the way lecturers on the *Sentences* are avoided. Nor can one hope to have an audience unless he chooses to offer the Bible or St Augustine or some other teacher of ecclesiastical authority. Farewell and pray for me. Monday after Easter V, 1517.

Brother Martin Luther.

I.3.G   After frustrating delay, the Elector responded to pressure from the faculty and implemented many of the proposed changes. In mid-1518 the brilliant young humanist Philip Melanchthon was appointed to teach classics. The Elector's secretary, Spalatin, was one of Luther's staunchest admirers and spoke for the faculty at court. (Latin text in Br 1, 153: 63.)

To his very good friend, Georg Spalatin.

Jesus.

Greetings. We have just been with the good Dr Carlstadt,[7] most excellent Spalatin, and we began to discuss the matter which you raised some time ago, namely the courses of study which are to be initiated or instituted in our school. The reason I have not written to you about them for some time was that we nearly all thought the situation was

---

[7] Andreas Bodenstein von Carlstadt (c. 1480–1541), dean of the theological faculty, an early champion of Luther who was nevertheless jealous of his brilliant younger colleague, and later left Wittenberg to become his extremist rival. (See III.3.B.)

looking desperate, especially since we were frightened that our illustrious Prince would feel such a great expense was excessive. Nevertheless, in order to meet your satisfaction and desire, I am sending this schedule in which you will be able to read what we decided. Even so, if such a curriculum could possibly be instituted, immortal God! what great glory this would be to us, and to the prince, and to scholarship! Moreover, it would really be the occasion for the reformation of all the universities —indeed, for the swifter elimination of the barbarism everywhere and a most abundant growth of all learning. Use your own judgement in the matter. Farewell. Wittenberg, March 11, 1518.

Brother Martin Luther, Augustinian.

II

THE BREAK FROM ROME

No PERIOD OF Martin Luther's career is so familiar, or has been subjected to such minute scrutiny, as the short years of sudden notoriety that led first to excommunication by the Pope and then to banishment by the Emperor. The steps by which an obscure Saxon theologian's local concern over a modest pastoral issue burgeoned into a struggle for authority permanently dividing the Christian West are an amazing study of the complexities of historical change. From the moment in late 1517 when unauthorised reprints of Luther's 95 Theses were distributed far and wide throughout Germany, his every small pamphlet rapidly attained a huge circulation. Yet Luther was not the first, nor the sharpest, of the critics of the ecclesiastical establishment. His initial protest was a scholarly attempt to draw the Church's attention to a local infraction of its own canonical principles. It was not yet a challenge to Roman authority or doctrine; but it rapidly became so as Luther discovered, to his bafflement, that the system would not tolerate correction, or even criticism. The dispute grew in dimensions as rival monastic factions and competing theological faculties used it as an occasion to enhance their own repute. Luther's persistent request for a considered response was met only with a disproportionate show of curial highhandedness. Under these pressures, his theological thinking underwent decisive new refinements. He moved beyond the intense experimental Augustinianism which had motivated his first protests to new formulations which differed fundamentally from Roman doctrine. His confidence in the Church's magisterium shattered, he first defined limits to papal authority, next admitted that both popes and councils could and did err, and finally concluded that the Pope's intractibility marked him as the very Antichrist. In short, Luther became the reformer in the press of his own Reformation, and he survived the resultant danger to his person only because political circumstance—above all the Elector Frederick's central position in the election of a new Holy Roman Emperor—created a temporary respite and accommodation at this crucial point. The sweeping human power of the evangelical doctrine, borne on the rushing stream of Luther's pastoral tracts, sustained not a cause but a movement. By the time Rome cast Luther from its communion, a new communion had already taken root.

II.1   THE INDULGENCE FUROR AND ITS AFTERMATH

Luther posted his 95 Theses on October 31, 1517. Their chief recipient, Albrecht of Mainz, on his theologians' advice referred the matter to Rome. On Tetzel's urging, the Dominican order also pitted its influence in Rome against Luther. The Pope persuaded the Augustinian General, Volta, to demand Luther's recantation at the Heidelberg Chapter meeting in April, 1518, where, however, Luther made a strongly favourable impression on his fellows, and was encouraged to publish his *Resolutions*. Thereupon the powerful Dominican theologian, Prieras, had Luther cited to Rome, where distorted and even forged versions of his teaching were circulating. In August, 1518, Leo X authorised Thomas, Cardinal Cajetan to take summary action against the German heretic. Luther's confrontation with Cajetan in Augsburg in October did not produce the desired recantation; but the infuriated Cajetan's attempt to arrest Luther was frustrated by the Elector Frederick's carefully considered intervention. The Elector was in a strong position owing to the prospective election of a successor to the Emperor Maximilian I. A papal nuncio, Charles von Miltitz, clumsily attempted to contrive a truce, which misled the Pope into supposing that Luther had submitted, and which Luther felt was immediately dishonoured. However, this attempt, together with Maximilian's death on January 11, 1519, produced a protracted lull in Rome's proceedings against Luther. The lull was shattered by the debate at Leipzig between Luther and Johann Eck in July, 1519, when Eck prompted Luther to challenge publicly the divine origin of papal primacy and the infallibility of general councils. Eck went triumphantly to Rome, where a series of papal commissions in early 1520 drew up the condemnation of Luther which Leo X promulgated in June, 1520, as the bull *Exsurge Domine*.

II.1.A   Long before Luther raised his voice against the peril of indulgences and the feverish hunt for merits, others had attacked abuses in the Church which opposed true godliness. In 1509, the nice, notorious scorn of Erasmus had turned against the pardon-traffic in *The Praise of Folly*. (Latin text in Erasmus, *Opera Omnia* (Leyden Edition), IV, 444 ff.; also translated in full in Erasmus, *The Praise of Folly*, trans. H. H. Hudson, Princeton, 1941, and other versions.)

What shall I say about those who so blissfully deceive themselves with fictitious pardons for sins, and measure out their span in purgatory as if with an hour glass, counting out the centuries, years, months, days, and hours as if from a mathematical table, beyond all error? What shall I say about those who, relying on magic charms or incantations which some pious imposter has dreamt up either for his soul's sake or profit, promise themselves anything: riches, honours, pleasures, abundance, perpetual good health, length of life, vigorous old age, and finally a seat next to Christ amongst the exalted. But they do not want the last unless it happens quite late in the piece—after the pleasures of this life have finally failed them, though they cling to them tooth and nail; then they will ascend to those heavenly delights. I picture to myself here some businessman or soldier or judge who, by laying down one single little coin from his huge plunder, thinks that the whole putrid bog of his life has been purified all at once and imagines that so many perjuries, so many lusts, so many binges, so many fights, so many murders, so many impostures, so many perfidies, and so many treacheries are bought off as by a contract, but bought off in such a way that he may start from scratch with a new round of sins. And who are sillier (yet happier too) than those who promise themselves more than the highest happiness by reciting their seven daily versicles from the sacred psalms? And these are the magic versicles which a certain demon is said to have pointed out to St Bernard. He was a facetious devil, to be sure, but more fatuous than clever, having been tricked into it against his will. These things are so foolish that I, Folly, am almost ashamed myself, and yet they are approved, not only by the crowd, but even by professors of religion. And is it not almost the same thing when various regions adopt some particular saint as their own, and when they assign particular character- istics to particular saints, and allot to each of them his own particular rites of worship, so that one brings succour for toothache, another is on hand for women in childbirth, yet another restores property which has been stolen, this one is propitious in shipwreck, and this one takes care of the sheep, and so on for the rest of them (for it would take far too long to run through them all)? There are some individual saints who are useful in many situations, especially the Virgin Mother of God, to whom common men attribute almost more than to the Son.

. . . The majority of the monks devote so much effort to their cere- monies and to human traditions that they regard a single heaven as scarcely worthy reward for such efforts—never reflecting that the time will come when, regardless of all these things, Christ will judge them according to his own precept, namely love. One monk will display his pot belly, distended with all sorts of fish. Another will pour out a hundred barrels of psalms. Another will count up his myriad fasts, and will attribute his almost bursting paunch to having only one meal so often. Another will produce a mountain of ceremonies so great that it could scarcely be carried by seven freight ships. Another will boast that he never touched money for sixty years, except when his fingers were protected by two pairs of gloves. Another will be wearing a cowl so foul and filthy that no sailor would let it touch his body. Yet another will recall that for more than fifty-five years he led the life of a sponge, always fixed to the same spot. Another will adduce a voice raucous with constant chanting; another a lethargy contracted from solitude; another a tongue grown dumb from the yoke of silence. And Christ, interrupting their otherwise unending boasts, will say: 'Where does this new race of Jews come from? There is only one law which I recognise as my own, and about that I hear nothing. Once upon a time, using no complex parables, I promised the inheritance of my Father not to cowls, or rituals, or fasts, but to the work of love. And I do not acknowledge those who acknowledge their own deeds too much.'

II.1.B   During the year before the furor broke out, Luther had preached against the abuse of indulgences on at least three recorded occasions. This was the theme of his sermon on Trinity X, 1516. (Latin text in WA 1, 65 f.; also translated in full in LW 51, 14 ff.)

Even if indulgences are the very merit of Christ and his saints and are therefore to be received with all reverence, in practice they have become the most disgraceful agency of avarice. For is anyone using them to seek the salvation of men's souls, rather than the cash out of their purses? This is plain and obvious from their own ministry: for the commissioners and ministers never preach anything else but to commend indulgences and to arouse the people to contribute. You will not hear from them who is to teach the people, or what indulgences are, or on what day they apply and cease to apply, but only how much they ought to contribute—in other words, they leave the people hanging in their ignorance, believing that they are immediately saved by getting these indulgences of theirs. For the grace by which a man becomes righteous or more righteous is not conferred by an indulgence, at least *per se*; all that is conferred is remission of an imposed penance and satisfaction, and it does not follow that a man who dies with such a remission will spring immediately to heaven. But a simple-minded man —like the majority of the people who have been deceived—believes that by 'plenary remission' sin is entirely removed so that he will immediately spring to heaven, and so he sins with impunity and binds himself even more tightly with the bonds of conscience.

It should be noted that grace is two-fold: the grace of remission and the grace of infusion, or extrinsic and intrinsic grace. Remission is the relaxation of the temporal penalty one is forced to bear here when it is imposed or to discharge the residue in purgatory (for example, at one time seven years used to be imposed for a single sin); but by this remission the concupiscence and sickness of the soul is in no way diminished, nor is love or any other interior virtue increased, even though all these things must happen before men enter the kingdom of God. For flesh and blood will not possess the kingdom of God, nor will anything defiled enter it. But how much this shortens the time in purgatory, no one knows. Moreover, it is by no means through the power of the keys that the Pope provides this remission, but only through the application of the intercession of the entire Church. There remains a doubt whether God will accept this in part or in whole. Of course, the Pope is able to release a soul from purgatory when he imposes or is able to impose the penance himself. As his bull declares: 'As far as the keys of Holy Mother Church extend, and from imposed penalties, we give merciful respite.' It is therefore the height of temerity to preach that souls are redeemed from purgatory through these indulgences, since the form of words is absurd, and they do not explain how they intend them to be understood. Otherwise the Pope is cruel, if he does not grant to wretched souls for nothing what he is able to grant the Church for the necessary fee.

Infusion is an inward illumination of the mind and inflaming of the will; it is a beam of the eternal into the soul, like a ray from the sun, and it does not come to an end because of 'plenary remission'. It is necessary for rooting out concupiscence to the point where it is rooted out completely. And it is complete only when a man, utterly weary of this life, sighs with longing for God and at last is released from the body by his yearning for God. Surely this is to be found in few men, and it is they who are fully absolved; indeed, plenary remission is conferred only upon those who are worthily contrite and have confessed.

II.1.c   This was also his theme on October 31, 1516 (exactly a year before the posting of the Theses), and again on St Matthew's Day, 1517. Here he displayed how his concern arose from his 'theology of the cross'. (Latin text in WA 1, 138 ff.; also translated in full in LW 51, 26 ff.)

Man hides what is his in order to deny it; God hides what is his in order to reveal it. For God hides it from the wise and the great to make them humble and foolish, and thus reveal it to babes: for this is pleasing in his eyes and is his highest will, just and right and holy. And what better will could there be than that which, by hiding what is its own, tries only to remove what prevents it from being revealed, that is pride? . . .

In an extraordinary manner, the very outpouring of indulgences produces a servile sort of justice. Indulgences do nothing but teach people to fear, flee, and dread the penalty for sins, but not the sins themselves. Accordingly, all too little results from the indulgences except for great security and a licence for sinning, so much so that unless people feared the penalty of sins no one would want these indulgences free of charge! Instead people ought rather to be exhorted to love the penalty and embrace the punishment. And I wish that I were lying when I say that perhaps indulgences are rightly so called, since to indulge is to permit, and an indulgence is an impunity, a permission to sin, and a licence to empty the cross of Christ. Or if indulgences are to be permitted, they should be given only to the weak in faith, so that those who try to achieve meekness and humility through the Cross, as the Lord enjoins here, will not be offended. For he says that it is not through indulgences but through meekness and humility that rest is found for men's souls. But there is no meekness except in penalties and the cross, the very things from which we are absolved by indulgences, which in fact they teach us to dread; and so make sure that we are never meek and humble, that is, never attain to true indulgence nor come to Christ. Oh, the dangers of our time! Oh, snoring priests! Oh, darkness deeper than the darkness of Egypt! How secure we are in all our worst evils!

II.1.D   The immediate occasion for publishing the disputation articles known as the 95 Theses was the success of the indulgence salesman Johann Tetzel in towns and villages not far from Wittenberg. Luther sent the Theses first of all to the prelate responsible, Albrecht of Mainz, with this covering letter. (Latin text in Br 1, 110–112: 48; also translated in full in LW 48, 45 ff.; Woolf I, 46 ff. The 95 Theses are translated in full in LW 31, 9–16; SW 1, 51–59; PE I, 29–38; Woolf I, 32–43; Wace and Buchheim 6–14. See also the important *Sermon on Indulgence and Grace of October 31, 1517*, in Woolf I, 50–55.)

To the Most Reverend Father in Christ, the most illustrious Lord Albrecht, Archbishop of the churches of Magdeburg and Mainz, Primate, Margrave of Brandenberg, etc., his most humbly revered and respected lord and pastor in Christ.

Jesus.

Grace and the mercy of God, and whatever is and can be! Forgive me, most reverend Father in Christ, illustrious prince, that I, the offscouring of men, have such temerity that I dare to consider sending a letter to your exalted Highness. The Lord Jesus is my witness that, conscious of my own insignificance and unworthiness, I have long delayed doing that which I now brazenly do, moved above all by the duty of loyalty which I know I owe your fatherly Reverence in Christ. May your Eminence therefore deign to glance at a mere speck of dust and understand my plea for clemency from you and the Pope.

Papal indulgences for the building of St Peter's are being distributed under your most distinguished name. I am not finding fault here with the declarations (which I have not myself heard) of those who are preaching these indulgences, but I grieve at the utterly false understanding which the people are deriving from them and which they are promoting everywhere amongst the populace. Plainly the unhappy souls believe that if they buy letters of indulgence they are sure of their salvation, and again that souls immediately fly from purgatory when they throw their contribution into the chest. Next, they believe that the grace of indulgences is so great that there is no sin so enormous that it cannot be forgiven, even if (as they say) against all possibility one were to rape the Mother of God. Again, they believe that through these indulgences a man is free from all penalty and guilt. O great God, souls committed to your charge, excellent Father, are thus educated for death! The very strict reckoning which you must render for all these things is thus established and augmented. I cannot therefore remain silent about these matters any longer. For a man can certainly not be sure of his salvation by any gift of a bishop when such certainty does not even come from the infused grace of God; rather the Apostle enjoins us always 'to work out our salvation with fear and trembling' [Phil. 2 : 12]. Again: 'Even the just will hardly be saved [Peter 4 : 18]. Finally, so 'narrow is the way which leads to life' [Matt. 7 : 14] that the Lord through the prophets Amos and Zechariah calls those who are to be saved 'brands snatched from the burning' [Amos 4 : 11; Zech. 3 : 2]. And everywhere the Lord warns of the difficulty of salvation. How, then, can they make the people sure and fearless through their false fables and promises of pardons? Indulgences confer absolutely nothing of value to souls for their salvation or holiness, but remove only an individual external penalty previously imposed canonically.

In short, works of piety and love are infinitely better than indulgences. And yet these are not the things they preach with so much pomp and zeal; indeed, they are silent about these things so that the pardons may be preached, even though the first and only duty of all bishops is this: that the people learn the gospel and the love of Christ. For Christ never ordered that indulgences be preached, but vigorously ordered that the gospel be preached. So what a horror it is, what a danger for a bishop, if while the gospel remains mute he allows literally a din of indulgences amongst his people, and is more concerned with them than with the gospel! Will Christ not say to him: 'You strain at a gnat and swallow a camel' [Matt. 23 : 24]?

To compound the matter further, my revered Father in the Lord, it is stated in the commissioners' instructions issued under your paternal title (but surely without your fatherly Reverence's knowledge and consent) that one of the principal graces is that inestimable gift of God by which a man is reconciled to God and all the punishments of purgatory are blotted out; and again, that contrition is not necessary for those who redeem souls or buy confessional letters.

But what can I do, most excellent prelate and illustrious prince, except beg you, most reverend Father, through our Lord Jesus Christ to deign at least to subject the matter to the scrutiny of your paternal concern, to remove the instruction booklet entirely, and to impose another form of preaching on the preachers of pardons, lest perhaps someone should emerge who by publishing books would confound them and their instructions, thereby bringing the sharpest censure on your illustrious Highness, an outcome from which I certainly shrink in horror, and yet I fear it will come unless help arrives quickly.

I ask your most illustrious Grace to deign to accept these loyal duties of my insignificant rank in a princely and episcopal way, that is, very mercifully; just as I for my part render them with a heart completely loyal and dedicated to your fatherly Reverence. For I, too, am a part of your flock. May the Lord Jesus guard your fatherly Reverence eternally! Amen. From Wittenberg, Eve of All Saints', 1517. If your fatherly Reverence please, you could look at these disputation Theses of mine to see what a dubious thing is the view of indulgences which they are disseminating as entirely certain.

Your unworthy son,

Martin Luther
Augustinian, by calling
Doctor of Sacred Theology.

II.1.E   Tetzel and his fellow Dominicans immediately struck back. At his
elevation to an honorary doctorate in January, 1518, Tetzel published a set of 95 Countertheses, but in a letter to Lang on March
21, 1518, Luther described what happened when the bookseller
from Halle brought copies to Wittenberg. (Latin text in Br 1,
154–155: 64; also translated in part in Smith I, 74 f.)

To his Reverend Father Johann Lang, STL, prior of the Augustinian Eremites at Erfurt, duly submitting himself in the Lord.

Jesus.

Greetings. Most Reverend Father, I had sent you several fascicles of Carlstadt's exposition of the book *Of the Spirit and the Letter*, as I also did to some others, and since my memory is confused I have no idea how many I showed to whom! So if you have seen them all, you ought to have nine—A, B, C, Cc, Ccc, Di, D, E, F; if fewer, write back and I shall ask for them, as we do have impressions of this much. For Dr Carlstadt was brought down, and is still laid low, by fever; he is there-fore interrupting and suspending his work.

The hawkers of pardons are fulminating against me wondrously from their platform, until they are finally running out of monstrous stories with which to label me. They are adding threats in which they promise the people that I will most certainly be burnt, one says within a fort-night, another says within a month; they are issuing counter-propositions against me; so much so that I am frightened that soon they will burst with the multitude and magnitude of their ire. As a result everyone is urging me not to go to Heidelberg, in case what they cannot achieve against me by force they will perhaps succeed in achieving by trickery. Nevertheless, I shall do my obedient duty and go on foot, and, God willing, I shall pass through Erfurt; but do not wait for me since I shall *scarcely* leave until three days after Quasimodogenti Sunday.[1] Our Prince, who supports our whole programme of theological study with astonishing warmth, unasked took Carlstadt and myself decisively into his own protection, and will by no means allow them to drag me to Rome, which really excruciates those that know about it!

However, to forewarn you in case some rumour has perhaps reached you about the burning of Tetzel's Theses, and so that no one will embroider the account unduly (as is usually the case), this is the story: The students, who are remarkably tired of such sophistic, antiquated scholarship but ravenous for the Holy Bible, and perhaps also anxious to gain my favour, when they learned that a man had arrived from Halle, sent by Tetzel the author of the Theses, they immediately gathered and terrorised the man for daring to bring such things here. Some of them bought copies, but others just snatched them and they burned all the remaining copies, almost eight hundred of them, having spread the word and given notice that if anyone wanted to be present at the burning and pyre of Tetzel's Theses he should come to the square at two o'clock; and this happened without the knowledge of the Prince, the Senate, the Rector, or any of us. Certainly I and everyone else were displeased by this injury done to the man by our charges. I am without blame, but I am afraid the whole thing will be attributed to me. A huge story is being made out of the incident everywhere, and their indignation is all the greater, not without justice. I do not know what the outcome will be, except that my perilous situation is made even more perilous by it.

Everybody claims that Dr Konrad Wimpina is the author of Tetzel's Theses, and I certainly think that is the case. I am sending you one snatched from the fire, so that you can see how they rave against me. For the rest, our school is proceeding in the hope, which we expect to realise very shortly, that we will have lectures in two or even three languages, on Pliny, mathematics, Quintillian, and some other excellent subjects, and the useless courses in Petrus Hispanus, Tartaretus, and Aristotle will be thrown out. Moreover, the Prince approves of this scheme and it has now been received for discussion in his council. Commend me to the fathers and brothers. I salute Father Usingen, and Father Johann Nathin too. Wittenburg, St Benedict's Day, 1518.

Brother Martin Luther.

[1] The first Sunday after Easter (Low Sunday), from the opening words of the Roman introit for the day, *Quasi modo geniti*, 'As newborn babes ...' (I Peter 2:2).

II.1.F   Tetzel's Countertheses, the object of this student demonstration,
were drawn up for him by an old rival of the Wittenberg faculty,
Dr Konrad Koch (known as Wimpina). The words in italics are
drawn directly from Luther's Theses. (Latin text in W. Köhler,
Dokumente zum Ablasstreit, Tübingen und Leipzig 1902, pp.
128 ff.)

1. *Our Lord Jesus Christ,* who wanted the sacraments of the new law
to be binding upon all men after his passion and ascension, also wanted
to teach all men those sacraments before his passion through his own
plainest preaching. Therefore anyone who says: *When Christ preached,
'be penitent', he intended by this interior penitence and the exterior
mortification of the flesh,* in such a way that he cannot also teach or
conclude that the sacrament of penance, and its component parts confession and satisfaction, are equally obligatory—he is in error.

2. Indeed, it is no help if *inner repentance* also *produces outward
mortification,* if confession and satisfaction are not also present by deed
or by vow.

3. Since God will not allow a fault to go unrequited, this satisfaction
is made through a penalty or its equivalent in the divine acceptance.

4. Whether this satisfaction is imposed by priests, *by their own
authority or that of the canons,* or whether it is something demanded by
divine justice, in both cases it is liable to payment here or in purgatory.

5. Just as no one is bound to repeat a duly-made confession of the
same sins (except in a few cases), and just as neither a cleric nor the
pope can demand that one repeat a confession however useful this
might be, so no one that has been absolved is bound to repeat a satis-
factory *outward penalty,* once duly discharged, for the same sins. To
urge the contrary is to err.

6. None the less, one is bound as long as one lives to grieve inwardly
by act or by habit, and always to detest the sin remitted, and not to be
without fear about the propitiation of sins.

7. This penalty, imposed because of sins regretted and confessed, the
pope is able to remit entirely through indulgences, whether it is imposed
by himself or by a priest, whether *by his own authority or by canon,* or
even if it is demanded by divine justice—to contradict this is to err.

8. But even if every penalty incurred as retribution for sins may be
remitted through indulgences, yet it is a mistake to think that therefore a
penalty which is curative and preservative is removed, since no time of
release is offered against that penalty.

9. Therefore, however much a man can be truly and completely
released through indulgences—and anyone who denies that it can be so
arranged is wrong—yet by no means ought he to neglect works of satisfaction as long as he lives, inasmuch as they are curative of the remnants
of sin, preservative from future sins, and meritorious.

10. As the Mosaic sacraments are merely rudimentary, neither removing guilt nor justifying, so the priests of the Jews possess neither the keys nor the authority and are thus unable to remit any guilt.

11. But the sacraments of Christians accomplish the grace which they signify, and hence they also justify their recipients. And Christian priests possess the true authority and the keys, and by them they are able to remit guilt.

12. They do this not only by *approving and declaring*, as the priests of the old law and the sons of Aaron used to do for lepers, but also by performing the act as ministers, instruments, and disposers.

13. Indeed, just as God possesses the keys of authority, and Christ the keys of supremacy, so the Christian priest has the keys of administration. Therefore anyone who says that the pope or even the least of priests has no power over guilt except *by approving* and *declaring* is in error.

14. In fact, he errs who does not believe that the least Christian priest has more power over sin than the whole synagogue formerly possessed.

15. Furthermore, he errs who thinks that Christ cannot remit sins or save a man without priestly confession, *approbation*, or *declaration* by means of his own key's superiority, in whose exercise he has not bound his power to the sacraments. . . .

93. For those who have confessed and are contrite and have been released through indulgences, *peace, peace* is a fact since every retributive penalty has been taken away—to contradict this is to err.

94. But the remnants of one's sins—one's proclivity and ease of relapse—remain; to heal them, so that they do not burst forth in new sins, curative penalties, *crosses* and castigations are demanded.

95. Thus when pardons have been duly obtained, there is *peace, peace* from past retributive penalties. But there remains *the cross, the cross* as a warning against future penalties—whoever denies this has no understanding, but errs and raves.

II.1.G In his *Resolutions* published in mid-1518, Luther gave an extended justification of his Theses on indulgences, and responded specifically to the Tetzel-Wimpina Countertheses. (Latin text in WA 1, 544, 9–33; translated in full in LW 31, 83–252.)

Our babbler in the lion disguise parades in glorious triumph around my sixth and seventh theses. In fact he sings his triumph song about me before the victory! Drawing from that stagnant well of opinions he distinguishes two sorts of punishments, one satisfying and retributive, the other healing and curative—as if we had to believe those who dream up such things even though they prudently hide this distinction from the people, so that the indulgences (or rather the money) do not fall off when the people realise that the punishments they remit are such trifling and sterile retributive (that is, fictional) punishments. So that everyone can see that he does not know what either the old or the new priesthood is, he introduces yet another verbal fog—a distinction of the keys, some of authority, some of supremacy, some of administration. Apparently even our illustrious masters, the inquisitors of heretical distortion and defenders of the catholic faith, have learned nothing except what they sucked from the stale and convoluted questions of the master of the Sentences. They wish, perhaps, that whatever Christ looses with the keys of supremacy in heaven (for he himself looses nothing on earth) will be loosed by God in a heaven above heaven! And so that God in turn may be high priest, another still higher God must be imagined, who will loose everything that God has loosed by his keys of authority in the heaven above heaven! But away with this nonsense: we know only one set of keys, those that have been given upon earth.

Again, they contend: 'He therefore errs who says that the priest of the new law looses only by approving and declaring.' (This, of course, was the rôle of the Jewish priesthood.) O sharpness of intellect and huge weight of erudition! These are plainly men most worthy to examine heretics and to defend the catholic faith—against sticks and stones! How much more accurately did the Apostle Paul assert that the old priesthood consisted in judging lepers, in rectifications and cleansings of the flesh, in food and drink and vestment and festival days and so on! These things all figuratively signified the justification in spirit and the cleansing of the heart which Christ effects in the Church by the ministry of the new priesthood.

II.1.H   The dedicatory epistle to the *Resolutions* was addressed to his superior Staupitz, acknowledging his rôle in shaping the concept of penitence which so decisively influenced him, and seeking Staupitz's mediation with the Pope. (Latin text in WA 1, 525–527; also translated in full in LW 48, 65–70.)

To his reverend and true Father Johann Staupitz, Professor of Sacred Theology, Vicar of the Augustinian Family, his disciple Brother Martin Luther gives both his greeting and himself.

I remember, Reverend Father, amongst your most delightful and salutary stories with which the Lord Jesus used to console me wonderfully, mention was sometimes made of the word 'penitence'. Then we who had grieved for many consciences, and for their tormentors who give endless and intolerable instructions in what they call a method of confession, received you as voice from heaven when you said that there is no true penitence except that which begins from the love of justice and of God, and that what they regard as the goal and consummation of penitence is really its beginning.

This statement of yours pierced me like the sharp arrows of the mighty. And then I began to collate it with passages of Scripture which teach about penitence—behold, what an utterly joyful pastime! Words on every side were joining me in the game and laughing and jumping in plain agreement with your outlook, to the extent that, whereas previously there had been scarcely a word in the whole of Scripture more bitter to me than 'penitence' (even though I sedulously pretended even to God and tried to squeeze out a contrived and coerced love), now nothing sounds sweeter or more agreeable to me than 'penitence'. For the commands of God become sweet when we understand that they are to be read not only in books, but in the wounds of the sweetest Saviour.

After this, it happened that through the zeal and favour of those very learned men who so effectively pass on to us Greek and Hebrew, I learnt that the Greek equivalent is *metanoia*, made up from *meta* and *nous*, that is, from 'after' and 'mind'. Penitence or *metanoia* thus means reconsideration and understanding of one's own evil, accepting the fault and recognising the error. It is impossible that this could happen without a change of disposition and love. All this agrees so well with the Pauline theology that virtually nothing else can illustrate Paul so well—at least in my judgement.

Then I progressed, and I saw that *metanoia* can be derived not only from 'after' and 'mind', but from 'across' and 'mind' (this may be forced, to be sure) so that *metanoia* means a transformation of the mind and the motion. This seemed to suggest not only a change of the disposition, but also the mode of this change, in other words, the grace of God; for that journey of the mind, the truest penitence, is found very often in Holy Writ. Thus Christ revealed that Exodus once symbolised, and long before that Abraham prefigured it when he was first called a 'Hebrew' (that is, 'wayfarer'), as he made his way into Mesopotamia, as Paul of Burgos learnedly teaches. The title of the psalm in which the singer is called 'Idithun', that is, 'one who leads over', has the same force. Holding fast to these discoveries, I dared to think that the people were wrong who attributed so much to works of penitence that they had left us scarcely a scrap of penitence itself, except some formal satisfactions and utterly laborious confessions. In short, they had been led astray by the Latin word, in that 'to do penance' sounds more like an action than a change of attitude, and by no means adequately renders the Greek *metanoein*.

While I was still aglow with this reflection, behold suddenly the din and racket of new bugles of indulgences and trumpets of pardons began around us; yet they did not arouse us to the strenuous effort of doing battle. Briefly, whilst the true doctrine of penitence was neglected, they presumed to magnify in this way not penitence itself, not even the paltriest part of it called satisfaction, but only remission of that paltriest part, as no one had ever heard it magnified before. They were teaching impious, false, and heretical things with such authority (I wanted to say temerity) that anyone who whispered a word against them was immediately a heretic destined for the fire and liable to eternal damnation.

Since I was unable to counteract the insanity of these men by myself, I decided to dissent from them modestly and to call their teachings into doubt, relying on the opinion of all the doctors and of the whole Church that it is better to make satisfaction than to have one's satisfaction remitted (that is, to buy indulgences instead). No one has ever taught anything else. So I disputed—in other words, I brought down on my own head from every source, high, middle, and low as well, as much malice as these zealots for money (oh no! I should have said 'for souls'!) could arouse and promote. So these complete gentlemen, employing the crassest artfulness because they cannot refute what I have said, pretend that the power of the supreme pontiff is violated by my theses.

This is the reason, Reverend Father, that I now step unhappily into the public arena—I who have always been a lover of privacy and prefer to be an onlooker at the grand pageant of the clever men of our age rather than to be looked and laughed at myself. But I see that some wild flowers have to be seen amongst the lettuces and some black has to be set amongst the white, for the sake of charm and prettiness, of course!

I ask, therefore, that you accept these inept explanations of mine and forward them with as much diligence as you can muster to the excellent Pope Leo X, so that they may play some sort of advocate's rôle for me there against the efforts of detractors—not that I want to involve you in my danger: my wish is that these events should bring danger only on myself. Christ will see whether my statements are his or mine; without his consent, the word of the supreme pontiff is no more on his own tongue than the heart of the king is in his own hand [cf. Prov. 21 : 1]. It is this judgement whose announcement I await from the Roman See.

All I can reply to those menacing friends of mine is Reuchlin's remark: 'He who is poor has nothing to fear, since he has nothing to lose.' I neither have possessions nor desire them; the man who loses fame and honour (if I had any) loses them for good; the one thing that remains is my poor weak body, exhausted by constant hardships, and if they take that away, either by force or by guile (in honour of God) they will make me poorer by perhaps one or two hours of this life. Sufficient for me is our sweet redeemer and propitiator, my Lord Jesus Christ, of whom I shall sing as long as I exist: but if someone does not want to sing with me, what is that to me? He may howl by himself if he likes. May the same Lord Jesus preserve you to eternity, my dearest Father. Wittenburg, Trinity 1518.

II.1.1   Meanwhile, a former friend who was to become Luther's most vocal adversary, Johann Eck of the University of Ingolstadt,

wrote some critical notes called *Obelisks* on Luther's propositions.
Luther received a copy from Wenceslas Link in Nürnberg, and
feeling betrayed sent back some outspoken *Asterisks* in response.
(Latin text in WA 1, 281–282.)

Since you have given me the *Obelisks* which our Eck has contrived
against my Theses, it seemed fitting to run through them one at a time
and to add some *Asterisks* to the arguments where they are a little
obscure. With this clarifying light shed on them, if you care to share
them with Eck, even he will easily understand how brash it is to condemn ideas that are strange, especially without understanding them, and
how it is by far the most insidious and iniquitous thing to speak with
such extremely venomous biterness against a friend who was not forewarned, and who expected from a friend that everything would be better
understood, or at least investigated. But the Scripture is true: 'All men
are liars.' We are men, and men we remain. And so he says:

ECK: I do not want to pursue the minutiae or matters which can be
attacked scholastically in the subject-matter of the current dispute
about indulgences, since in this case I should have first attacked the
conclusion.

LUTHER: With such a generous (I shall not say proud) preface he
addresses the subject—except that he modestly says 'attack', rather than
'vanquish', the small and scholastic issues. Perhaps he will vanquish the
larger issues! Who would not be terrified by his trumpetings? But I was
reminded of Horace's remark: 'What can this boaster say to match the
size of his mouth?'[2] I scarcely restrained a laugh. He does not want to
dispute or to join battle scholastically, an expression from which I get
the strong impression that our Eck contrived his *Obelisks* during the so-
called carnival days, wearing his cleverness as a mask. For throughout
the mess of *Obelisks* there is nothing from Holy Writ, nothing from the
church fathers, nothing from the canons, but everything is wholly
scholastic and wholly conjectural, he is making up sheer fantasy—in
short, the very things against which I am disputing. So if I too wanted
to play the philosopher, I should scatter all this gossamer of his with a
single breath by repeating his own master's injunction: 'Begging the
question is the besetting vice of disputation and argument.'[3] For I was
hoping that he would fight me on the basis of the Bible or the church
fathers or the canons. But it is with the chaff and husks of Scotus,
Gabriel, and the rest of the scholastics (his belly is stuffed quite full of
them) that he opposes me who now at last refute them. Nevertheless, let

[2] Horace, *Ars Poetica* 138.
[3] 'His own master' was Aristotle: see *Topica* VIII, 12.

us listen how this rhetorical gentleman, pretending not to oppose the first conclusion, none the less opposes it. For he says:

ECK: For since 'the kindom of heaven' in Christ's terminology seems to signify the present church and the fullness of time for the gospel then drawing near, it is not obvious how penitence could occupy the whole life of the faithful.

LUTHER: This is a scholastic (that is, ludicrous and self-deluding) argument. I do not know whether it is by the logic of reason or by the logic of faith that he arrives at this conclusion—that the kingdom of heaven is now, therefore the whole life of the faithful is not penitence—as if there were even one of the men in that kingdom who does not sin persistently, and thus does not persistently need penitence. The conclusion which follows from this sort of penitence is the basis of my statement. But perhaps Eck is chattering about sacramental or ritual penitence. However, to say that man is sometimes without sin and thus does not need penitence (granted that Bonaventure, who was sometimes wrong, has said so), St Augustine dealing with the heretical Donatist party says in many places: 'Rather, it is only the faithful who are penitent. . . .'

II.1.J   Whilst Luther received support from his fellow-Augustinians at Heidelberg in April, 1518 (see II.2.E below), the machinations of the Dominicans against him grew more vicious. They forged a set of theses on excommunication purporting to be Luther's, and a fictional violent attack on Rome's rapacity. In July, 1518, Luther innocently stepped into a trap at Dresden, as he later described to Spalatin in a letter of January 14, 1519. (Latin text in Br 1, 301–302: 135; also translated in part in Smith I, 149 ff.)

Jesus.
    Greetings. The fact that some people claim that I was conquered at the banquet in Dresden should not surprise you, my Spalatin—for a long time they have been saying whatever else they liked! Actually I, together with our friend Johann Lang and our prior at Dresden, were virtually forced by Jerome Emsser, rather than invited, to a late-starting drinking party. Here, where I thought I was amongst friends, I soon discovered that I had fallen right into a trap. There was one little Leipzig teacher, a slip of a Thomist, who was marvellously confident he knew everything. This fellow, who was full of spleen against me, received me amicably at first, but eventually when an argument began inveighed against me bitterly and noisily. All the while, unknown to me, the friar who was the district preacher was standing outside the door listening to everything; and I heard later that he boasted that he was fit to be tied, and could scarcely contain himself from bursting in and spitting in my

face and heaping every foul name upon me, he was so tormented to hear me thus refute Thomas for that little teacher. He is the same man who even today is boasting everywhere that I was so overcome that I was unable to reply in either Latin or the vernacular. Because we were arguing (as usual) in a mixture of German and Latin he has confidently announced that I do not know Latin! Anyway, the argument was about the trifling nonsense of Aristotle and Thomas. I demonstrated that neither Thomas nor any of the Thomists had understood a single chapter of Aristotle. In the long run, when he was becoming boastful, I asked him to gather all the power of his Thomistic erudition and define for me what it means to fulfil the commands of God. 'I am sure,' I said, 'that there is no Thomist who knows that.' This fellow, still remembering his crudities from junior school, exclaimed: 'Give him some fodder!' (which is what they call a play-leader's pay). What else could someone say who did not know anything else? We broke up in laughter at this insulting answer and left.

Later the Prior of Dresden wrote to me how they were bragging, and how in the Prince's court they were also denigrating me as unlearned, proud, and I do not know how many other names. Moreover, he said they were twisting the sermon which I preached in the castle into every guise except the truth. I had adduced an entirely theological story about three virgins; later they prattled in the Prince's court that the three virgins had been disparaged by me. In short: I have first-hand experience of this generation of vipers who want to do everything and are able to do nothing, imagining that it detracts from their own glory, if they let anything at all of mine go unreproved. Despising their masquerades, I wrote back that the Prior should keep his peace, and should let my Cain, my Judas remain just mine. But then Jerome Emsser earnestly exonerated himself. Similarly when he met me most recently at Leipzig, he swore that he had not plotted against me with any ambush. I replied that I despised such ados about nothing, as I do today. If they are so learned, they have type and paper, let them publish something and let them display the glory of their magnificent erudition. My sermon was about St James the Great, whose feast day it was, on the gospel: 'You know not what you ask' [Matt. 20 : 22]. Accordingly, I rebuked the stupid vows men make when they are praying to God, and taught what a Christian man ought to ask for. . . .

Martin Luther.

II.1.K   Luther's summons to Rome as a rebel and heretic was modified for reasons of political expedience, and Cardinal Cajetan, papal legate in Germany, was given summary powers to demand a recantation. Luther later published a full report of their October meeting (*Proceedings at Augsburg* in LW 31, 259–292), but sent

this graphic account to Spalatin on the day the meetings abruptly
ended, October 14, 1518. (Latin text in Br 1, 214–215: 99; also
translated in full in LW 48, 83–87.)

Jesus.

Greetings. I write with some reluctance to our illustrious Prince, my
Spalatin, so please, as one close to him, take care of transmitting this to
our most clement Prince. The lord Legate is now dealing with me, or
rather against me, for the fourth day in a row. He promises, of course,
that he will do everything leniently and paternally for the good name
of the illustrious Prince, but in fact he does everything by sheer inflex-
ible force alone. He has been unwilling that I should answer publicly in
disputation, and he has been unwilling to dispute with me in private.
There was just one thing which he repeated over and over: 'Recant,
acknowledge your error, the Pope wants it so and not otherwise, whether
you like it or not!' and other things of that sort. But most strongly of all
he pressed me with the decretal of Clement VI which begins *Unigenitus*.
'Look, look,' he said, 'you see here the Pope rules that the merits of
Christ are the treasury of indulgences, Do you believe it or do you not
believe it?' He would not permit any statement or response, but relied
on the force of his language and shouting. At last, barely prevailed upon
by the pleas of many, he gave permission for me to submit an argument
in writing. I did this today and Dr Philipp von Feilitzsch, admitted to
represent the title and office of the Prince, was present to submit the
Prince's request a second time. Eventually, he thrust my pages away
with contempt and again clamoured for a recantation. And he thought
he had beaten me and put me in check with a long-winded discourse
drawn from the fairy stories of St Thomas. I started to speak almost
ten times, but as often as I did he began to thunder again and kept sole
control. Eventually I began to shout too, and said: 'If it can be demonstrated that that decretal teaches that the merits of Christ are the
treasury of indulgences, I shall recant as you wish.' At this, O God,
what gesturing and jeering there was! Suddenly he grabbed the book,
and read with breathless excitement until he came to the passage where
it says that Christ by his passion acquired a treasure, and so on. At this
I said: 'Oh! Reverend Father, notice the word "acquired"! If Christ by
his merits acquired a treasure, then his merits are not the treasure: but
the treasure is what his merits merited, that is, the keys of the Church.
Therefore my conclusion is correct.' This abruptly threw him into confusion, and since he did not want to seem confused, he, prudent man,
passed vigorously on to other subjects and wanted to forget this. But I,
quite irreverently to be sure, burst out passionately: 'Let your Reverence
not imagine we Germans are also deficient in grammar! It is one thing
to *be* a treasure, quite another to *acquire* a treasure.' And this had the
effect of shattering his confidence, even though he was still clamouring

for a recantation. I left when he said to me: 'Go away and do not come back to me any more unless you are prepared to recant.' Lo and behold, soon after dinner he called to him our reverend Dr Staupitz and plied him with all sorts of flattery to urge me to recant (I was not present), also asserting that I did not have a better friend than himself; and although Staupitz replied that he had urged me, and was still urging me today, to submit humbly to the Church (as I myself had earlier declared in front of them all), he nevertheless claimed that in his own opinion he was no match for me in sacred letters and ability, so he suggested the Legate himself, as the representative of the Pope and all our local prelates, should urge me in person! The final outcome was that he is drawing up articles to guide my recantation, a process I am supposed to relish. And this is where the matter stands. But I have neither hope nor confidence in him. However, I am daily preparing my appeal, since I certainly do not intend to recant a syllable. And I shall publish the response which I offered to him so that he will be confounded throughout the world if he proceeds, as he has begun, by force. Farewell in haste. Augsburg, St Calixtus's Day, 1518.

Friar Martin Luther, Augustinian.

II.1.L   As the Elector Frederick considered Cajetan's demand that he banish or surrender Luther, the university added its voice to Luther's own appeal for a fair hearing in this petition to Frederick. The rediscovered first draft of this letter reveals that it was largely phrased by Luther himself! (Latin text in DB 4, 585–586.)

Jesus. Grace and peace from our Lord Jesus Christ, with his commendation! Most illustrious and clement Prince, venerable Sir: Friar Martin Luther, Master of Arts and Theology and regular lecturer, a noble and most celebrated member of our university, has related to us how the very reverend Lord Legate of the Apostolic See, Thomas, Cardinal Presbyter of St Sixtus, has written to your illustrious Lordship and has made plans either to send the said Martin to the city of Rome or to banish him from the country on account of certain propositions disputed by him and offered to the supreme pontiff some time ago. In addition, he also described how he had offered himself for public disputation or for private reply by letter. He had begged that the errors in his writings should be indicated to him by direct arguments and by the authority of Scripture and of the holy fathers. Enlightened by this means, he could have seen and recognised his errors. Yet he was unable to obtain any of these things, but said that he was simply placed under demand to recant his erroneous statements, nor was there shown to him that faithful pastoral duty which should give a reason to one who asks for it, and which is commanded to be applied not only to those who are willing to learn, but even to the unwilling, favourably or unfavourably. He has therefore asked and obtained that we should intercede with your illustrious Lordship and should beseech you, as far as your illustrious Lordship deigns, to write to the said very reverend Lord Legate or to the supreme pontiff himself, and graciously intervene so that the articles and points of error in his writings may be pointed out to him and that either arguments or authorities be adduced by which he may recognise that he has erred, and thus recant. Moreover, that he should not be forced to condemn his opinions before he knows which of them deserve condemnation. This was the practice of the ancient Church, and the example of the fathers also teaches that they urged the correction of errors by citing reasons and authorities. However, they did not condemn anyone's statements simply by their own assertion and authority. Therefore, most illustrious Prince, even though we are unable to reject this man's request (since believing his account we regard it as most just), it is nevertheless our desire above all that he should refer the honour of the holy Church simply and directly to your illustrious Lordship and to the supreme pontiff. Nor do we advise any other course. Finally, may we add that if we discover this man to have concluded wrongly in any respect, we shall be the first to hold him a stranger? For we regard nothing as more venerable than the judgement of the holy Roman Church. Accordingly, this is all we ask, most excellent Prince and sole support of this our school now flourishing by the favour of God and your efforts, since your illustrious Lordship may not wish to be burdened; and then he will display by letter his most humble and devoted reverence for the Roman Church (a reverence we know he will embrace as firmly as possible without any instruction from us). What is more, especially for the sake of the revelation of truth and the purity of effort, this man's petition should not be ignored: it is proper to ask for light for him whom they say is in darkness, especially since he does not himself deny that he is in darkness. Rather, he hopes for that most just and for Christians most worthy discipline, so that when the light has shone in and testimonies of the truth have been given, he may be led out of the darkness and not thrust down into even deeper darkness. Not because he expects that the most holy lord Leo X would ever do this, but because he abhors the pursuit of wickedness or the devising of anything under the name of the holy Church which the Church would do its best to be rid of, if it knew about it. May the Lord Jesus Christ preserve your illustrious Lordship in happiness for us and His whole Church for a long time. Amen. Wittenberg, November 22, 1518. Signed: The Rector, Masters, and Doctors of your Illustrious Eminence's university school of Wittenberg.

II.1.M Frederick was not prepared to abandon his protégé, but was prepared to allow von Miltitz to seek an accommodation. On January 5 or 6. 1519, Luther reported to his patron the result of his meeting with the nuncio. However, Luther soon concluded that Miltitz's agreement had been breached. German text in Br 1, 293–294: 130; and translated in full in LW 48, 97–98.)

Most illustrious, high-born Prince, gracious Lord!

Let me humbly inform your Grace, the Elector, that Sir Charles von Miltitz and I have finally reached an agreement, and have concluded our negotiations with two articles:

First, a common injunction has been placed upon both parties, and both sides will be forbidden to preach, write, and dispute further about this subject.

Secondly, Sir Charles is to write shortly to the Holy Father, the Pope, describing all aspects of the situation as he has found them, and also to see that his Holiness the Pope commissions some learned bishop to adjudicate the question and to point out the erroneous articles which I should recant. And when I have thus been apprised of my error, it will be my duty and pleasure to recant them gladly and do nothing to diminish the honour and power of the Holy Roman Church.

II.1.N   Over many months, Eck negotiated with Carlstadt and Luther for a decisive public disputation, finally held at Leipzig in July. Eck skilfully manœuvred Luther into a minor rôle at first, but when the two leading figures did confront each other, Eck elicited Luther's most extreme challenge to papal authority. Here is Luther's account to Spalatin. (Latin text in Br 1, 422: 187; also translated in full, with the disputation articles, in LW 31, 313–325.)

. . . For the second week Eck debated with me. First he argued very bitterly about the primacy of the Roman pontiff. He rested the strength of his case on the statements: 'You are Peter' and 'Feed my sheep, follow me, and strengthen your brethren', and many additional authorities from the fathers. What I replied you will see shortly. Then with the discussion coming down to my last proposition, the whole issue rested on the Council of Constance, which had condemned the article of Hus who said that the papacy, which claimed to exist by divine right, really existed by virtue of the emperor. At this Eck pressed in boldly as if he were on his own ground, reproaching me with the Bohemians and upbraiding me as an open heretic and patron of the Bohemian heretics. For as a sophist he is no less impudent than rash. In a marvellous fashion these accusations titillated the Leipzig people more than the debate itself. In rebuttal I cited the Greeks for the past one thousand years and the ancient fathers, neither of whom had been under the power of the Roman pontiff, even though I did not deny him a primacy

D

of honour. And last we disputed about the authority of the Council, too. I openly declared that some articles had been impiously condemned, articles which were taught by the plain, clear words of Paul, Augustine, and even Christ himself. But at this the viper swelled up and magnified my heinous deed and almost went wild, to the adulation of the Leipzig crowd. Finally, I proved from the words of the Council itself that not all the articles there were condemned as heretical and erroneous, so he had accomplished nothing with all his proofs. And there the question rests.

For the third week penitence, purgatory, indulgences, and any priest's power to absolve were debated between us (since Eck was not anxious to debate with Carlstadt, but was after only me). Indulgences really did go down completely: he agreed with me on almost every score, and his defence of indulgences turned ridiculous and slippery, whereas I had hoped this would be the high point of the dispute. Finally he stated his position in public sermons in such a way that even the common folk realised he had no stake in indulgences. He is even said to have declared that if I had not disputed the power of the Pope he could easily have agreed with me in every respect. . . .

II.1.o Claiming victory, Eck proceeded to Rome to press for curial action against Luther. In June, 1520, Leo X's bull *Exsurge Domine* gave Luther sixty days in which to recant, and condemned all his writings to be burned. At the end of this period, Luther dramatically burned the bull, and his excommunication was decreed to be final. The break was complete. (Latin text in *Bullarium diplomatum et privilegiorum s. Romanorum pontificum*, Turin edition, Vol. V, pp. 748 ff.)

Leo, bishop, servant of the servants of God, for perpetual recollection.

Arise, Lord, and judge your cause! Be mindful of the trespasses against you which are committed every day by foolish men; incline your ear to our prayers, for foxes have arisen who seek to demolish the vineyard where you have trod the winepress alone; and when you were about to ascend to the Father you committed the care, government, and administration of this vineyard to Peter, its only head and your vicar, and to his successors as the image of the Church Triumphant. A roaring boar of the forest is trying to devastate it, a single wild beast is devouring it. . . .

For a long time now we have heard from the reliable testimony of worthy men and widespread public report something that we are scarcely able to express without anguish and agony of soul. Indeed truly—oh grief!—we have seen and read with our own eyes many and various errors, some of them already condemned by the councils and rulings of our predecessors, expressly containing even the heresies of the Greeks and Bohemians; others in turn heretical or false or scandalous or offensive to pious ears or seductive to simple minds, from the cultivators of a false faith who covet worldly glory by their arrogant prying, and contrary to the apostle's teaching desire to be wiser than they ought; whose chattering (as Jerome says) is faithless, lacking Scriptural authority, even if they seem to bolster their perverse teaching with divine (though ill-interpreted) testimonies; from whose eyes the fear of God has departed at the prompting of the enemy of the human race; errors newly contrived and now spread by lesser men throughout the renowned nation of Germany. That this should have happened there is all the more painful to us because both we and our predecessors have always borne love for that nation in our hearts. . . . Therefore, for the sake of the responsibility of the pastoral office we bear, entrusted to us by divine grace, we can by no means tolerate the pestilential poison of the aforesaid errors any longer. And by these presents we have caused some of those errors to be included in the following list. . . . [Here follow 41 articles declared to be erroneous.]

Above all, since these stated errors and many others are contained in the books or writings of Martin Luther, we similarly condemn, reprove, and totally reject the said books and all the writings of the said Martin, whether in Latin or other tongues, in which one or more of these errors are to be found. We repeat, we want them condemned, reproved, and rejected for all time, forbidding each and every faithful Christian, man or woman, in the power of the holy obedience and under the threat of every punishment, to presume to read, protect, preach, praise, print, or defend such writings, books, sermons, or broadsheets or any chapter of their contents, in person or by agent or agents, directly or indirectly, tacitly or expressly, publicly or secretly, or presume in any way to retain them in their homes or in any other place, public or private. Rather, immediately upon the publication of this decree, they are to be searched out diligently, wherever they are, by the ordinaries and other officers named above, and publicly and solemnly burnt in the presence of clergy and people, under pain of each and every aforementioned penalty.

As for Martin himself, dear God! what have we neglected, what have we not done, what fatherly love have we omitted in order to recall him from his errors? For after first summoning him, we then invited him in a desire to deal with him more gently, and both by various treatises drawn up with our legate and by our own letters exhorted him to abandon his aforementioned errors, and with the offer of safe-conduct and the necessary funds for the journey to come here without any of the fear or anxiety which perfect love casts out, and to talk with us not in hiding but openly and face to face, after the example of our Saviour and the Apostle Paul. Had he done so, he would certainly (we believe) have changed his heart and acknowledged his errors; and he would not have found in the Roman curia as many errors as he so severely censures, paying more heed than he ought to the empty rumours of spiteful men; and in a clearer light we should have taught him that the holy Roman pontiffs, our predecessors, whom he injuriously impugns without any moderation, never erred in the canons and rulings which he is trying to erode. For as the prophet says: 'Is there not a balm in Gilead? Is there not a physician there?' [Jer. 8 : 22].

But he persistently refused to obey, and spurning our citation and each and every one of these efforts he disdained to come, and to the present day has stood his ground arrogantly and with a heart impervious to criticism for more than a year; and what is worse, piling evils upon evils, in full knowledge of our citation he has burst out, raising his voice in a rash appeal to a future council, contrary to the ruling of our predecessors Pius II and Julius II warning that those who thus appeal are to bear the punishments due to heretics. In any case, it is vain for one who openly professes that he does not trust councils to appeal to a council for help. . . .

We therefore wholeheartedly exhort and beseech Martin himself and all his adherents, patrons and protectors, by the bowels of mercy of our God and the sprinkling of the blood of our Lord Jesus Christ, by and through whom the human race is redeemed and Holy Mother Church edified, that they cease disturbing the peace of this Church for which the Saviour prayed so urgently to the Father, and abstain completely from the pernicious errors we have named; and if they comply effectively, and notify us by sworn affidavits that they have complied, they will discover in us a response of fatherly love and a flowing spring of gentleness and mercy.

Nevertheless, from now on we command the said Martin for the time being to desist altogether from preaching and the preaching office. Otherwise, if perchance the love of justice and virtue does not draw Martin back from his sin, and the hope of indulgence does not lead him to repentance, in order that fear of the penalties may drive him to discipline, by these presents we charge and warn the said Martin, and his adherents, accomplices, protectors and patrons, in the power of the holy obedience and under each and every stated punishment incurred by him; we give clear forewarning and command that within sixty days . . . Martin, his said accomplices, protectors, adherents and patrons are to desist altogether from their errors and from preaching, publishing, and promulgating them, and also from defending or issuing books or writings about them or any part of them; and they are to burn or have burnt each and every book and writing in any way containing some or all of these errors. Martin himself is also to revoke entirely his errors and assertions, and is to certify this revocation to us within sixty days. . . .

Let no man whatsoever infringe this our decree of damnation, repro-
bation, rejection, resolution, declaration, inhibition, will, mandate, exhortation, obsecration, requital, warning, assignment, withdrawal, condemnation, subjection, excommunication and anathema, or by brash
daring contravene it. But if any man presume to tamper with it, let him
know that he shall incur the wrath of Almighty God and his blessed
apostles Peter and Paul.

Given at St Peter's, Rome, June 15 in the year of the incarnation of
the Lord 1520, in the eighth year of our pontificate.

II.2   THE DEVELOPMENT OF LUTHER'S THEOLOGY: JUSTIFICATION

The mature shape of Luther's Reformation doctrine was forged in the
heat of the Church struggle. It was not yet complete when the indulgence
dispute began; and Luther himself looked back with chagrin on what he
had published before 1520. Yet the foundations of the later theology
were already well laid even in the earliest lectures on the Psalms (1513–
15). He knew his sins were forgiven; he knew that 'the justice of God'
could mean the justice by which God justifies the sinner; he was
already developing a fresh new approach to exposition which broke the
shackles of allegorical exegesis. The new power of his biblical insight
was displayed in his lectures on Romans (1515–16), Galatians (1516–
17), and Hebrews (1517). His deeply empirical stress on the humility
of faith which accepts God's negative judgement, but finds God's Yes!
hidden beneath his No!, was the burning motive behind his onslaught
on the indulgence traffic and the deep affinity he felt with the German
mystical tradition. Yet the shock of the Church's response brought a
new clarity on the alien character of the justice of Christ by faith, and a
resulting rejection of purgatory, the treasury of merits, the intercession
of the saints, and the medieval doctrine of the sacraments. It is not surprising that Luther regarded his pre-1520 publications as 'a crude and
inchoate muddle'.

II.2.A   At the end of his life, Luther was persuaded against his will to
issue an authorised edition of his earliest works. He used the
autobiographical *Preface* of 1545 as an opportunity to issue a
caveat lector against any reliance on his first books. (Latin text in
WA 54, 179–187; also translated in full in LW 34, 327 ff.; SW 1,
17 ff.)

Martin Luther greets the sincere reader.
I have resisted long and hard the people who have wanted an edition of
my books, or better, my confused lucubrations. . . . The fact that these
events took place in no particular order had the (quite unavoidable)

effect that my books are a crude and inchoate muddle, which now I myself cannot easily put in order. . . .

Above all I pray the sincere reader, and I pray for the sake of our Lord Jesus Christ himself, that he will read these things judiciously, with much pity. He should realise that I was a monk and a raving papist when I initiated that cause, so drunk—indeed submerged—by the pope's dogmas that I should have been quite prepared, if I could, to slay all who detracted even one syllable of obedience from the pope, or to give help and consent to their slayers. . . . Accordingly, you will find in these earlier writings of mine how I very humbly conceded to the pope many weighty matters which in later years, including the present, I regard and execrate as the height of blasphemy and abomination. Therefore, dear reader, you will ascribe this error (or, as my slanders say, contradiction) to the times and to my inexperience. For I was alone at first, and certainly quite inept and uninstructed in prosecuting such great matters. God himself is witness that I stumbled into these turmoils by accident, not by intention or desire.

Thus in the year 1517 indulgences were being sold—I meant to say promulgated—in these areas for very shameful gain. At that time I was a preacher, a junior professor of theology as they say, and I began to dissuade the people: I urged them not to listen to the preaching of the indulgence hawkers; they had better things to do. And I felt sure that in doing so I should have a protector in the pope, on whose trustworthiness I relied strongly at that stage. For his decrees very clearly condemn immoderation on the parts of the quaestors, as he calls the indulgence preachers.

Shortly afterwards I wrote two letters. One went to Albrecht, the Archbishop of Mainz, who got half of the money from the indulgences. (The pope got the other half, which I did not know at the time.) The other went to the ordinary of the district (as he is called), Jerome, the bishop of Brandenburg. I begged them to stop the impudence and blasphemy of the salesmen. But this poor little friar could be treated with contempt! Ignored, I published the Theses, and at the same time a *Sermon on Indulgences* in German, and a little later the *Explanations*, in which, in honour of the pope, I argued that indulgences were not indeed to be condemned, but good works of love were much more desirable. But this was to smash heaven and consume the earth with fire! I was accused by the pope, a summons to Rome was issued against me, and the whole papacy rose up against me alone. . . .

In the course of that year [1519], I had returned to the Psalter to interpret it a second time. I was confident of the fact that I was more practised after treating in lectures St Paul's letters to the Romans and Galatians, and the letter to the Hebrews. I had suddenly been possessed with an unusually ardent desire to understand Paul in the Epistle to the

Romans. It was certainly not cold blood about the heart, but just one phrase in chapter one—'in the gospel the justice of God is revealed' [Rom. 1 : 17]—that had so far stood in my way. I hated that phrase 'justice of God', which according to the usage and custom of all the teachers I had to understand as what they called the formal or active justice with which God himself is just and punishes unjust sinners.

But for myself, even though I was living irreproachably as a monk, I felt that before God I was a sinner with an utterly disquieted conscience, and I could not believe that He was placated by my satisfactions. I did not love, indeed I hated, that God who punished sinners; and with a monstrous, silent, if not blasphemous, murmuring I fumed against God, and said: 'As if it is not enough that wretched sinners are eternally damned by original sin and crushed by every sort of calamity through the law of the decalogue, without having God add sorrow upon sorrow by the gospel, that the gospel too should threaten us with his justice and wrath!' Thus a fierce battle raged in my troubled conscience. Yet I knocked persistently upon Paul in this passage, most earnestly wanting to know what St Paul intended. At last as I meditated night and day, God had mercy on me. I realised the significance of the context, namely: 'In it the justice of God is revealed, *as it is written, "He who through faith is just shall live."* ' I began to understand that 'the justice of God' meant that justice by which the just man lives through God's gift, namely by faith. This is what it means: the justice of God is revealed by the gospel, a passive justice with which the merciful God justifies us by faith, as it is written: 'He who through faith is just shall live.' Here I felt that I was altogether born again and had entered paradise itself through open gates. Immediately the whole face of Scripture was totally transformed for me. I ran through the Scriptures from memory, looking for analogies in other terms, such as 'the work of God', by which he works in us; 'the power of God,' by which he makes us strong; 'the wisdom of God', by which he makes us wise; 'the strength of God', 'the salvation of God', 'the glory of God'.

Now I exalted in that sweetest phrase with as much love as I had previously hated the words 'justice of God'. So this verse in Paul was truly for me the gate to paradise. Afterwards I read Augustine's *On the Spirit and the Letter*, and contrary to expectation I found that he also interprets the justice of God in a similar manner: the justice in which God clothes us when he justifies us.[4] And even though this was still expressed imperfectly, and concerning imputation Augustine did not explain everything clearly, yet it was a delight to find a justice of God by which we are justified being taught.

Equipped more fully with these reflections, I began a second time to

---

[4] Augustine, *De Spiritu et Littera* Book I, chapters IX–X (sections 15–16), in MPL XLIV, pp. 208 ff.

interpret the Psalms. And the work would have grown into a large commentary, if I had not been forced to interrupt what I had begun when in the following year the Emperor Charles V convened the Diet of Worms. I tell this story, most excellent reader, so that if you become a reader of my little works you will remember that (as I said above) I was one of those who have gained proficiency (as Augustine writes about himself) in the course of writing and teaching. I was not one of those who suddenly come from nowhere to the very top even though they are nothing, and with a single glance at Scripture draw out its whole spirit without effort, trial, or practice.

II.2.B   When did the so-called 'tower discovery' of justification take place? Melanchthon seems to place it vaguely in the early monastic years—perhaps as early as 1508 (see I.2.A above). Luther's 1545 *Preface*, on the other hand, suggests a date as late as 1518–19 (see II.2.A), and he once commented that when he became a doctor he did not yet know the truth. Yet some of the early lectures on the Psalms do tentatively reflect a passive understanding of God's justice. This is Luther's comment on Psalm 71 : 19 (Vulg. 70 : 19) during 1514. (Latin text in WA 3, 457, 38.)

'Your justice is in the heights.' In this verse the right distinction between God's justice and man's is described. For the justice of God reaches, and makes one reach, to the heaven of heavens. It is a justice 'in the heights', a justice of attainment; but human justice is not so, it is rather in the very depths. Since this is the case, he who exalts himself will be humbled, and he who humbles himself will be exalted. So now the justice of God is wholly this: that a man should humble himself into the depths. For such a man reaches the very highest point because he has first descended to the very lowest. Properly, this describes Christ, who is the power of God and the justice of God by the way of the greatest and most profound humility; so now he is in the heights by the way of sheer glory.

Accordingly, anyone who wants to understand the Apostle and the rest of the Scripture aright should understand all these things tropologically: truth, wisdom, power, salvation, justice—namely the means by which God makes us strong, saved, just, wise, etc. So also the works of God, the ways of God; Christ is all these things literally, and morally they are all the faith of Christ.

II.2.C   Luther's notes for his lectures on Romans were not published until their rediscovery this century. Comparison with extant student notebooks shows that Luther did not deliver all the material he had prepared. On the theme of justice, his notes speak movingly of Christ as our justice, and clearly distinguish between the active and passive senses of *iustitia dei*. (Latin text in WA 56, 204 and 218–220; also translated in full in LCC XV.)

Certainly we have nothing but accusing thoughts from our conscience, since before God (unless he himself works in us by his grace) our works are nothing. For even though we excuse ourselves readily in our own eyes, just as we also readily approve ourselves, what difference does that make except that we are convicted by this very fact of knowing the law? Such complacent thoughts are thus witnesses that we have done good or avoided evil, but we have not yet satisfied God nor completely fulfilled the law. From whence, then, shall we receive thoughts to defend us? Nowhere but from Christ and in Christ. For when the heart of the man who believes in Christ reproaches and accuses him by testifying against his wrong-doing, he quickly shifts his gaze and turns to Christ and says: 'But he has made satisfaction, he is just, he is my defence, he died for me, he made his justice mine, and he made my sin his. So if he made my sin his, I myself have it no longer and I am free. And if he made his righteousness mine, I am just with the same justice as he is. My sin is not able to swallow him up but is swallowed up in the infinite abyss of his justice, for he is God himself, blessed forever.' In this way 'God is greater than our heart' [1 John 3 : 20]. Our defender is greater than our accuser to an infinite degree. God is our defender, and our heart is our accuser. What sort of a proportion is this? Yes, yes, indeed yes! 'Who shall lay anything to the charge of God's elect?' No one. Why? Because 'it is God who justifies. Who is it that condemns?' No one. Why? Because 'it is Christ Jesus (who is also God) who died, yea rather was also raised', etc. But then 'if God is for us, who can be against us?' [Rom. 8 : 31–34]. . . .

We conclude, then, that God cannot become wise, just, true, strong, good, etc., in his words unless we, believing in him and yielding to him confess that we are unwise, unjust, lying, weak, and evil. So humility and faith are needed. And the whole purpose and content of these words is that we should become nothing in the depths of our being, divest ourselves of everything, empty ourselves, and say with the prophet: 'Against you only have I sinned, that you may be justified in your words [Ps. 51 : 4; Vulg. 50 : 4]. To you I am unwise and weak so that you may be wise and strong in your words.' Indeed, all creatures teach this. It is only the ill who need a physician, it is only a lost sheep that needs to be sought, it is only the captive who needs to be set free, it is only the pauper who needs to be enriched, it is only the weak who needs to be strengthened, it is only the humble who needs to be exalted, it is only a vacuum that needs to be filled, it is only what is in pieces that needs to be assembled. And as the philosophers say: Form cannot be imposed except where there is a lack of form, or preceding forms are removed. Again, the *intellectus possibilis* [the intellect as we know it] cannot receive a form unless in its origin its essence is bare of all forms, like a *tabula rasa*.

Since, then, all creatures declare this, it cannot be that a man full of his own justice can be filled with the justice of God, who fills no one but those who hunger and thirst. Thus he who is filled with his own truth and wisdom has no capacity for the truth and wisdom of God, which can only be received in a vacuum and emptiness. So let us say to God: 'Oh, how gladly we are empty, that you may be full in us! How gladly I am weak, that your power may dwell in me; how gladly I am a sinner, that you may be justified in me; how gladly I am unwise, that you may be my wisdom; how gladly I am unjust, that you may be my justice!' See, this is what it means to say: 'I have sinned against you, that you may be justified in your words.'

In summary, then, God is justified in three ways:

First, when he punishes the unjust; for then he demonstrates that he is just and his justice is manifested and commended by the punishment of our injustice. But this is a meagre commendation, because even the ungodly punish the ungodly.

The second way is accidentally or relatively, just as opposites placed alongside each other are made clearer than when they stand alone. Thus God's justice is the more beautiful, the more loathsome our injustice. But in this passage the apostle is not dealing with this, which is the internal and formal justice of God.

Thirdly, when he justifies the ungodly and infuses grace, or when he is believed to be just in his words. For by being believed in this way, he justifies; that is, he reputes men to be just. Hence this is called the justice of faith and of God.

II.2.D   A 'passive justice of God' where a man in humility and self-abasement acknowledges the justice of God's condemnation, so justifying God and receiving Christ's justice in return, demands a faith—a 'courage to be'—which seeks life hidden in death, grace hidden in wrath, access to heaven hidden in resignation to hell. Here is Luther's comment on Hebrews 7 : 1. (Latin text in WA 57, 187–188; also translated in full in LW 29, 109 ff.; LCC XVI, 29 ff.)

'Melchizedek, king of Salem, etc.': '*Melech*' in Hebrew means king, '*Salem*' means peace, and '*Sedech*' means justice. One must note carefully that these words 'justice' and 'peace' in Scripture are everywhere to be understood of the divine justice and peace; and thus it becomes clear that 'justice' is that grace by which man is justified, namely faith, hope, and love. As Psalm 30 [1 Vulg.; AV 31 : 1] says: 'Deliver me in your justice.' . . . Hence the rule is to be observed that grace, which the scholastic teachers call 'justifying grace' or '*fides formata*', may in Scripture be called 'the justice of God', 'the mercy of God', 'the salvation of God', 'the power of God', and similar phrases. And this is the justice which Romans 1 [: 17] declares to be from faith, as the verse says: 'In the gospel the justice of God is revealed from faith to faith.' It is wrong to expound this of that justice of God by which he himself is just—unless it is understood to mean that faith so exalts the heart of man, and carries him out of himself into God, that God and the heart become a single spirit; and thus the divine justice may be said to be the justice of the heart, 'informing' the heart, as the scholastics say, just as in Christ the humanity, by its union with the divine nature, has become one and the same person. It follows that this Melchizedek could not have been 'king of justice' except as a representation of Christ in name and figure, since Christ alone is 'sun of justice' and 'king of justice', justifying all the just men there are. 'Taking our sandals off our feet' [cf. Exod. 3 : 5] is also to be explained in this way, that is, the removal of the illusion of a human justice acquired by 'elicited acts'. Similarly, 'peace' does not mean that peace which can be stated, described, and thought by man or granted by any creature, but is rather that peace 'which passes all understanding'—that is, which exceeds the mind, and is hidden under the cross and death as the sun is hidden beneath a cloud.

II.2.E   This view of justification as an inner transaction in which faith discovers God 'hidden beneath the opposites' was the impelling motive of Luther's attack on indulgences. He expounded his *theologia crucis* to his fellow-Augustinians in the articles for the *Heidelberg Disputation* of April, 1518. (Latin text in WA 1, 362; also translated in full in LW 31, 39 ff.; SW 1, 65 ff.; LCC XVI, 276 ff.)

> 21:   *The theologian of glory calls bad good and good bad;*
>   *the theologian of the cross calls each what it really is.*

This is obvious, for as long as a man does not know Christ, he does not know the God hidden in sufferings. So he prefers works to sufferings and glory to the cross, power to weakness, wisdom to foolishness, and generally good to bad. These are the sort of people whom the Apostle calls enemies of the cross of Christ. They are so because they hate the cross and sufferings, but they love works and the glory of works, and thus they call the good of the cross evil and the evil of a work good. But as I said before, God cannot be found except in sufferings and the cross. Therefore the friends of the cross say that the cross is good and the works are evil, for through the cross works are cast down and Adam, who by contrast is built up by works, is crucified. For a man cannot possibly help being puffed up by his own good works, unless he has first been completely emptied and brought down by sufferings and evil until he knows that he himself is nothing and that his works are not his own, but God's.

II.2.F To his delight, Luther discovered this self-denying piety already expressed in the German mystical tradition. In 1516 he published a partial version of the anonymous fourteenth-century *Theologia Deutsch*. In 1518 he found a complete version of the tract, and republished it with this preface. (German text in WA 1, 378–379; also translated in full in LW 31, 75 f. The *German Theology* itself is translated in LCC XIII, 327 ff.)

One reads that St Paul, a humble and despised person, nevertheless wrote bold and authoritative letters, and he prided himself that his language was not bedecked with ornate and flowery words, yet fully displayed the riches of all the skill of wisdom. In the same way, when one gazes upon God's wonders, it is clear that he always refuses to choose fine, pompous, and brilliant preachers for his words, but as it is written: 'Out of the mouths of infants'—by the mouths of the inarticulate and sucklings you have proclaimed your praise best of all [Ps. 8 : 2; Vulg. 8 : 3] Again: 'The wisdom of God makes the tongues of the inarticulate to be the most articulate of all' [cf. Isa. 32 : 4]. Moreover, he smites high-minded people who are offended and annoyed by such simple folk: 'You would confound the plans of the poor' [Ps. 14 : 6; Vulg. 13 : 6]—you have downgraded good advice and doctrine because they were given to you through poor and obscure men.

I say this because I want to forewarn everyone who reads this booklet not to incur such disgrace by being annoyed at its homely German or its ungarnished, ungarlanded vocabulary; for this noble little book, however poor and unadorned it is in language and human wisdom, is by the same measure far richer and more priceless in skill and godly wisdom. And if I may boast like my 'old fool', apart from the Bible and St Augustine I have not encountered any book from which I have learned or could learn more about God, Christ, man, and everything. And now I discover for the first time the truth that some highly educated men amongst us Wittenberg theologians are talking nonsense, when we want to initiate something brand new, as if there was nobody else before us or in other places. Yes, indeed, there have been such people, but God's wrath incurred by our sin has prevented our deserving to see or hear them, for it is as plain as daylight that the sort of material this book contains has not been dealt with in the universities for a long time, with the result that the holy Word of God has not only been shoved under the bench, but has almost rotted away in the dust and the dirt. Let anyone who wishes read this booklet and then say whether the theology we teach is new or old, for this book is certainly not new. But should they perhaps say, as they have said before, that we are *German* theologians, we are content with that. I thank God that in the German language I hear and find my God in a way in which I (and they with me) have not found him before, whether in the Latin, Greek, or Hebrew tongues. God grant that this booklet gain a wider reading, and then we shall find that the German theologians are doubtless the best theologians! Amen.

Dr Martin Luther
Augustinian at Wittenberg.

II.2.G How the theology of the cross led directly to his offence at contemporary penitential practice is the burden of Luther's extensive
Resolutions upon the 95 Theses. (Latin text in WA 1, 540–543;
also translated in full in LL 31, 83 ff. See also II.1.H above.)

When God undertakes to justify a man, first he condemns him—just as whom he wants to build up, he destroys, whom he wants to heal, he smites, whom he wants to make alive, he kills, as he says in 1 Samuel 2 and Deuteronomy 32: 'I kill and I shall make alive,' etc. Now, he does this when he crushes man and humbles him to the recognition of himself and his sins and makes him tremble, so that the wretched sinner says: 'There is no peace for my bones in the face of my sins, there is no health in my flesh in the face of your wrath' [Ps. 38 : 3; Vulg. 37 : 4]. For so the mountains flee before the face of the Lord, so he sends his arrows and routs them: 'By your rebuke, Lord, and by breathing out the breath of your anger' [Ps. 104 : 7; Vulg. 103 : 7]. So sinners are turned back to hell and their faces are filled with ignominy [Pss. 9 : 17, 83 : 16; Vulg. 9 : 18, 82 : 17]. In many different psalms, David confesses with groans that too often in his own experience he had been perturbed and distressed. But in this very alarm salvation begins; for 'the fear of the Lord is the beginning of wisdom' [Ps. 111 : 10; Vulg. 110 : 10]. . . .

In truth, then, a man knows so little about his own justification that he thinks himself very close to damnation, and he thinks that this is not an infusion of grace, but an effusion of God's wrath upon him. Yet blessed is he if he sustains this trial, since it is when he believes that he has been consumed that he will arise like the morning star. However, while this wretched confusion of his conscience persists he has neither peace nor consolation, unless he flees to the power of the church and begs for comfort and cure for his sins and miseries disclosed through confession. For he will not be able to give himself peace through his own counsel or help; indeed, his grief will be finally swallowed up in despair. Here the priest, in the fullest confidence of the power given to him for exercising mercy, will step in when he sees such humility and sorrow, and will loose him and pronounce him loosed, and thus give him peace of con- science. But at all costs let a man who needs absolution beware of doubt- ing that his sins are forgiven him before God, and let him be at peace in his heart; for if, because of the confusion of his conscience, he is uncertain (as must usually be the case if the sorrow is real), yet he is bound to abide by the judgement of another—not by any means on account of the prelate himself or his power, but on account of the Word of Christ who cannot lie when he says: 'Whatever you loose upon earth . . .' [Matt. 16 : 19, 18 : 18]. For trust in this Word will create peace of conscience, so long as the priest absolves in accordance with it. But he who seeks peace by another way, for example by inward experience, certainly seems to tempt God and to want to have peace in fact, not in faith. For you will have peace only in so far as you believe the Word of him who promises: 'Whatever you loose,' etc. For Christ is our peace—but in faith. Anyone who does not believe this Word, even if he is absolved a million times by the pope himself and confesses to the whole world, will never find rest.

This, then, is that sweetest power for which we ought to thank God exceedingly from the botom of our hearts because he has given such power to men, the only consolation for sinners and miserable consciences, if only they will believe that Christ's promises are true. . . .

We can tell that this understanding of the power of the keys is widespread amongst the people, since they seek and receive absolution in simple faith. But some men who are more learned try to create peace for themselves by their own contrition and works and confessions; and they achieve nothing except to go from disquiet to disquiet because they trust in themselves and their own works, whereas when they experience an evil conscience they ought to believe in Christ who says: 'Whatever you loose.' The theologians of recent days all too readily enhance this evil of conscience by treating and teaching the sacrament of penance in such a way that the people learn to trust that they can blot out their sins by their own contritions and satisfactions—an utterly vain presumption which can have the effect only of making them worse and worse, like the woman with an issue of blood whose whole fortune was spent upon doctors [Matt. 9 : 20]. First of all they must be taught faith in Christ, the free bestower of pardon, and they must be urged to despair of their own contrition and satisfaction, so that in certainty and joy of heart they may be sure of the mercy of Christ, and at last gladly hate their sins and be contrite and make satisfaction. The jurists, too, are scarcely reluctant authors of the same torture, since in extolling the power of the pope with so much zeal they have caused the power of the pope to be more esteemed and revered than the Word of Christ to be honoured by faith; whereas men ought to be taught that if they really want to be consoled in conscience they should learn to trust not in the power of the pope, but in the Word of Christ who gives the promises to the pope. For it is not because the pope gives that you have anything, but if you believe that you receive it, you have it: you have only as much as you believe in accordance with Christ's promise.

However, if the power of the keys were valueless at producing this sort of peace at heart and remission of guilt, then truly (as some people say) indulgences would be regarded as worthless. For what is conferred of great moment when remission of sin is granted, since it is a Christian trait even to despise death? . . .

II.2.H   During 1518 and 1519 Luther's doctrine of faith underwent many refinements. The notion of passive justification was overshadowed by the theme of alien justification—Christ's own justness becomes ours as we are united with him by the external Word and sacraments. Human justice ceases to be part of salvation; the law/gospel dialect becomes central. These themes, which reach decisive expression in the mighty *Freedom of a Christian* (1520) are sounded in this *Sermon on the Twofold Justice* on Palm Sunday, 1519. (Latin text in WA 2, 145–147; also translated in full in LW 31, 297 ff.; Dillenberger 86 ff. *The Freedom of a Christian* is translated in LW 31, 333 ff.; SW 2, 9 ff.; PE II, 301 ff.; *Three Treatises* 251 ff.; Wace and Buchheim 95 ff.; Woolf I, 356; Dillenberger 42 ff.; and other sources.)

The justice of Christian men is twofold, just as the sin of men is also twofold.

The first is alien justice, infused from without. This is the justice by which Christ is just and also justifies through faith, as 1 Cor. 1 [: 30] says: 'God has made him to be our wisdom and justice and sanctification and redemption.' Indeed, He himself says the same thing in John 11 [: 25]: 'I am the resurrection and the life; he who believes in Me shall not die eternally.' And again John 14 [: 6]: 'I am the way, the truth, and the light.' This justice is given to men in baptism and at every time of true penitence, so that a man can boast with confidence in Christ and say: 'What Christ lived, did, said, suffered and died, is mine, not less than if I myself had lived, done, said, suffered and died.' Just as a groom has everything which belongs to his bride, and the bride has everything which belongs to the groom (for since they are one flesh everything is common to both), so Christ and his Church are one spirit. . . . Thus everything that Christ possesses is ours, given to us freely and without our desert from pure mercy, even though we deserved wrath and damnation instead, and hell as well. So even Christ himself, who said that he came to fulfil the most sacred will of his Father, became obedient to him, and whatever he did, he did for us, and wanted it to be ours, as he said: 'I am amongst you as one who ministers' [Luke 22 : 27]; and again: 'This is my body which is given for you' [Luke 22 : 19]; and in Isaiah 43 [: 24]: 'You have made me serve in your sins, and you have forced me to toil in your iniquities.'

Therefore through faith in Christ, the justice of Christ becomes our justice, together with everything that is his—indeed, he himself be-comes ours. Hence the Apostle Paul's statement in Romans 1 [: 17]: 'The justice of God is revealed in the gospel, as it is written "he who is just from faith shall live." ' . . . Thus this alien justice, infused in us without any action of ours through grace alone as the Father draws us inwardly to Christ, is set over against original sin, which is similarly alien, having been inbred and contracted by us without our actions through birth alone. And thus Christ drives out Adam more and more from day to day, in proportion to the growth of that faith and knowledge of Christ. For it is not all infused at once, but he begins it, continues it, and in the end finally perfects it through death.

The second justice is our own proper justice, not because we produce it on our own, but because we co-operate with that first alien justice. This justice is our present upright manner of life in good works: first, towards oneself in mortification of the flesh and crucifixion of the lusts; . . . secondly, towards one's neighbour in love; and thirdly, to-wards God in humility and awe. The apostle, and all Scripture, are full of these things, but Paul briefly sums them all up in Titus 2 [: 12] when he says: 'Let us live soberly (towards oneself in crucifixion of the flesh) and justly (towards one's neighbour) and piously (towards God) in this world.' This justice is the work and fruit and sequel of the first justice.

III

LUTHER AND THE
GERMAN NATION

THE POLITICAL EFFECTS of the Reformation in Germany were both
devastating and obvious; yet Luther's own rôle in German national development has been an oddly controversial topic. He himself said, in
retrospect, that he could have grasped public leadership at Worms, if
that had been his calling. But he believed his task was to give theological,
not political, leadership. This decision has earned him the criticism
(graphically repeated in John Osborne's play *Luther*) that he incited
both the lesser nobility and the peasant classes of Germany to rise in
search of liberty and redress of grievances, only to abandon and betray
them when they put their aspirations into action. Accordingly, the
romantic nationalists of nineteenth-century Germany found Luther less
worthy than the impetuous, headstrong knight, Ulrich von Hutten;
while Marxist historians have found him less worthy than Thomas
Müntzer, the religiously potent and socially violent prophet of the
peasants. From 1525 to the present, Luther's injunction to the princes to
'stab, smite, slay' the rebellious peasants has seemed shockingly immoderate; yet in his defence he was able to claim justly that his position
was at least consistent. He had tried to mediate the just demands of the
oppressed class, but he had a deep horror of the social effects of anarchy.
It is not unfair to say that his concern for the common people was moved
by compassion, but not respect. Though his social theory was remarkably liberal, the very high value he placed upon order sometimes led
him to exalt offices over persons. It has even been suggested (somewhat
imaginatively) that Luther's stress on civil obedience, submission to
governmental authority, and acquiescence in the *status quo* was a factor
in the German disaster of the twentieth century. Though this is far-
fetched, the misapplication of Luther's teaching was certainly an
element in the German church's moral paralysis under the Third Reich.
What complicates the study of Luther's judgements on national issues,
be they peasant insurgency, the threat of Turkish invasion, or the formation of princely alliances, is that they were always intended as theological
judgements. It is often hard to accept them in a day when religious

orthodoxy is no longer a matter of public policy, and when heresy can no longer be identified simply with subversion.

III.1 NATIONAL ASPIRATION

The capture of his beloved Germany for the gospel was one of Luther's fondest hopes. His masterful appeal for a national reformation, *An Open Letter to the Christian Nobility of the German Nation* (1520), is an essential introduction to our topic. (It is available in full in SW 1, 259 ff.; PE II, 61 ff.; *Three Treatises* 9 ff.; Woolf I, 109 ff.; Wace & Buchheim 17 ff.) His hopes were to be desperately clouded in the years that followed. It is true that political factors allowed the Reformation to survive and spread; and that Luther's heroic stand provided opportunity for Germany to demand a response to its grievances. But it is also true that the evangelical cause was sullied by national calamities—the knights' war, the peasants' revolt, the Pack affair—and that Germany (though threatened by Turkish invasion) split into two armed camps over Luther's doctrine. Rather than a glorious reformation, Luther came to expect God's judgement on his Germans.

III.1.A The hot-headed, patriotic knight Ulrich von Hutten was one of the first to see the nationalist potential of Luther's revolt. Though little interested in Luther's doctrine, he sprang to his defence by publishing a translation of the bull *Exsurge, Domine* with this foreword. (German text in Ulrich von Hutten, *Opera* (E. Böcking, ed., Leipzig, 1859), I, 430: ccv.)

Urich von Hutten, knight, to all Germans: greeting!
Behold Leo X's bull to you, men of Germany. Here he tries once more to stamp out resurgent Christian truth which he attacks and opposes, as our freedom raises its head again after long repression, lest it gain strength and revive for all to see. Shall we not withstand him as he contrives such plots? Shall we not be thoroughly forearmed, by taking public counsel against his intruding further and making headway by means of man's insatiable cupidity and boldness? I ask you by the immortal Christ—when was there a more opportune moment, when did a better occasion present itself as one worthy of bearing the name 'German'? See, everything points to the fact that there is a greater hope than ever before that this tyranny will be wiped out, and this disease find a cure. Dare to attempt it at last, and accomplish it! It is not just Luther who is involved in this business, but whatever the issue, it affects us all; the sword is not thrust at any one individual, but we do public battle. They do not want to be deposed from their tyranny; they do not want their frauds to be detected, their deceits brought to light, their frenzy resisted, their depredations to meet any opposition. This is pre-

cisely what they are angry about, and they rail against it so much that they behave with utter lack of dignity. You who see this happening under your nose, what will you do at last? Do you want advice? If you will heed mine, you will surely remember that you are Germans. This alone should be sufficient motive for you to vindicate these things. I am now assuming this risk in your name and the common name, but I do so gladly: first, because I am convinced it is the most fitting thing to do; secondly, I now not only hope, but I am perfectly sure, that you will all sooner or later join me in daring these high deeds. I have made myself responsible for publishing this bull now in the hope that when you read it, you will all be willing to take instruction from a single source. Farewell.

III.1.B   Luther himself chose to exercise his national rôle by advice and teaching. The limits of secular authority in religious matters, and the Christian duty of civic obedience, were the subjects of his 1523 treatise *On Temporal Authority*. (German text in WA 11, 261–264; translated in full in LW 45, 81 ff.; SW 2, 271 ff.; PE III, 225 ff.)

Here we come to the chief point of this discourse. For when we have learnt that there must be temporal government on earth, and how we should use it in a Christian and salutary way, we must then learn how long its arms and how far its hands reach, if it is not to stretch too widely and to encroach upon God and his kingdom and realm. And it is essential to know this. For unbearable and terrible danger results if we give it too much scope; yet damage is also done if it is too narrowly constricted. In the first case it punishes too much, in the second it punishes too little. Even so, it is more tolerable to err on this side and to punish too little, for it is always better to let a scoundrel live than to put an upright man to death, seeing that inevitably the world will always have scoundrels left, but it has few upright men.

First, it is to be noted that the two groups of Adam's children, the one in God's kingdom under Christ, the other in the world's kingdom under the government (as I described earlier), have two sorts of law. For every kingdom must have its laws and statutes, and without law no kingdom or realm can stand, as daily experience sufficiently demonstrates. The temporal government has laws whose scope extends no further than to the body and to property and to external matters on earth. For God can and will allow no one to rule over the soul except himself alone. Therefore when the temporal power presumes to issue laws for the soul, it encroaches upon God in his realm, and only misleads and destroys souls. We want to make this clear enough for everyone to grasp, so that those gentlemen of ours, the princes and bishops, will see what fools they are when they set out to force people with their laws and commandments to believe thus and so.

If someone imposes a human law on the soul, to believe this or that as the imposer dictates, God's Word is certainly not present there. If God's Word is not present, it is quite uncertain whether he will have it so. For one cannot be certain that what God has not commanded is pleasing to him. On the contrary, one is certain that it does not please God. For he wishes our faith to be grounded utterly and entirely on his divine Word alone. . . . Further, each individual takes his own risk in what he believes, and has to see for himself that he believes rightly. For no one else can believe or not believe for me any more than he can go to hell or heaven for me, and he can no more drive me to belief or unbelief than he can lock or unlock heaven or hell for me. For it rests on the conscience of the individual, how he believes or does not believe—a fact which subtracts nothing from the temporal power, which should be content, look after its own business, and let anyone believe this or that as he is willing and able, and constrain no one by force. For to have faith is a free act, and no one can be forced to it. Yes, it is a divine work in the Spirit, so it is nonsense to say that an external power could enforce or produce it.

III.1.c The Edict of Worms, outlawing Lutheran teaching, was later compromised by the Diet of Nürnberg in 1522/23 and by expectation of a council. By 1526, hostile alliances had begun to form, and that year's Diet of Speyer reached a stalemate: execution of the Edict was left to the discretion of each Estate. Here is the vital fourth article of the Recess, August 27, 1526. (German text in St L 16, 210: 809.)

Now, therefore, we, the Electors, Princes, and Estates of the Empire and their representatives here present at this Diet, have unanimously agreed and resolved that, pending the convening of a council or a national assembly, each one of us with our subjects will so live, govern, and act in the matters treated by the Edict issued by His Imperial Majesty at the Diet held at Worms as he hopes and trusts to answer for it to God and His Imperial Majesty.

III.1.d With the territorial principle thus tentatively sanctioned, Catholic and Lutheran princes continued to build partisan alliances. Mutual suspicions were aggravated in 1528 by the Pack Affair, when Philip of Hesse reacted violently to a fabricated threat of attack by Catholic princes. Duke John of Saxony sought the advice of Luther, who replied to the Duke's Chancellor, Brück, on March 28, 1528. (German text in Br 4, 421–424: 1246; also translated in full in Smith II, 436 ff.)

Honourable, learned Lord Chancellor, etc. In accordance with yesterday's command of my most gracious lord, I am here forwarding a statement of my opinion.

First, so that my most gracious lord may confidently retain a good conscience in the face of violations by the hostile princes (should it prove necessary to defend himself), it should be remembered, as no one can deny, that His Grace, as an elector of the Empire, has over him no superior with the right and authority to punish or judge His Grace except only His Imperial Majesty himself. For all other princes and kings are either His Grace's equals or his inferiors in rank, and have no right or authority over His Grace.

Secondly, His Grace is responsible for protecting his subjects against such princes, and for ruling so that (as Paul teaches in Romans 13) the temporal government is God's servant for punishing the guilty and protecting the innocent. And if he is responsible for protecting them against a single or lowly murderer, he is equally responsible for protecting them against many or great murderers; there is no difference among murderers, whether they are princes or tramps.

Thirdly, if these murderous princes or enemies allege any command from His Imperial Majesty to attack His Grace, His Grace should again direct his conscience as follows:

1. His Grace is not obliged to believe or accept any such order, but to interpret it as a false, unlawful, and insubordinate deception, on the grounds that His Imperial Majesty has promised to be His Grace's gracious lord and to undertake nothing against His Grace without a prior recusation (as the answer has come from Spain, I hear). His Grace should and must stand as fast by this promise of His Imperial Majesty, just as those princes on their part are duty bound by loyalty to regard His Imperial Majesty as truthful and honourable, and not let themselves be deflected from this promise by any commandment until His Imperial Majesty himself countermands it. For His Grace is bound to believe His Imperial Majesty himself more than all princes, especially more than such dubious enemies, even if they boast of a command as much as they like.

2. It is in fact the case, and there is no room for doubt, that the attack of these hostile princes has been undertaken apart from and without the knowledge, will, and command of His Imperial Majesty, since they themselves testify that they will produce such an order only after their association (or gang) is established; from which one has to suppose that this undertaking springs from neither a divine nor a human ordinance, but from a jealous, seditious, vicious source, for which they wish to use His Imperial Majesty to cloak their infamy. All true and upright followers of His Imperial Majesty should take lawful action to counteract this attack; for what they are doing is not their duty to His Imperial

Majesty—rather His Imperial Majesty is to be the cloak for what they are wickedly undertaking.

3. It is openly acknowledged throughout the Empire that the decree issued at Worms was not agreed to by all the Estates of the Empire, but evoked dissent from even the highest and most influential Estates, so there is no doubt that it should be regarded as the decree of the priestly crowd and not of the Emperor or the Empire—especially as afterwards it was suspended, and then at Speyer it was resolved that it be suspended by His Imperial Majesty's order as well. So it is out of sheer malice that this princely crew bases itself on the decree—a groundless pretext which the whole world sees through. Accordingly, with a good conscience before God and the world, every command which might be brought forward on the basis of such a groundless decree should without any doubt be regarded as unlawful, and as an order which His Imperial Majesty has not issued, nor is able or willing to issue; and whatever action the princely crew takes on this basis is to be deemed a real revolt and insurrection against the Empire and His Imperial Majesty, and before God and the world is not only to be shown no obedience, but rather to be withstood in every way.

4. Then there is available Appeal and Protestation. If this should become necessary (which God forbid), it could be presented in a manner entirely favourable to my gracious lord, and altogether unfavourable for the horde of priests and princes, representing them as deceivers of His Imperial Majesty and disrupters of the whole realm, and anything else that serves this purpose as need and right provide. Meanwhile much water will flow under the bridge, and the time of grace will grow from a night to a year, if God wills. We hope and pray, however, that because God has given us his Word it will not come to an appeal to need and right.

But to attack or wish to anticipate such an association of princes by means of war is in no way advisable, but to be avoided at all costs. For the Word of God insists: 'He who takes the sword shall perish by the sword' [Matt. 26 : 52]. Now here there is no command to use the sword, since the guilt and the deed of our opponents have not yet been proved nor brought to light, nor are the hostile princes concerned under our most gracious lord's authority. Furthermore, that would be to punish openly—indeed, to attack outrageously—those who had not done anything openly or been convicted, and thus they would gain not only the finest excuse, but even the unquestionable right, to protect themselves as of necessity against those who were attacking the innocent in a seditious manner without His Imperial Majesty's command; for God can still forestall their secret plans. But if they were to attack in this way, it could not be prevented any more, and would confer a right for the first time. For just as our claim and confidence is now that the enemy crowd will attack my gracious lord as insurgents without any basis in preceding right or hearing, so they in turn would have exactly the same claim—that they had been attacked without any preceding basis in right as innocent men who had not yet deserved anything, and thus forced to defend themselves. Oh, may God protect us from this abomination! That would really be fishing for the hook and using might for right! No greater shame could come upon the gospel; for out of it would come not a peasants' revolt, but a princes' revolt which would topple Germany, and Satan would be gratified to see it.

If, however, my lord the Landgrave is not willing to be guided, but intends to proceed, my most gracious lord is not bound to maintain the alliance; for one must obey God rather than men. All alliances must thus be and remain subordinate to God and the right, so that they engage in no act of undertaking against them. But if my gracious lord the Landgrave, or the people of Magdeburg, were thus attacked, my most gracious lord is bound by the provisions of the alliance to stand by them as if it were His Grace himself, and to proceed in the above-stated way; for God wants loyalty and faithfulness maintained.

III.1.E   At the Diet of Speyer in February, 1529, the Catholic majority revoked the earlier Recess and demanded compliance with the Edict of Worms. The Lutheran princes protested. Out-voted, they began the legal process of Appeal and Protestation (which gave 'Protestantism' its name). Here is their protest, as recreated for the formal document containing the appeal. (German text in Julius Ney, *Die Appellation und Protestation der evangelischen Stände aufdem Reichstage zu Speier 1529* (Leipzig, 1906), 50–53.)

Protestation read openly before the Electors, and submitted to the official records of the realm.

Your Worship, and you, dear lords, cousins, uncles, friends, and associates; you know what sort of grievance we caused to be presented, both orally and in writing, on the final day of the recently held Diet, against certain points in the article about 'the preservation of peace and unity, in light of threatened divisions over religion in the realm, until a council is held to deal with it'. And although, in our presentation, we deliberately referred to nothing but what was demanded on the one hand by our consciences, for the honour and praise of God and the hallowing of his name, and on the other by the inescapably urgent need of the said 'peace and unity' of the realm, Your Worship and you others ought to have searched for a way whereby with good conscience and without complaint we might have reached agreement with Your Worship and you all in interpreting the last Recess of Speyer, if that Recess had indeed been 'abused' through differing interpretations. In this way the said last Recess, which otherwise has everywhere been regarded as just (and until now unanimously so), would continue its essence and substance; as indeed we, Duke John, Elector of Saxony, had suggested, when we responded to the resolution drawn up by the high commission with a cordial opinion dealing with the alleged abuse and the aforesaid preservation of peace; and afterwards we presented it to the commission a second time, and then had it presented on yet another occasion to Your Worship and to you all, in expectation that this suggestion would be regarded by Your Worship and by you others as a balanced and cordial clarification, and would be accepted.

But since we have found that Your Worship and you all insist on maintaining your point of view; and since you reject our recital of the pressing causes and grievances which we want immediately restored and repaired everywhere, both for conscience's sake, and because it appears that Your Worship and your excellencies will make no concessions, either officially or in any other way, for 'preserving peace and unity pending a council, in light of threatened divisions', nor take any action in which we can participate and assent; furthermore, both because of the way the business was conducted, and, before that, because of the last Recess of Speyer cited above: we are not bound by this decision—especially since our consent was lacking, in light of the following stringently binding clauses and terms from the said last Recess, executed and sealed here at Speyer, namely the statement recorded at the end of that Recess, beginning 'Hereby we, Ferdinand, Prince and Infant in Spain, etc., and we electors, princes, etc., prelates, counts and lords do declare and promise . . .', etc. We therefore conclude that, on the basis of our oft-repeated complaints, our extreme and inescapable necessity demands that we openly protest to your excellencies against the declaration of Your Worship and of you all as void and without authority in light of the said last Recess, and as not binding on us and ours, individually and collectively; and we do so protest by these presents. And we have hereby protested to Your Worship and to you all that for similar reasons we cannot, may not, and know not how to acquiesce in the said resolution of Your Worship and of you others, but regard it as void and not binding. We wish nevertheless in the matter of religion, pending the said 'general and free Christian council or national assembly', with the help of the godly assistance, authorisation, and provisions of the much-cited last Recess of Speyer, 'so to act, live, and rule' in our governments, and also by and with our subjects and kinsmen, 'as we trust to give account before God Almighty and His Roman Imperial Majesty', our most gracious sovereign. In addition, the decisions concerning spiritual taxes, rents, fees, and tithes, and those concerning peace drawn up and published in the oft-mentioned last Recess of Speyer we wish to apply and retain everywhere unaltered. Similarly, we wish it known that we are of one mind with Your Worship and with you all on what the following article asserts concerning re-baptism and its suppression, as we have obviously been throughout this Diet; and that we hold the provisions of this article to be entirely appropriate.

There remains, above all, our friendly plea to Your Worship and to you all, and a cordial disposition which hopes that this protestation of ours will be attributed to our inescapable need. Its purpose and character is to see whether by this means the resolution adopted by Your Worship and by your excellencies as the Recess of this Diet can be set aside as quite unacceptable to us, in order that our necessary protest against its content may thus and with your concurrence be incorporated and recorded, and that the protest we have now executed, together with the complaints we have brought forward against the relevant articles in the latest writing, may be brought to the attention of His Imperial Majesty, and be made public in other ways also, so that one and all may have knowledge and understanding that we have not consented to this judgement, and why, but instead have openly protested against it before Your Worship and before you all. Furthermore, we anticipate extending our repeated complaints and protests further, and having them accepted as owing to our pressing need, both before Your Worship and before you others and elsewhere.

So that Your Worship and you others will understand all this in the most favourable light and owing, as we have said, to our extremely urgent need and nothing else, we declare ourselves disposed to serve Your Worship amicably and to acknowledge you others with favourable and cordial goodwill.

III.1.F The Emperor himself returned to Germany in 1530 to seek a settlement at the Diet of Augsburg. After frustrating delays, four Protestant groups presented confessions of faith. Waiting impatiently for news at near-by Coburg Castle, Luther relayed this report of the reading of the Augsburg Confession at the Diet. Despite Luther's optimism, the Diet refused to legalise Protestantism. (Latin text in Br 5, 440: 1625.)

To that venerable man, lord Nicholas Hausmann, faithful and sincere bishop of the church at Zwickau.

Grace and peace in Christ! Our friend Februarius [Hornung] will report to you better than I can write, good sir, everything that happened both at Augsburg and here with me. Yet after he had arrived here to see me, Dr Jonas wrote that our Confession (which our Philip prepared) was read publicly in the imperial palace itself by Dr Christannus [Beier], our Prince's Chancellor, before the Emperor and the princes and bishops of the whole empire, with only a crowd of commoners excluded. And the following subscribed the Confession: first, the Prince Elector of Saxony; then Marquis Georg of Brandenburg; Prince

Johann Frederick, Jr; the Landgrave of Hesse; Ernst and Franz, Dukes of Lueneburg; Prince Wolfgang of Anhalt; and the cities of Nürnberg and Reutlingen. Now they are deliberating about the imperial response. Many bishops are inclined to peace, and despise the sophists Faber and Eck. In private conversation one bishop is reported to have said: 'This is the pure truth—we cannot deny it.' Mainz especially is said to be anxious for peace. Similarly, Duke Henry of Brunswick, who familiarly invited Philip to a meal as a sign of friendship, testified that he certainly could not deny the articles about two kinds in the sacrament, priestly marriage, and unimportant distinctions of foods. Our people report that no one in the whole Assembly is more accommodating than the Emperor himself. New beginnings are signalled thus. The Emperor deals with our Prince not only mildly, but also reverently; so Philip writes. It is marvellous how everyone is burning with love and goodwill for the Emperor. Perhaps, if God wills, just as the Emperor was the worst of men at first, so here at last he will be the best of men! Let us only pray, for the power of prayer is seen openly. You will inform Cordatus and all the brethren of these things, because they are true. I believe that meanwhile you have received my letter to you and your brother. The Lord be with you, Amen. Greet all our friends. From the desert, July 6, 1530.

Your Martin Luther.

III.1.G Total Protestant compliance was demanded by April, 1531. But this date passed without incident, and the religious truce effected by the Peace of Nürnberg (1532) permitted a decade of far-reaching Protestant consolidation. Yet Luther was not impressed by this outward success; in his last years he grew increasingly distressed at Germany's inner failure to respond to the gospel—as he wrote to his friend Lauterbach in 1541. (Latin text in Br 9, 547: 3685.)

To that excellent man Dr Anton Lauterbach, bishop of the church at Pirna, and most faithful inspector of the churches of the area, beloved brother in the Lord.

Grace and peace! Since I had nothing to write, my Anton, I wanted to write this to you all the same to say that I had nothing to write, rather than not reply to your letters at all! May God strengthen Prince Maurice in true faith and sound government. Perhaps you have heard all the news about the Turk. I have almost despaired of Germany because it has accepted amongst its household gods the *real* Turks, the cruel demons of avarice, usury, tyranny, discord, and that whole swamp of perfidy, malice, and profligacy amongst the nobility, in the palace, in the councils, in the towns, in the countryside, but above all its contempt of the Word and its unheard-of ingratitude. With these fiercest and cruellest Turks roaring amongst us, how can we make headway against the physical Turks? God have mercy upon us and lift up the light of his countenance upon us! [Ps. 4 : 1 and 6]. For when we pray against our enemies the Turks, there is a risk that the Spirit will understand that we are unwittingly praying our prayer against the true Turks, and so answer against us—yet at the same time for us. For I foresee that unless he frightens and humbles our nobles by the tyranny of the Turk, we shall suffer from them a tyranny more terrible than the Turk's. For their whole concern is to impose snares and chains on the hands of the princes, and fetters on the citizens and countryfolk, but most of all on literature and writers. Thus they avenge papal servitude with a servitude of the people under the hand of the nobility. But enough of this. My Kate greets you and your two girls, and so do we all. And let us beseech and pray the Lord together if he will perhaps grant us repentance and avert the Turkish scourge. For without God's special help our arms and men will achieve nothing. The eve of St Martin, 1541.

Your Martin Luther.

III.2 SOCIAL UNREST

The most tragic public event of the Reformation's first decade was the Peasants' Revolt of 1525. It was not the first such outbreak; it was one of a long series of peasant insurrections which repeatedly shook late medieval Europe. But in this uprising, the leaders of the huge peasant mobs claimed a radical evangelical basis for their demands. In the ensuing tragedy, thousands upon thousands of hapless peasants were slaughtered, religious tensions were aggravated, hostile alliances formed, and Lutheranism was accused of destroying the social order. On the basis of his doctrine of 'the two kingdoms', Luther denied that armed revolt, even in a just cause, was ever Christian, and won lasting opprobrium by the harshness of his condemnation of the rebels.

III.2.A Luther had tried vainly to avert a confrontation by his urgent counsel to both sides. In the spring of 1525, Luther wrote his *Exhortation to Peace* as a commentary on the Twelve Articles, the peasants' demand for civil rights. He warned rulers against refusing just demands, and the peasants against the horror of armed revolt. (German text in WA 18, 293–333; also translated in full in SW 3, 308 ff. and PE IV, 210 ff., where the text of the Twelve Articles is also given.)

To the Princes and Lords

First of all, for the current unrest and uproar we have no one else on earth to thank but you princes and lords—especially you blind bishops and raving priests and monks. Till this very day you are stubborn and you will not stop ranting and raving against the holy gospel, even though you know perfectly well that it is right and that you cannot counteract it. Moreover, in your secular government all you do is fleece and tax to maintain your own pride and splendour, until the poor common man can no longer sustain the burden. The sword is at your neck, yet you imagine you are sitting so firmly in the saddle that no one can unseat you. Such smugness and obstinate arrogance will break your necks, you will see. . . .

If it is still possible at this point to give you advice, my lords, make a little allowance for their anger for the sake of God's will. 'A hay cart should make way for a drunken man': how much more should you leave your ranting and headstrong tyranny, and deal reasonably with the peasants. Deal with them as you would with drunken, deranged men— do not begin a fight with them, for you do not know where it will end. First proceed gently, because you do not know what God intends to do. Do not apply the spark and engulf the whole of Germany in a fire which no one can quench. . . .

They have set forward twelve articles. Among them, there are some so fair and just that they take away your good name before God and the world, and make the Psalm about 'pouring contempt upon princes' [Ps. 107 : 40; Vulg. 106 : 40] come true. . . . Their first article, where they petition for the right to hear the gospel and to choose a pastor, you cannot refuse with any glimmer of justice. . . . The other articles, pointing out such physical hardships as probate taxes, imposts, and the like, are surely also fair and just. For government is not instituted to provide wantonly for its own needs at its subjects' expense, but to make provision for those subjects and to seek their best interest. . . .

To the Peasants

St Paul says in Romans 12 [: 19]: 'Do not avenge yourselves, be- loved, but give place to the wrath of God.' Similarly, he praises the Corinthians in 2 Corinthians 11 [: 20] because they suffer gladly if anyone smites or robs them. But in 1 Corinthians 6 [: 1–7] he criticises them because they had gone to court about property and would not suffer the injustice. Indeed, our ruler Jesus Christ says in Matthew 1 [5 : 44] that we should seek the good of those who do us wrong, pray for our persecutors, love our enemies, and do good to our abusers. . . . These are our Christian laws, dear friends. Now you can see how far the false prophets have led you away from them, and yet they still call you Christians even though they have made you worse than heathen. From these statements even a child could easily grasp that the Christian law is not to strive against injustice, not to stretch after the sword, not to protect oneself, not to avenge oneself, but rather to give up body and property, and let whoever wants to steal it, steal it—we still have enough in our Lord, who will not leave us, as he has promised. 'Suffering, suffering, cross, cross,' is the Christian law, and no other. But now you struggle like this for the sake of temporal property. You are not prepared to have your coat follow your cloak—instead you want your cloak back! How, then, do you propose to die, or give up your body, or love your enemy, or do him good? O listless Christians! Dear friends, Christians are not so common that such a large number could possibly be gathered into a single band; a Christian is a lonesome bird. Would that there were more of us who were good, upright heathen, who kept the natural law, let alone the Christian law! . . .

Not that I intend, by saying this, to justify or defend the authorities in the intolerable injustice which you suffer at their hand. There are unjust rulers and they act with cruel injustice, that I know. But my intention is this: if both sides refuse to allow yourselves to be instructed, and set upon and smite one another (which God forbid), then neither side will deserve the name of Christian, but one group will simply be fighting another in the usual fashion of the world; and as they say, 'God will punish one knave with another. . . .'

Warning to both Rulers and Peasants
Since, dear sirs, there is nothing Christian on either side, and there is no Christian issue pending between you, but both lords and peasants are concerned about heathen or worldly justice and injustice, and about temporal goods; since, moreover, both parties are acting against God and stand under God's wrath, as you have heard: for the sake of God's will let yourself be counselled and advised, and grasp these issues as such issues deserve to be grasped—that is, with justice and not with violence or strife, so that you do not produce endless bloodshed in Germany. . . . You lords have against you both Scripture and history, describing how tyrants are punished. . . . You peasants also have Scripture and experience against you, declaring that no rabble has ever come to a good end, and God has always held firmly to this word: 'He that takes the sword shall die by the sword' [Matt. 26 : 52]. . . . Accordingly, my faithful counsel would be that some counts and lords should be chosen from the nobles, and some councillors from the cities, and the issues dealt with in a friendly fashion and resolved.

III.2.B But the revolt was not averted, and peasant uprisings broke out in Swabia, Franconia, and Thuringia. Luther's *Against the Robbing and Murdering Horde of Peasants* (May, 1525) urged the princes to fierce retaliation as a Christian act of mercy. (It is translated in PE IV, 248 ff.) A month later, Luther replied to critics of his harshness in this *Open Letter about the Harsh Booklet against the Peasants*. (German text in WA 18, 386–400; also translated in full in PE IV, 259 ff.; SW 3, 363 ff.)

If people think that my answer is too harsh, and claim that its purpose is to be violently outspoken and to stifle dissent, I answer: That is right! For an insurrectionist does not deserve to be answered with reason, since he does not accept it. One should answer such mouths with the fist—that brings the sweat to their faces! The peasants will not listen, they will not let anyone say anything at all, so one must unplug their ears with buck-shot, so that their heads jump in the air. Such pupils deserve such a rod. He who will not heed God's Word with gentleness must heed the executioner with his blade. If anyone says I am utterly without gentleness and mercy in this, I answer: 'Mercy is neither here nor there—we are speaking now about God's Word, which wants the king to be honoured and insurrectionists destroyed; and he is just as merciful as we are.'

. . . There are two kingdoms: one is God's kingdom, the other is the kingdom of the world. I have written this so often that it amazes me that there is anyone who has not yet learnt it or become aware of it. For anyone who knows how to distinguish correctly between these two kingdoms will certainly not be annoyed by my little book, and will easily understand the passages about mercy. God's kingdom is a kingdom of grace and mercy, and not a kingdom of wrath or punishment, for in it there is sheer forgiving, caring, loving, serving, doing good, possessing peace and joy, and so on. But the worldly kingdom is a kingdom of wrath and severity, for in it there is sheer punishing, restraining, judging, and condemning, to crush the evil and protect the upright. For this reason it both possesses and wields the sword, and in Scripture a prince or lord is called God's wrath or God's rod. . . .

In this respect the Scriptures have fine, clear eyes and view the worldly sword correctly, namely, that it is out of an even greater mercy that it must be unmerciful, and for the sake of sheer good must exercise wrath and severity. As Paul and Peter say, it is God's servant for vengeance, wrath and punishment upon the evil, and for protection, praise, and honour to the upright. It looks upon the upright and is merciful towards them, and so that they may not undergo suffering it guards, bites, stabs, cuts, hews, and kills, in accordance with the command of God whose servant it knows itself to be. . . . Now, the fact that the evil are thus punished without grace is not because the punishment of the wicked is an end in itself, or to satisfy some blood lust, but so that the upright may be protected and peace and security maintained; and without doubt these are precious works of great mercy, love, and gentleness, since there is no more wretched thing on earth than turmoil, insecurity, repression, violence, and injustice. For who either could or would remain alive if this came about? And so the wrath and severity of the sword is just as necessary to a people as eating and drinking—yes, as life itself! . . .

They say that the lords are misusing their swords and slaying far too cruelly. I answer: 'What has that got to do with my booklet? Why do you lay someone else's guilt on me?' If they are abusing their power, they have certainly not learnt it from me. They will discover their reward, for the supreme Judge, who punishes the headstrong peasants by their hand, has not forgotten them; they will not escape him in their turn. My booklet does not say what the lords deserve, but what the peasants deserve; and how one should carry out this punishment I have had no pretentions to describe. If on occasion an issue should demand that I do so, I will deal equally firmly with the princes and lords, since so far as my office of teacher is concerned, a prince has the same value as a peasant. . . .

I was writing only for those rulers who wanted to act in a Christian or otherwise honest way, to instruct their consciences in handling such a situation, namely, that they should strike swiftly against the mob of insurrectionists, irrespective or whether the blow fell upon the guilty or the innocent; that they should not have an evil conscience if it fell upon the innocent, but confess by it that God is responsible for what they do in his service; but afterwards, if they won, to show grace not only to those whom they regard as innocent, but also to the guilty. But fanatical, raving and senseless tyrants who even after the onslaught cannot have enough blood and have virtually never asked a question about Christ in their whole life, I have not undertaken to instruct; for it is all the same to such bloodhounds whether they smite the guilty or the innocent, whether it pleases God or the devil—they hold the sword only to satisfy their own lust and wantonness. I leave them for their master, the devil, to lead, as indeed he does lead them. For instance, I heard that at Mühlhausen, under some of these bigwigs, one of them had the poor wife of Thomas Müntzer, now a widow and great with child, brought before him, and he fell down on his knees before her and said: 'Dear lady, let me —— you.' Oh, what a chivalrous, noble deed, inflicted on a wretched, forsaken, pregnant woman! Indeed he is a valiant hero, easily worth three knights! What would I write for such knaves and pigs?

III.2.c Luther's severity obscured his real compassion for the peasants' plight (see V.1.B below). One critic was Ulrich Zwingli of Zürich, who chided Luther's harshness in *A Friendly Exegesis* (1527), his first published attack on Luther's sacramental doctrine. Its introduction is this open letter to Luther. (Latin text in CR 96, 78: 602.)

To that learned man, Martin Luther, his revered brother in the Lord: Grace and peace from the Lord.

You have compelled us, most learned Luther, really quite unwillingly to write this *Exegesis*, in which we have taken you up with somewhat greater freedom than before but without any reproach at all. For I have always respected you so much that I could not have respected a father more, even if I say so by writing you a letter at a time when the course of events may suggest the contrary; and I shall not stop respecting you—unless you stubbornly refuse to bring your resistance to the truth to an end. (For I intend to deal quite openly with you throughout my letter.) Once you used to search the Scriptures diligently, and whatever you uncovered, you confessed and defended before all men and against every sort of enemy. In all this, there was a strain of bitterness, unbearable to your enemies, but which we on our part swallowed for a while, during the early stages of the affair; and as your opponents argued back with daily increasing sharpness, your own unwillingness to endure it also grew and drove you in an opposite direction, to the point where you now admit not a few of the very things which you were condemning in the enemy a little while before. Once you wished that everything should be subject to the judgements of the Church; but now, if the things that are written and said about you are true, you advise whoever you can that our opinion about the Eucharist should not even reach the churches. In that case, when can 'the one sitting by in church' [I Cor. 14 : 30] speak? Once you used to condemn the papists' frenzy and slaughtering; now you advise the princes and their class, even in the absence of the ring-leaders, to rage even more tyrannically, not to say madly, against the wretched slaves with flame and sword, laying waste and slaying not only the rioters, but also innocent masses who only believe that what they see is true. You even threaten, as fiercely as you can, a new Arian age; but on what grounds? You advise the princes to settle the matter with the sword, just like those good-for-nothings Faber, Eck, and that bunch of centaurs. Why did you write to the Prince of Hesse that now the dispute must be settled by the sword? These things, most learned Luther, have brought us to the very depths of sorrow, not because we are melting with fear, but because (whether you admit it or not) we fear that your intolerance has changed into fury, and that you despair of carrying your case by Scripture and have therefore turned to force of arms. But there is still no one anywhere—at least, no one who has been allowed to speak freely on the subject—who shares your conviction; and if we had not disagreed, there would have been no one to stop the magistrate from dealing just as severely with us, too, if we refused to come to our senses. Now then, since you are publishing material worthy neither of yourself nor of the Christian religion, and knowledge of the truth is increasing daily whilst your own gentleness and humility are not, but only your boldness and cruelty, there are very many people who suppose that you share the fate of those whom the Lord is repudiating. But may Luther be far from this! For if he is

really so fully assured about the rightness of his cause, then I myself
and many others guarantee that he will not lose sight of his own limits.
There never was anyone so completely learned that he had nothing to
learn, never forgot anything, never made a mistake—hence the ancient
dictum: 'Mighty Homer sometimes sleeps.' I believe, my Luther, that
you reached this self-knowledge a long time ago and are aware that
there are many things you do not know, even though you possess the
friendly and favourable spirit of the Lord. So, say to yourself in this
case: 'What if I am not looking at this matter rightly or not seeing
clearly?' lest you are forced to yield in this case because you have defended it for the wrong reasons and lest you bring down everything you
have taught, if not to ruins at least into suspicion. What you are hoping
for is leading you completely astray. You ask: 'What is this I am hoping
for?' I shall speak plainly. You hope that in return for the efforts you
are now exerting, in which you leave natural eating of flesh behind you
and are converted into living flesh in a mystery by the power of the
divine Spirit—I am afraid to say you hope that when you produce
these marvellous and magnificent works, a smoke-screen will be stirred
up by them which will so capture and hold the attention of both princes
and insurgents that they will say: 'The Lord's body must not be taken
completely away from the Supper!' But you hope in vain. For you will
never get anything than that the body of Christ is present, whether in
the Supper or in the minds of the godly, simply and solely by con-
templation, and as we progress we shall bring to light all the illusions.
For you have reached such a point of authority that you believe that the
one matter depends upon the other. And even though we have no desire
at all to diminish that authority, yet if there is no other way, we must
detract from it a little. My voice has directed these appeals to you from
my heart. Your erudition, power, and acumen are known and respected
by us; but at the same time, we also know the truth. If for any reason
you persist in obscuring, or at least obstructing, the truth, we shall deal
with you fearlessly. And shall there be no battles of this sort for the
good of the Church of Christ? There shall; for the Spirit of truth will
be at hand, who will lead us into all truth [John 16 : 13], and thus it
will also come to pass that anything carried out too uncautiously or
imprudently will be corrected. You yourself have written to the Prince
of Hesse that this business is to be submitted to God the Judge. Certainly I acknowledge this; but at the same time I hope that this Judge
will also deal with those who substitute their own judgements for divine
judgements, and that he will beat back any hypocrite who leads his
poor little flock astray. Many men use the high-flown—that is, magnilo-
quent and bombastic—mode of discourse on God's behalf; few men
either experience or perform magnificent things for God. Unless I am
mistaken, then, it seems right (together with you) to submit such bloated

E

language and pretence to that Judge; it seems good to expunge the things which have been said too wildly and poured out in public; it seems proper to strip away the pretence from those who have been raised by God's goodness but have begun to neglect him and worship themselves. It will be our part, most learned Luther, to do nothing out of emotion, to extort nothing by being abusive, to support nothing on our own authority, in order to await his verdict more confidently. Since we do not want to give the papists breathing space by our dissension, we shall not trust the sharp point of the pen. For others too have their spikes, not very sharp to be sure, but very solid! For this reason, my Luther, whatever you decide in the long run, nevertheless temper your violence, and if there is anything in this exposition of ours that should be charged to us as sin, admonish us publicly if you are not prepared to do so privately. But listen! Take care that you do not attempt anything harsher still, for we shall not let it pass.

Farewell, and occupy your mind in contemplating the death and resurrection of Christ. For if you want to make use of the natural body, do not put your trust in its clothing; and do not hope for a world to come which is so silly that it makes no difference between the verbal trappings and the fundamentals of truth. Be sure that we shall always revere you most deeply if you in your turn continue to be what you hear, namely, *katharos*—that is, pure, clean, untainted by self-esteem, and counting as less than nothing the foul abuse of your advisers. Again farewell, and fear not.

Zürich, April 1, 1527.

> H. Zwingli, yours from the heart,
> as long as sincerity of the heart and
> zeal for the truth remain yours.

III.3   RELIGIOUS DISSENT

Those who stood to Luther's left, whether moderates like the Swiss theologians or radicals like Thomas Müntzer, early accused Luther of refusing them the same liberty of conscience that he had demanded for himself. It is true that his opposition to sectarianism was, if possible, even more determined than his opposition to Rome. He saw in the religious dissent which the Reformation soon unleashed a repetition of the apostles' experience: no sooner had the pure light of the gospel dawned than Satan caused factions and horrid enthusiasms to obscure it. Though the state neither could nor should force anyone to believe, it was entitled to silence such emissaries of Satan, not as heretics, but as a threat to the security of the realm.

III.3.A   While Luther was in hiding in the Wartburg in 1521, Wittenberg itself was the scene of a radical outbreak, provoked by the

'Zwickau prophets', Mark Stübner and Nicholas Storch, and encouraged by Luther's colleagues, Zwilling and Carlstadt. Luther finally came out of hiding to denounce these disruptions, as he described to Nicholas Hausmann of Zwickau on March 17, 1522. (Latin text in Br 2, 474–475; 459; also translated in full in LW 48, 400 ff. and Smith II, 110 f.)

To the faithful evangelist of the church at Zwickau, lord Nicholas Hausmann, his dearest brother in Christ.

Jesus.

Greetings. Although I have been occupied in various ways by our great disturbances here, my Nicholas in Christ, yet I could not fail to write to you, especially when the occasion itself prompted it and the friend of yours who bears this letter requested it. And I hope that you are firm in the faith and are growing daily in the knowledge of Christ. These 'prophets' of yours who have come from Zwickau are in labour and giving birth to monsters I do not like. If they come to birth, the harm they do will not be mild. This spirit of theirs is extremely insidious and specious, but the Lord be with us. Amen.

Satan has attempted great evils here in my fold, to such an extent that it will be difficult to counteract him without scandalising both sides. You should certainly see that you do not permit any innovation to be made by popular decree or force. The things which our people attempted by violence and force are to be withstood only by the Word, overthrown by the Word, destroyed by the Word. It is Satan who makes them act thus. I condemn masses regarded as sacrifices or good works. But I am unwilling to lay a hand on those who are reluctant or unbelieving, or to prohibit them by force. With the Word alone do I condemn; he who believes it, let him believe and follow it, he who does not believe it, let him not believe and go his way. For a person is not to be constrained to faith and the things which are of faith, but is to be drawn by the Word so that he comes spontaneously in willing belief. I condemn images, but with the Word, not so that they will be burned, but so that trust will not be placed in them, as has happened so far and still happens. They would fall of their own accord if an instructed people knew that they were nothing in God's eyes. I similarly condemn the laws of the pope on confession, communion, prayer, and fasting, but with the Word, so that I may free consciences from them. When their consciences are free, then they can use these laws for the sake of others who are weak and still entangled in them, and in turn not use them when people become strong, and in this way love will reign in such external works and laws. But now no one disgusts me more than this mob of ours which has abandoned the Word, faith, and love, and boasts that it is Christian only because they can eat meat, eggs, milk before the eyes of the weak, use both elements [in the sacrament], and give up fasting and prayer.

I beg that you, too, will adopt this position in your teaching. Certainly everything is to be proved by the Word, but hearts are to be led on a little at a time, like the flocks of Jacob [Gen. 33 : 14], so that first they take up the Word gladly, and later, when they are strong, do all things. But perhaps it is superfluous to tell you this, all of which you know. Yet concerned love prompted this duty. Farewell in Christ, and aid the gospel with your prayers. Wittenberg, March 17, 1522.

Your Martin Luther.

III.3.B Andreas Carlstadt, smarting from Luther's rebuke, abandoned academic life and in 1523 became pastor of Orlamünde. There, growing ever more radical, he violently attacked Luther's sacramentalism. Expelled from Saxony in 1524, he took his grievances to south-west Germany, provoking Luther's *Letter to the Christians at Strasbourg against the Fanatic Spirit*. (German text in WA 15, 393–395; also translated in full in LW 40, 65 ff.)

Some of you have written to me that Dr Carlstadt has raised an uproar among you with his fanaticism about the sacrament, images, and baptism, as he has also done elsewhere, and he blames me for driving him out of the country. . . . Dr Carlstadt has not been prepared to justify any one of these points, nor is he capable of it, as I now see from his writings—I really never imagined, and was quite shocked, that the man was still so deeply entrenched. And as I assess his performance, he falls on external things with such vehemence as if the whole strength of the Christian enterprise rested on smashing images, overthrowing the sacrament, and hindering baptism; and with this sort of smoke and vapour he wants to blot out the whole sun and light of the gospel and the vital issues of Christian existence, so that the world would forget everything it had learnt from us so far. And yet he does not come forward to demonstrate what a genuine Christian existence is. For smashing images, denying the sacrament, and attacking baptism is a poor craft, of which even a knave is capable, and it will certainly never make anyone a Christian. So this is a clumsy devil who afflicts me little.

Now, my sincere advice and warning is that you be on your guard and persevere in the single question, what makes a person a Christian? On no account let any other question or skill be as important as this. And if anyone brings something up, begin by saying: 'Friend, does this make one a Christian, or not?' If not, ignore it as certainly not a vital point deserving your undivided concern. But if anyone is too weak to react thus, let him take time and wait until he sees what we or others say about it. So far my own handling of the vital issues has produced right and good, and if anyone says otherwise, he cannot be a good spirit.

I hope I will do no damage even in these outward issues which capture the whole energy of such prophets.

I confess that if Dr Carlstadt or anyone else had been able to convince me five years ago that in the sacrament there was nothing but bread and wine, he would have done me a great service. I was at the time undergoing such severe trials, wrestling and struggling with myself, that I would have escaped gladly, because I saw clearly that I could have struck the papacy my heaviest blow in this way. I also had two correspondents who wrote to me on the subject more skilfully than Dr. Carlstadt, and did not torture the Word according to their own fantasies, as he does.[1] But I am caught, I cannot escape, the text is too powerful and will not allow itself to be wrenched from its meaning by mere words.

Indeed, if it happened today that someone should argue on stronger grounds that mere bread and wine were present, he need not assail me with such spleen—I myself am altogether too inclined to do that, in so far as I know my old Adam! But the way Dr Carlstadt raves on affects me so little that my opinion is only strengthened all the more by it. Even if I did not already think so, such loose, lame spite, without any scriptural warrant and based only on his reason and fancy, would have made me believe that his opinions must amount to nothing, as I hope everyone will see when I now answer. . . .

That he accuses me of driving him out, I would have to endure, were it true; but if God will, I shall answer that, too. I am, however, glad that he is out of our country, and I wish too that he was not in yours. And he should have told himself to withhold such accusations. For I fear that my exoneration will become quite a sharp indictment of him. Protect yourself from the false spirit, if you can! That is my advice— nothing good will come from that source. At Jena, he himself almost convinced me, on the basis of a treatise, that I should not confuse his spirit with the seditious, murderous spirit of Allstedt.[2] But when I was visiting among his Christians at Orlamünde at the Prince's command, I certainly found out what sort of seed he had sown, to such an extent that I was glad that I was not driven out with stones and dung, and some of them gave me their blessing like this: 'Go away in the name of a thousand devils, so that you break your neck before you get out of the city'—although they have dressed themselves up quite beautifully in the booklet they published about it. 'If the ass had horns'—that is, if I were prince of Saxony—Dr Carlstadt would not be banished unless I were petitioned. At least he should not despise the kindness of the princes.

[1] One of these correspondents was Cornelius Hoen, a humanist lawyer at the court of the Netherlands, who wrote a letter in 1520 proposing a symbolist view of the sacrament; Luther was brought a copy in 1521 by two emissaries from Hoen, Hinne Rode and George Saganus. The identity of the second correspondent is not known.

[2] That is, Thomas Müntzer of Allstedt (see III.3.c.)

Yes, dear friends, I pray that you will be wiser than us, seeing we have
become fools and have written about our own deeds. I quite realise that
the devil is only seeking occasion for people to write and read about us
men, whether we are godly or wicked, and thus the vital issues of Christ
will be silenced and the people kept agog with new reports. Just let each
person watch the straight path, what the law, the gospel, faith, the
kingdom of Christ, Christian freedom, love, endurance, human law and
the like are; we have enough here to keep up learning for eternity. . . .
And ask your evangelists, my dear lords and brothers, to turn you away
from Luther and Carlstadt, and direct you ever to Christ.

III.3.c Most extreme and exceptional of the dissenters was Thomas
Müntzer of Allstedt, the radical who first self-consciously rejected
Luther's 'laxity' in the name of the Spirit. By 1524, he was
threatening the rulers of Saxony with godly war if they rejected
his apocalyptic vision of the kingdom of God. Examined for his
iconoclastic views, he sent this unsubmissive 'appeal' to Frederick
the Wise in August, 1524. (German text in Thomas Müntzer,
Schriften und Briefe, Kritische Gesamtausgabe, ed. Franz and
Kirn, Gütersloh 1968, 430–432.)

To the diligent father and lord, Frederick, Elector of the beloved land
of Saxony.
The unalloyed upright fear of God with the unconquerable Spirit of
godly wisdom, in place of my greetings! Since sheer necessity demands
that all unfaith should be openly confronted—unfaith which hitherto has
assumed the guise of the Christian Church and will now be displayed in
the lying shape of carnal and fictitious kindness—by God's command, I
am (as Ezekiel says [13 : 5 ff.]) set before a wall of wretched, corrupt
Christianity, which is not merely, as some imagine, to be mildly rebuked, but is even to be torn up completely by the roots, as indeed God
in a fitting manner has partly done in some places. Now, however, it is
the godless theologians whom Satan drives to their downfall as before it
was the monks and priests, for they have betrayed their guile by mocking
the Holy Spirit of Christ most contemptuously and denouncing him as a
devil in many of the elect, as the lying Luther now does in the scandalous
letter against me which he has sent to the Dukes of Saxony, where he
blasts forth so grimly and maliciously without any brotherly warning,
like some splendid tyrant. Therefore I pray you, for God's sake, to consider earnestly what a ludicrous situation would arise, were I to requite
him for his slander, which I am not inclined to do, yet since it has
offended many godly men from foreign lands and cities who have
heeded my teaching, such slander can hardly be left unanswered.
I therefore loyally beg that Your Excellency will not prevent or forbid
me from serving, preaching, or writing to poor Christendom to avoid

the new risk that Christianity may be distorted again under Luther's label, and afterwards restored to unity only with difficulty.

In short, this is my earnest intention: I preach the sort of Christian faith which does not harmonise with Luther, but which is identical in all the hearts of the elect upon earth (Ps. 67) [Vulg. 68]. . . . I have promised my dear lord, Duke John your brother, to submit my books for examination before printing, but I submit not merely to the venomous and pompous judgement of the scribes, but even to him who reckons the coming of faith to the crushed heart. Accordingly, if you will be my gracious lord and prince, then I will let this Christian faith go forth, in the clear light of day before the whole world, both in speech and writing, and make it known with all devotion. But if this plea receives no satisfaction from Your Excellency, then you will have to take account of the aversion and despair of the common folk against you and the others. For the people have pinned great hopes on you, and God has granted you foresight in advance of other lords and princes. But if you abuse it in this case, then it will be said of you: 'See, here is a man who was not willing to have God as his defence, but has abandoned himself to worldly arrogance.' . . .

Given at Allstedt, August 3, in the year of Christ 1524.

Thomas Müntzer, a sincere bondsman of God.

III.3.D At about the same time, Müntzer received two letters of encouragement from the growing circle of Zürich Anabaptists led by Conrad Grebel. Here is their second letter. Their warning against belligerence went unheeded: Müntzer was executed at Mülhausen in June, 1525, for inciting the peasants to revolt. (German text in Thomas Müntzer: *Schriften und Briefe*, ed. Franz and Kirn, 97–101: 69b; also translated in part in LCC XXV, 83 ff.)

Beloved brother Thomas: Just as I had hurriedly written in all our names and was thinking that this messenger would not wait while we also wrote to Luther, he had to stay and wait because of the rain. So I have written to Luther, too, for myself and the others, my brothers and yours, and urged him to abstain from false leniency towards the weak (namely, themselves). Andreas Castelberg has written to Carlstadt. Meanwhile, Hans Hujuff of Halle, our fellow-citizen and brother who was with you recently, has received a letter and a shameful booklet by Luther, unfit for anyone to write who intends, like the apostles, to be 'firstfruits'. Paul teaches that 'the servant of the Lord' should act differently [2 Tim. 2 : 24]. I see that he wants to denounce you for outlawry and to hand you over to the prince, to whom he has bound his gospel, just as Aaron had to have Moses for a god [Exod. 4 : 16]. On the basis of your booklets and protests I find you without guilt, for I cannot infer from them that you reject baptism entirely, but that you condemn infant baptism and the misunderstanding of baptism. What the word 'water' in John 3 [: 5] means, we shall examine closely both in your text and in the biblical text. Hujuff's brother writes that you have preached against the princes that they should be attacked with physical force. If this is true, or if you are so prepared to defend war, carved tablets, hymn-singing, or other things which you do not find a clear text for, as you do not for these points I have mentioned, then I exhort you by the salvation common to us all: if you will abstain from them and from all conceits now or hereafter, you will be completely pure, and besides you have pleased us more on other points than anyone else in Germany, or in any other land. If you fall into the hands of Luther and the Duke, let the articles I have mentioned drop and stand by the others as a hero and champion of God. Be strong. You have the Bible (from which Luther has made 'bible, bauble, babel') as defence against that idolatrous Lutheran leniency which he and the learned shepherds about us have cultivated throughout the world, a defence against a beguiling, permissive faith, against their preaching in which they do not teach Christ as they ought. They have even opened the gospel to the whole world for all to read for themselves—or they ought to read it, but not many do when everyone is depending on them instead! With us there are not twenty men who believe the Word of God; now they trust persons— Zwingli, Leo [Jud], and others elsewhere who are regarded as similarly learned. And if you must therefore suffer, you know well that there is no other alternative. Christ must yet suffer more in his members. But he will strengthen them and hold them fast to the end. God give grace to you and to us when our shepherds wax so furious and frenzied against us, inveighing against us in the public pulpit as knaves and Satans changed into angels of light. And in time we shall see persecution directed at us through them. Therefore pray for us to God. We exhort you once again, and we do so because we love you so dearly and honour you for the clarity of your word, and dare to write to you in trust: do not act, teach, or set up anything according to human conceit, your own or anyone else's, and what has been set up, suppress it again; but set up and teach only the divine, clear Word and usage, together with the discipline of Christ, unalloyed baptism and unalloyed Supper (as we have touched on in our first letter, and on which you are far better informed than a hundred of us). If you and Carlstadt, Jacob Strauss and Michael Stiefel are not willing to be rigorously and completely pure (as I, however, and my brethren hope that you will be), it would be a wretched gospel which had come into the world. But you are far purer than our fellows here and those at Wittenberg, who daily stumble from one distortion of Scripture to another and from one blindness into another greater blindness. I believe and think that they want to become

true papists and popes. No more now. May God our leader with his Son
Jesus Christ our saviour and his Spirit and Word be with you and us all.

> Conrad Grebel, Andreas Castel-
> berg, Felix Mantz, Heinrich Aberli,
> Johann Broedli, Hans Ockenfuss,
> Hans Hujuff your countryman from
> Halle, your brethren and seven new
> young Müntzers for Luther.

If freedom is granted you to oppose the preachers and nothing
happens to you, we wish to send you a copy of our treatise against
Luther and the answer which he has written against us. We have admon-
ished him as well as our preachers here. In this way, if God does not
prevent it, we wish to point out their shortcomings and not fear what
will happen to us as a result. Besides this we have kept no other copy,
except some letters we have written to Martin, your adversary. Therefore receive our unskilled, rough-hewn writing kindly, confident that
you have shown us true love if we are one in the Word and tribulation
and opponents, even though you are so much more learned and forthright in the Spirit. For the sake of this unity we have said or written
enough to you. If you, God willing, will cordially write back to us your
greetings in a long letter, you will arouse in us great joy and heartfelt
love towards yourself.

III.3.E The deepest dissension in infant Protestantism was that between
the Lutherans and the Swiss over the eucharist. Luther and
Zwingli did not clash directly until 1527, but in 1526 Luther had
reviewed the dispute in his preface to Johann Brenz's *Swabian
Syngramma*. (Latin text in WA 19, 457–461.)

Martin Luther to all dear friends in Christ.

Grace and peace in Christ, our Lord and Saviour. This is a Latin
booklet called *Syngramma*, published by the preacher in Swabia against
the new rabble who are introducing novel dreams about the sacraments
and disrupting the world. I find the book so pleasing that I was prepared to translate it into German, since, with many other things to write
and do taking precedence, I have not been able to write a special treatment quickly. But now that my translation in turn has been delayed, a
German version has been produced by my good friend, Master Johann
Agricola, teacher at Eisleben, and I have been spared the trouble. Even
when I wrote against the heavenly prophets and attacked Carlstadt's
'*touto*', I anticipated that others in succession (especially educated men)
would follow with '*est*' and '*significat*'; yet this is really such a childish,
incompetent argument. There is no example of it in Scripture, and even

if there were examples, it could not thereby be proved that the words, 'This is my body', should and must be so taken. They will never prove it—that I know for sure. For it is a completely different thing to say: 'It *may* mean this' and to say: 'It *must* mean this and cannot mean anything else.' The conscience cannot rely on the first version, but it can rely on the second. I thought, and I still think, that in my book against Carlstadt I had established this point sufficiently well that no one could refute it; and I still do not see that the principle I stated there has been genuinely assailed or shaken. But what I wrote is so despised by these exalted spirits that they do not even look at it, and after a mere glance in its direction conclude that it is all worthless, and that I must offer something quite different. Well, then, since I did not have time to write against this spirit in particular, I will bear witness to my faith with this foreword, and sincerely counsel those who will let themselves be warned to beware of these false prophets who call our God a 'baked God', a 'breaden God'; they call us 'God's flesh-eaters', 'God's blood-drinkers', and I know not how many other horribly blasphemous names, and yet they stay amongst patient, meek people who suffer great persecution and confess Christ aright. But the devil rules the patient and meek who overthrow the faith! I hope that such horrible blaspheming will come to a swift end, and he along with it. Even so, we have really deserved such pitiful beings and sects through our own ingratitude and persecution of the gospel, and through our wickedness we deserve still more the even greater distress to come.

First, this sect is so prolific that it has grown five or six heads within a single year.[3] The first was Dr Carlstadt with his '*touto*'. The second was Ulrich Zwingli with his '*significat*'. The third is Johann Oecolampadius with his 'figure of the body'. The fourth is transposing the word-order of the text. A fifth is on the way, which rearranges the words. A sixth is now being born, who tosses the words like dice. Perhaps a seventh will show up as well and shuffle cards! Each individual wants to come out on top here. Look, has God's Spirit not forewarned us enough about such sects which divide up like this from the start? Where else does this portrait belong but with the beasts of the Apocalypse, where there are also beasts with one body and many heads

---

[3] The 'six heads' are the following new interpretations of 'This is my body which is given for you': 1. Andreas Carlstadt: When Christ said 'This (*touto*) is my body', he was pointing to his own body, not the bread. 2. Ulrich Zwingli: 'This is my body' meant 'This signifies my body' (*est = significat*). 3. Johann Oecolampadius: 'This is a figure of my body (*figura corporis*)', a logical refinement of Zwingli's position. 4. A view, attributed in a letter of Luther's only to 'C——': 'That which is given for you is my body.' 5. Caspar Schwenkfeld and Valentin Krautwold: 'My body, which is given for you, is this (namely, spiritual food).' 6. Melanchthon had heard by letter of yet another arrangement, attributed to a citizen of Cologne, but Luther had no specific information.

[Revelation 13]? These sects hold precisely the same thing in the long run, like one body, but in motives and basis each individual gang has proclaimed its own head and its own style, even though they are all set up to blaspheme one and the same Christian truth. Anyone who by now is not repelled or forewarned by such a horrible picture and God's admonition deserves to have to believe not only that there is mere bread and wine in the sacrament, but that it is mere mushroom or morel!

Secondly, the true Spirit not only takes care to avoid rebellious arguments and to present always a single ground of belief to all the world throughout his preaching (for he is not a God of duplicity, but of simplicity); no, he presents unwavering arguments, so that the longer one resists them, the stronger they become and grow. But with this beast it is quite different. Its first head, Carlstadt's *'touto'*, is drooping already and has not been able to sustain a single blow; so even they have to admit themselves that he was wrong, and the Spirit could not have dwelt there. The excuse that holy people sometimes stumble in faith and life does not help here, even though it is true. No, the Spirit has never let his own teachers err in promulgating the fundamentals of doctrine, especially when new ones are springing up as they are now. Certainly, he lets the arguments be weak, but he does not let them fail or be overthrown. Rather (as I said) he makes them grow and prevail—not like Carlstadt's *'touto'*, lying prostrate. The same thing is true of Zwingli's *'significat'*; its head, too, has drooped and faded right away. For there is no single instance in Scripture where 'signifies' can be derived from 'is'; and if, after all, some instance were produced (which it cannot be), they will still never be able to derive 'signifies' from 'is' in the Supper. So here, too, his spirit has erred and fallen. That makes two major cautions and warnings from God to all who fear him and wish to believe truly. In fact, there is no surer way to recognise the devil than by lying and duplicity in the faith, and there is no better way to recognise the Spirit of God than by the truth. But this does not help: the world must and will be seduced, just as in Arius's day, when the same sorts of lies should also have served as warnings but did not help.

Thirdly, this spirit is above all a fickle, volatile spirit which does not stand still on any issue, as I have proved both orally and in writing. If one demands of them that they demonstrate that the saying, 'This is my body' or its parallels, used to be understood in their sense, and otherwise than the plain, common, natural words indicate, they take up another little tune—they are simply full of words and ideas! Here they explain from John 6 that there are two kinds of eating, spiritual and physical, as if no one knew that before; or sometimes they praise themselves for being so pious and enduring so much; or they deny that there is any need to insist that Christ's body and blood are present; or else they snatch at something to the effect that 'they do not have to stick to the

words anyway'—otherwise they would be caught! In this way they fill
up pages and ears with fruitless words, so that one cannot fail to see how
Satan twists and changes himself into every shape to avoid being
ensnared in his own lie. I say, then, that such falderols and flights of
fancy have nothing to do with the case; I say they should stick to the
words and demonstrate their understanding from the self-same passage
of the text—oh yes, now they take me back to John 6 or to the monkey's
tail, and in the meantime the issue is lost in the babble and still nothing
is settled. It is the true mark of Satan's skill to flicker in this way, like
night fires in the fields at evening.

I therefore state my judgement; however intensely it displeases them,
I am nevertheless sure that it is true, for in this case I am thoroughly
conversant both with the faith and with the devil. Their error rests on
two grounds; first, it seems such an ungainly idea by rational standards,
and secondly, it seems unnecessary, that Christ's body and blood should
be in the bread and wine—that would be absurdity, not necessity. They
have clung to these two points, and through Satan's temptation it has
so penetrated into them—'as oil soaks into bone' (Ps. 109) [: 18; Vulg.
108 : 18]—that they cannot get rid of it. Accordingly, now they wear
such distorting glasses before their eyes that they come toddling to
Scripture to see how can they drag their own opinion in and force the
Scripture to their interpretation. In this way the Word may not be
understood to mean what it says; you have to mould it and produce
here a 'touto', there a 'significat', here a 'figura', now transpose the
words, now rearrange the text, now shuffle the text like a pack of cards.
See, this is where the sects come from; but if they stuck to the words as
they stood, or demonstrated from the text and sequence, or on other
good grounds, that the words were to be understood differently from
what they say, they would not give rise to any such factions.

If, now, they want to establish their interpretation, they will really
have to take a different sword in hand; the treatises they have submitted,
if they are like the *Subsidium* or the *Antisyngramma*,[4] will not do it;
they can lead many astray, but they can settle nothing fundamentally.
Hereby I also wish to warn all pious Christians to be prepared for these
sects, and to abide by the pure, unalloyed words of Christ; indeed, we
have the advantage that we dare not twist or bend the words as they do.
I also ask that you will read this booklet diligently. If God gives me
time, I will write specifically on this subject, but meanwhile I thank my
God that he does not let the devil produce more potent lies than these
are. God's grace be with us all.

[4] Ulrich Zwingli, *Subsidium sive coronis de eucharistia*, August 1525; Johann
Oecolampadius, *Antisyngramma*, February 1526, a reply to the Latin first edition
of Brenz's *Syngramma*.

III.3.F Luther's rejection of other views may seem at first hidebound and
sweeping. In fact, it was only after agonised heart-searching and
self-doubt that Luther reached his theological judgements upon
them. Here is what he told his students, during the dark days of
1527, in lectures on 1 John 2 : 19 and 4 : 2–3. (Latin and German
text in WA 20, 673–674 and 726–727.)

It is a deplorable and yet a consoling thing that we are blamed for
whatever evil happens in the world—sedition, insurrection, and all the
rest. However grave the sin, the taunt is always: 'If only the pope had
gained control, perhaps so many heretics would not have rebelled, or
perhaps the present turmoil would not have broken out among the
peasants.' Indeed, it is true that heretics have not been put to death since
we burst through, and that we constructed the path of liberty on which
the fanatics have fallen flat. This is true; should it make us afraid? I
have often wondered whether it would have been better to have preserved the papacy than to see so much tumult; but it is better that the
errors of the papacy should be illuminated and snatched from the devil's
jaws than that all should perish. How did it come about that Christ was
crucified? Out of his own little band of disciples! If Judas had not been
there, he would not have been crucified. So we, too, have a Judas among
us who scatters us. This is why we are blamed. We are not able to deny
that 'they went out from us', but our consolation is that 'they were not of
us' [John 2 : 19]. The apostles heard themselves called 'these men who
turned the world upside down' [Acts 17 : 6]. Wherever there were riots
and crowds, the apostles had to hear the charge: 'Before, the Roman
realm was at peace, but now these fellows wickedly condemn it with
their gospel.' So we hear today: 'What good has come from it? Monks
take wives, and secession has begun.' In this way the Gentiles were
caused to stumble, as the Jews were by faith. So today it is a very great
stumbling-block—and I regard it as the greatest evil—that we are at
logger-heads amongst ourselves. Who began it? Our boast is that we
have not sought our own advantage. First Müntzer, and then the Sacramentarians, wanted to have a better spirit. They have gone out from us:
since they have created the stumbling-block, let them make the excuses,
let them reply to the charge. . . .

I have encountered spirits who have confessed Christ so fervently that
I have scarcely set eyes on such confession and such experience—they
seemed flawless, as we say. But what were they doing? They worked
themselves up into an ecstasy so that truth would be revealed to them,
but afterwards nothing came of it except that God and certain voices
were to be heard 'by inspiration'! When I reached this point I knew
what was happening. These men 'come in spirit to God'; and if a man
wants to create his own access to God, it is Satan at work. For the whole
Christ is in the flesh. We acknowledge the existence of no God except

him who is in the man who came down from heaven. I begin with the swaddling clothes and I receive him who comes, and I seek him who dwells, in that flesh. The stairway which I ascend is not prepared by me. They started by eliminating things—'water and wine are nothing'—and eventually they went so far in this direction that Müntzer closed his eyes to our Christ because he was something external! . . . A like spirit, he also denies that Christ has come into the flesh. For he says that 'the flesh profits nothing'. On the ground that the bodily word is nothing and that the sacrament is the outward sign, they simply snatch away the flesh of Christ because 'it profits nothing', and instead one must possess a versatile spirit!

III.3.G When Luther wrote against Anabaptism in 1528, baptist lay preachers had not yet infiltrated Electoral Saxony; but soon they did appear, and in this 1532 *Open Letter about Skulking and Furtive Preachers*, Luther condemned them on both religious and civil grounds. (German text in WA 30 III, 518–520; also translated in full in LW 40, 383 ff.)

To the able and worthy Eberhart von der Tanne, magistrate at the Wartburg, my gracious lord and friend.

Grace and peace in Christ, our Lord and Saviour. Amen. I have heard, my dear lord and friend, how the Anabaptists are trying to worm their way into your area too, and to infect our people with their poison. Even though I know that you have been sufficiently informed and forewarned by Justus Menius's book, and that you have discharged your duty against these messengers of the devil justly and commendably, yet because the devil does not willingly give up, and there are many who, having once glanced at a book, fling it into a corner and forget everything they have been warned about and really need a constant daily reminder, by this letter to you I wish to beseech and warn anew all other magistrates, cities, and lords to beware of such infiltrators, so that we may do our part.

And first, this is how to convict them properly and easily: If they are asked about their call, who has told them to infiltrate here or to come and preach in hidden corners, they will be unable to give an answer or to point to their authority. And I tell you the truth: if such infiltrators possessed no other fault and were absolute saints, yet this single fact (that they come skulking without authorisation and unbidden) would prove abundantly that they are the devil's messengers and teachers. For the Holy Spirit does not sneak about, but flies down openly from heaven. Serpents slither, but doves fly. So such sneaking is truly the devil's progress, that is sure.

I have heard about how these infiltrators attach themselves to labourers during the harvest and preach to them in the fields while they work, and also to charcoal-burners and solitary people in the woods, and everywhere sow their seed and spread their poison, diverting the people from their parish churches. There, indeed, you see the true hand- and footprint of the devil, how he shuns the light and noses around in the dark. Who is so dull that he cannot recognise that they are the devil's messengers? If they were from God and were honest, they would go first of all to the pastor and come to terms with him, indicating their call and making clear what they believe, and asking him if he would let them preach openly. Then if the pastor would not let them, they would be blameless before God, and could then shake the dust from their feet, etc. [Luke 10 : 11]. For the pastor has charge of the pulpit, baptism, and the Sacrament, and the care of all souls devolves upon him, but now they want secretly to displace the pastor with all his authority, and yet not disclose their own secret authority. That makes them real thieves and murderers of souls, slanderers and enemies of Christ and his Church.

There is no other remedy here than that both offices, the spiritual and the temporal, should take action with all diligence. The spiritual office must certainly instruct the people constantly and diligently, impressing upon them the points I have mentioned: to admit no infiltrators, to recognise them clearly as the devil's messengers, and to learn to ask them: 'Where do you come from? Who has sent you to me? Who has told you to preach to me? Where are the seals and letters you have from the men that sent you? What signs do you perform to show that God sent you? Why do you not go to our pastor? Why do you sneak along to me so secretly and cower in a corner? Why do you not step forward openly? If you are a child of the light, why do you shun the light?' With such questions (I believe) one can guard against them easily. For they cannot prove their call, and if we could bring the people to this understanding of calling, such infiltrators would be readily controlled. . . .

The temporal office must also look to this matter. For since such infiltrators are the devil's messengers to preach sheer poison and lies, and the devil is not only a liar but also a murderer, his purpose cannot fail to be also to stir up rebellion and murder through these messengers of his (even if he appears to act peaceably for the time being), and thus to overthrow both the spiritual and the temporal governments against the will of God. He cannot do otherwise, for it is his nature to lie and murder. Thus those who are his, who are possessed by him, do not control themselves, but must act as he impels them. Thus magistrates, judges, and those concerned with government should be instructed and aware that they are right to suspect such infiltrators not only of false teaching, but also of murder and rebellion, since they know that these people are driven by the devil. . . .

IV

PROTESTANT POLITY

LUTHER'S REJECTION OF the authority of Rome, and his sweeping criticism of the ecclesiastical system, had an inescapable corollary—the task of reordering the structures of authority, worship, oversight, and moral order for the newly independent evangelical churches. Here the fundamental document is the shattering 1520 treatise, *The Babylonian Captivity of the Church*, which deserves to be read in full. (It is readily available in English in LW 36, 11 ff.; SW 1, 363 ff.; PE II, 170 ff.; Woolf I, 208 ff.; *Three Treatises*, 119 ff.; Wace and Buchheim 141 ff.) In his *Appeal to the German Nobility*, Luther had assailed the triumphalism and pastoral dereliction of the hierarchy; now, in this dignified but devastating sequel, he plunged to the heart of the Church's control over the laity—the system of sacramental grace. He rejected transubstantiation; he assailed the Roman view of the mass as a sacrifice; he insisted that the laity should receive 'both kinds' in the eucharist, the cup as well as the bread; he denied that baptism automatically effected grace apart from faith, and that the sacrament of penance was essential as the 'second plank' of salvation from sin after baptism; he rejected any special priestly powers of absolution; and he repudiated as human invention the sacramental graces of confirmation, marriage, orders, and extreme unction. His learned attack, accompanied by fierce comments on the human suffering imposed by tyrannical canon laws, did more than any other writing to undercut the longstanding clerical dominance of the Church. For by liberating the grace of the dominical sacraments from the control of the clergy, and by rejecting the efficacy of other churchly graces, Luther sought to free the laity from priestly autocracy, and to demolish the sacerdotal system of merits and sanctions, regulations and fees, penances and vows. He achieved such success that in coming years the signal for reformation in region after region was abolition of the Roman Mass, the emptying of monasteries, and the exaltation of preaching to the central place in worship.

IV.1   REORDERING THE CHURCH

Demolition of the sacerdotal system was one thing; its replacement with a workable Church order was quite another. However sweeping his criticisms, Luther was in fact conservative in seeking to retain whatever he held to be good and catholic in traditional practice, and in making changes slowly to avoid unnecessary offence. The most dramatic vacuum was created by his onslaught on monasticism (see I.2.D), for the monks had long supplied the work-force of the Church. Here, however, we shall concentrate on Luther's proposals for choosing clergy, improving worship, and reforming the state of the parishes.

IV.1.A Luther's approach to Church government was flexible, permitting an episcopal, synodical, or congregational polity as local need dictated. He outlined the ideal implications of 'the priesthood of all believers' in his 1523 treatise, *That a Christian Congregation . . . Has the Right and Power to Call, Appoint, and Dismiss Teachers.* (German text in WA 11, 408–414; also translated in full in PE IV, 75 ff.; SW 2, 325 ff.)

In the business of judging teaching and appointing and dismissing a teacher or pastor, one must pay absolutely no attention to any human law, regulation, tradition, usage, or custom, even if it is a law of pope or emperor, prince or bishop, or has been observed by half the world or all of it, or has existed for one year or a thousand years. For the soul of man is an eternal thing, and above everything that is temporal. It must therefore be governed and shaped only by the eternal Word. For it is utterly ludicrous to govern the conscience for God with human laws and long-standing custom . . . Christ establishes exactly the opposite: he takes away from bishops, scholars, and councils both the right and the power to judge teaching, and he gives them to everyone and to all Christians in common. He says so in John 10 [: 1–18]: 'My sheep know my voice.' Again, 'My sheep do not follow a stranger, but flee from him, for they do not know the voice of strangers.' Again, 'All who came before me are thieves and robbers; but the sheep do not heed them.'

Here you see clearly who has the right to judge teaching. Bishop, pope, scholar—everyone has the right to teach; but the sheep should judge whether it is Christ's voice teaching or the voice of strangers . . . Christ says again in Matthew 7 [: 15]: 'Beware of false prophets, who come to you in sheep's clothing but inwardly are ravening wolves.' See, here Christ commits the judgement not to the prophets or the teachers, but to the pupils or the sheep, for how could you beware of false prophets if you had no right to assess, adjudicate, and judge their teaching? Certainly there can be no false prophet amongst the hearers, but only amongst the teachers. Therefore all teachers should and must be subject to the judgement of the hearers, and so should their teaching. . . .

So now we conclude that where there is a Christian congregation which has the gospel, they not only have the right and power, but are

obliged for their souls' salvation, according to the duty that they undertook to Christ in their baptism, to shun, flee, set aside, and forsake the
authority which the bishops, abbots, cloisters, seminaries, and the like
are now exercising, since it is quite obvious that they are teaching and
ruling against God and his Word. . . .

But because a Christian congregation should not be without God's
Word, and cannot be, it follows directly enough that it must have
teachers and preachers who promote that Word. Yet in this accursed
last time, the bishops and the false spiritual government are not and will
not be such teachers. They are also unwilling to provide or allow such
teachers. And as God is not to be asked to send a new preacher from
heaven, we must act according to Scripture, and from amongst ourselves
call and appoint those that are found fit for it, men whom God has
enlightened with understanding and has equipped with the necessary
gifts. For no one can deny that every individual Christian has God's
Word, is taught by God, and is his anointed priest. As Christ says in
John 6 [: 45]: 'They will all be taught by God.' And Psalm 44 [: 8,
Vulg; A.V. 45 : 7]: 'God has anointed you with the oil of gladness
above your fellows.' These 'fellows' are Christians, Christ's brothers,
who are consecrated priests with him. As Peter also says in I Peter 2
[: 9]: 'You are a royal priesthood, that you should make known the
praise of him who has called you into his wonderful light.'

But if it is the case that they have God's Word and are anointed by
him, then they are also obliged to confess, teach, and spread it. . . . You
will say: 'How so? If he has not been called to it, surely he dare not
preach, as you yourself have often taught?' Answer: Here you should
consider the Christian man in two different situations. First, in a situation where there are no other Christians, he needs no other calling than
that he is a Christian, inwardly called and anointed by God, and it is
his duty under the obligation of brotherly love to preach and teach the
gospel to erring heathen or non-Christians, even if no one calls him to
it. . . . Secondly, however, when he is in a situation where there are
Christians who share with him this power and right, he should not push
himself forward, but let himself be called and set up, so that he preaches
and teaches in the stead, and by the mandate, of the others . . . 1 Corinthians 14 gives abundant authority to a Christian congregation to
preach, license preaching, and issue calls. In case of special necessity,
Paul himself calls each Christian in particular apart from the call of
men. Accordingly, we should have no doubt that a congregation which
has the gospel must and should choose and call from amongst itself
someone to teach the Word on its behalf. . . .

Moreover, even if our present bishops were men of integrity who
wanted to have the gospel and wanted to appoint preachers with
integrity, they could not and should not do even this without the con-

gregation's consent, choice, and calling, except where they are forced by necessity so that souls will not be lost for want of God's Word. For in such necessity (as you have heard), not only may the individual provide a preacher, either through prayer or through the power of temporal authority, but he should also offer himself to step forward and teach, if he can. For necessity is necessity, and has no bounds—just as everyone should move and act when fire breaks out in the city, and not tarry until someone asks him! Otherwise, where there is no such necessity, and people are available who have the right, power, and grace to teach, no bishop should appoint anyone without the choice, consent, and call of the congregation, but should ratify the one whom the congregation has elected and called.

IV.1.B Luther early saw the need and value of evangelical forms of worship. His greatest contribution was the creation of Protestant hymnody. He adapted much old Church music for congregational use, and composed words and music for many rousing hymns, of which this 1523 hymn is typical. (German text in WA 35, 422–425; also translated in full in LW 53, 219 f.)

1. Rejoice, dear Christians, now rejoice,
   And let us leap for gladness.
   Exult and sing we in one voice,
   With love and free from sadness,
   What God for our sakes hath decreed,
   And with his own sweet, wondrous deed
   Hath won at cost so precious.

2. The devil's bondsman low I lay,
   A slave of death beleaguered.
   My sin assailed me night and day,
   In sin was I conceived.
   In ever deeper sin I fell,
   In all my life was nothing well,
   But sin had overcome me.

3. 'Good works' of mine were valueless,
   Their goodness was all painted.
   'Free will' abhorred God's righteousness,
   For good it was too tainted.
   Distraught and driven to despair,
   There was no hope but dying there,
   To sink in hell my ending.

4. Then God took pity from above
   To see my bitter grieving,
   And thought on his own tender love,
   And purposed to relieve me.
   He turned his father's heart to me;
   For that he bore no meagre fee,
   The dearest price it cost him.

5. He spoke to his beloved Son:
   'The time is here for mercy.
   Go down, my heart's most precious crown,
   And save him from his misery,
   And help him from sin's bondage grim,
   And strangle bitter death for him.
   So let him live, beside thee.'

6. The Father's Word the Son obeyed,
   And from a pure young mother
   Himself on earth a man was made:
   He came to be my brother.
   Now all his strength in secret lies:
   He took upon him my poor guise,
   For he would snare the devil.

7. He said to me: 'Hold thou to me
   And thou shalt be successful.
   I freely give myself for thee:
   And in thy place I wrestle.
   For I am thine, and mine thou art,
   And thou from me shalt ne'er depart:
   The devil shall not part us.

8. 'The enemy will shed my blood
   My very life to plunder.
   All this I suffer for thy good:
   From that thy faith ne'er sunder.
   My life is mingled with thy death,
   Thy sin my pureness swalloweth.
   So thou becomest blessed.

9. 'From this life to my father's side
   I go, and heaven inherit.
   Thy master there I shall abide
   And send to thee my spirit.

In trouble he will comfort thee,
And teach thee how to learn of me,
And into truth will lead thee.

10. 'What I have done and I have taught
Be that thy deed and story,
So that God's kingdom spreads abroad
To his own praise and glory.
Of man's devices be thou ware:
For they besmirch the treasure rare.
With this last word I leave thee.'

IV.1.c Luther revised the major worship services to express the evangelical message. In 1523 he issued a revised Latin Mass, and in 1526 a *German Mass and Order of Worship* with this preface. (German text in WA 19, 72–75; also translated in full in PE IV, 170 ff.; SW 3, 397 ff.; Woolf II, 316 ff.)

Before everything else I wish, amicably and for the sake of God's will, to beg all those who see this Order of Divine Worship of ours, or wish to follow it, not to make any binding regulation out of it or to bind or compel anyone's conscience with it, but to use it as they like in Christian liberty how, where, when, and as long as the situation allows and requires it. For on our part, we are not publishing this with the intention of lording it over anyone or subjecting him to regulation by this means, but because there is widespread pressure for German masses and services, and much complaining and annoyance over the disparate character of the new masses which everyone is making for himself, some with good intentions, but others from an itch to produce something novel and to shine amongst men, not to be mere teachers; for that is always the way with Christian liberty—there are few who use it except for their own pleasure or advantage, instead of for God's honour and their neighbour's edification. But while it is up to the individual's conscience how he uses his liberty, which is not to be refused or forbidden anyone, we are nevertheless bound to see that liberty is and shall be the servant of love and of our neighbour. Where, then, it turns out that men are muddled or led astray by this variety of usage, we are really obliged to forgo our liberty, and as far as possible to see that what we practise or permit edifies other people and does not offend them. For since this is an outward order and has no bearing on our conscience before God, and yet can be of help to our neighbour, we should strive for love, as St Paul teaches, so that we may be of one mind [2 Cor. 13 : 11], and maintain as best we can a common practice and ceremonial, just as all Christians have one baptism and one sacrament, and no one has received a special one of his own from God.

. . . Such orders of service are necessary for the sake of those who are not yet Christians, or need to be strengthened; for a Christian does not need baptism, the Word, and the sacraments as a Christian, since he already possesses all things, but as a sinner. Above all, they are needful for the sake of the simple and the young folk, who should and must be trained and instructed daily in Scripture and God's Word, so that they become familiar with Scripture, skilled, fluent, and knowledgeable in it, in order to defend their faith and in time teach others and help advance the kingdom of Christ. For their sake one should read, sing, preach, write, and compose, and if it were helpful or necessary to achieve this, I should let all the bells peal and all the organs play and let everything that can ring, ring! For this is why papal services are so damnable: they make laws, works, and merits out of worship, and thus suppress faith. They do not use them to lead the young and the immature to become familiar with Scripture and God's Word, but to entrench themselves in their services and regard them as intrinsically useful and necessary to salvation—that is the devil! This was not the reason the ancients arranged or instituted them.

We can distinguish three kinds of service and mass. The first is the Latin mass which we published previously, called *Formula Missae*. I have no intention now of withdrawing or altering this, but just as we have retained it among us so far, we shall continue to feel free to use it where and when it suits us or occasion demands. By no means do I wish the Latin language to be completely excluded from divine service, since my whole concern is for the young. And if I could, and Greek and Hebrew were as common among us as Latin and possessed as many fine hymns and songs as Latin has, we should hold masses, sing, and read in all four languages, German, Latin, Greek and Hebrew on various Sundays. I do not hold at all with those who confine themselves to only one language and despise all others. I should rather train the sort of young people and others who could be of use to Christ in other lands and converse with the people. . . .

The second is the German mass and service, which should be drawn up with the simple layfolk in mind. But we must allow both these methods to continue side by side and to be maintained openly in the churches for all the people, for amongst them are many who do not yet believe and are not yet Christians, and usually just stand there and gape, looking for something new—as if we were holding a service amongst Turks or heathen in an open square or field! This is still not an organised stable congregation in which Christians could be governed according to the gospel. This service is an open invitation to faith and to Christianity.

But the third style, which should possess the true character of evangelical order, must not happen so openly, in the public square and amongst all sorts of people. Rather, those who want to be Christians in earnest and to confess the gospel by deed and word should enrol their names and gather alone somewhere in a house to pray, read, baptise, receive the sacrament, and practise other Christian works. In this order, those who do not walk Christianly could be known, chastised, corrected, expelled or excommunicated in accordance with Christ's rule in Matthew 18 [15–20]. Here, too, the alms of Christians could be collected in common, to be willingly given and distributed amongst the poor after the example of St Paul in 2 Corinthians 9. Here there would be no need for much grand singing. Here one could maintain a short, refined style for baptism and the sacrament and build everything on the Word and prayer and love. . . . But as yet I cannot and do not wish to organise or establish such a communion or congregation, since I do not yet have the people or staff for it, and in fact I do not see many who are anxious for it. But if it happened that I had to do it, and were convinced that I could not refuse with a good conscience, I should do my part gladly and help to the best of my ability. Meanwhile, I shall let the two styles I have described suffice, and in addition to preaching I shall help promote amongst the people the sort of services which train our youth and invite and attract others to believe.

IV.1.D To instruct the young in doctrine and worship, Luther placed great store by catechetical training. (Consult his two famous works, *The Small Catechism* and *The Large Catechism*, available in Lenker 24, 16 ff.; *The Book of Concord*, 158 ff.; and in separate Lutheran editions.) This passage is the continuation of IV.1C above. (WA 19, 76–77.)

The first necessity for German worship is a plain, straightforward, good, simple catechism. 'Catechism' means an instruction in which heathen who want to become Christians are taught and shown what they should believe, do, avoid and remember as Christians: hence young candidates who were admitted to this instruction and were learning the faith before they were baptised used to be called 'catechumens'. I know no plainer or better way to present this instruction or preparation than the way it has been presented from the beginning of Christianity and has remained to the present, namely in these three parts: the Ten Commandments, the Creed, and the Our Father. These three parts contain, in a brief and simple form, virtually everything that a Christian needs to know. In the absence of a special gathering for the purpose, this instruction should be preached from the pulpit, either occasionally or daily as necessity demands, and rehearsed or reread at home morning and evening with the children and servants to make Christians of them; and not so that they merely learn to recite them by heart, as has been the case up to now, but they should be questioned on each point and answer what it means and how they understand it. If all the questions cannot be answered at one time, one part can be taken up one day, another the next. For if the parents or guardians of the young will not make this effort, either themselves or through others, no catechism will ever be successfully instituted. Then a special gathering for this purpose would have to be organised, as I said.

For instance, they should be questioned as follows: 'What do you pray?' *Answer:* 'The Our Father.' 'What does it mean when you say: Our Father, who art in heaven?' *Answer:* 'That God is not an earthly but a heavenly Father, who will make us rich and blessed in heaven.' 'What then is the meaning of: Hallowed be thy name?' *Answer:* 'That we should honour his name and prevent it from being profaned.' 'How is his name profaned or dishonoured?' *Answer:* 'When we, who should be his children, live sinfully or teach and believe wrongly.' And so on; what God's kingdom means, how it comes, what God's will means, or daily bread, etc. So also with the Creed: 'What do you believe?' *Answer:* 'I believe in God the Father,' down to the end. Thereafter from point to point as time allows, one or two questions at a time. Thus: 'What does it mean to believe in God, the Father Almighty?' *Answer:* 'It means that the heart trusts him wholly, and confidently looks to him for all grace, favour, help and comfort in this world and eternally.' 'What does it mean to believe in Jesus Christ his Son?' *Answer:* 'It means that the heart believes that we would all be lost eternally if Christ had not died for us,' etc. So too, in the Ten Commandments, one should ask what the first means, what the second, what the third, and the others mean. One may take such questions from our *Small Prayer Book*, where the three sections are briefly expounded, or make up others of one's own, until one has finally deposited the whole sum of Christian truth in the heart in two parts (as in two purses), faith and love.

. . . Let no one imagine here that he is too clever, and disdain such child's play. When Christ wished to draw men, he had to become a man. If we wish to draw the children, we too must become children with them. Would to God that such child's play were actively pursued!

IV.1.E   The hopeful tone of Luther's early writings on evangelical polity was soon dampened by the discovery of sad decay in the parishes. He turned to the prince to be 'emergency bishop', and to appoint visitors to restore the parishes. He wrote as follows to Elector John Frederick on November 22, 1526. (German text in Br 4, 133–134; also translated in full in Smith II, 383 ff.)

Grace and peace in Christ! Serene, highborn Prince, gracious lord! I have brought Your Grace no petitions for a long time, and they have now accumulated. I hope Your Grace will be indulgent—it is not your nature to be otherwise.

First, gracious lord, the complaints of the pastors nearly everywhere are quite beyond all measure. The peasants will simply not give any more, and the ingratitude amongst the people for God's holy Word is such that without doubt a great plague is in the offing. And if I could do it with a good conscience, I might well help see to it that they had neither pastors nor preachers, and lived like swine—as in fact they do! There is no fear of God or discipline left, because the pope's ban has been removed, and everyone does just what he likes.

But because we all (and especially the government) are commanded to see to all the needs of poor children, as they are born each day and as they grow up, and to train them in the fear of God and by discipline, we must have schools and preachers and pastors. Of course, they may always go to the devil if adults do not want them. But if the young are neglected and remain untrained, that is the government's fault, and the land will be full of wild and dissolute people. Thus not only God's command, but also our own common necessities, force us to devote our efforts in this direction.

Now that papal and hierarchial rules and regulations no longer apply in Your Grace's principate, and all the cloisters and foundations fall into Your Grace's hands as head of state, the duty and onerous task of regulating these matters comes with them. For no one assumes the task, and no one person can or should assume it. Accordingly, as I have discussed with Your Grace's chancellor and with Sir Nicholas von Ende, it will be necessary for Your Grace in particular, as the one whom God has appointed and commissioned to act in such cases, to have four persons visit the land, two who are experts on taxation and property, two on teaching and moral training. On Your Grace's instructions, these men should have the schools and parishes set in order and provided for wherever necessary.

When, however, a town or village is capable of it, Your Grace has power to compel them to maintain schools, pulpits, and parishes. If they are unwilling to do this, or to consider doing so for their own salvation, then Your Grace's rôle is that of supreme guardian of the young and of all who need protection, and should force them to do it compulsorily— just as they are required by force to provide compulsory contributions and labour for bridges, footpaths, and roads, and whatever else the country happens to need.

It is proper that what a country lacks or needs should be provided and contributed by those who use and enjoy the country. Now there is nothing more needful than the nurture of the people who will come and run things after us. However, if the towns do not have the resources and are overburdened in other directions, there are monastic properties which were founded especially for this purpose, and still ought to be so used, that the common man may be spared a further burden. For Your

Grace can readily imagine that in the long run evil gossip would arise, quite justifiably, if schools and parishes were to crumble while the nobles were to appropriate monastic properties to themselves, as is reported already; some of them are certainly doing it. Since, then, such properties do not benefit Your Grace's exchequer, and were after all established for the service of God, it is only right that they should be applied to this purpose first of all. Your Grace may then apply whatever is left over to the pressing needs of the country, or give it to the poor. . . .

The Thursday after St Elizabeth's Day, 1526.

Your Grace's obedient servant, Martin Luther.

IV.2 MAINTAINING THE MAGISTERIUM

Clearly, the most urgent issue was the question of doctrinal authority. Luther, it has been said, dethroned the pope and enthroned the Bible; he took the Word of God as the sole supreme authority, above every council, pope, bishop, and theologian, and above reason itself. But almost overnight it became clear that Scripture, freed from traditional interpretation by the Roman magisterium, was liable to all manner of private interpretations. We now examine Luther's efforts to find practical means of protecting the clarity of the Word from repeated distortions.

IV.2.A The Word of God usually came to men not as the written word of Scripture, but as the living voice of preaching. The clarity of the Word gave each Christian the authority to judge whether the preaching he heard was faithful, Luther explained in this Whit Tuesday, 1522, sermon on John 10 : 1–10. (German text in WA 10, I 2, 289–290; also translated in full in Lenker 12, 377 ff.)

'He that enters by the gate is the shepherd of the sheep; to him the doorkeeper opens, and the sheep hear his voice.' The doorkeeper here is the preacher who teaches the law correctly, namely, that it exists only to show us what weeds and venomous worms we are, and that the works of the law do not help us, yet they must be done. For he opens the door to the shepherd, that is, to the Lord Christ, and lets him alone pasture the sheep. His own task is complete now that the law has accomplished what it was sent to accomplish—it has revealed to the heart its sinfulness and completely overwhelmed it. Then Christ comes and makes a lamb out of it, pastures it with his gospel, and tells it what it should do to recover a joyful heart. Then the lamb hears this voice gladly, follows after it, and feeds in a choice pasture; it recognises the voice of the shepherd, but a strange voice it neither heeds nor follows. . . .

So understand clearly that the sheep have to judge what people put before them, and say: 'We have Christ as our Lord, and we have his Word before the words of all devils and men. We intend to determine and judge whether the pope, the bishops, and their associates are doing right or not. For Christ says here that the sheep judge and recognise which is the right voice and which is not. Now let it apply here: if they have decided on something, we wish to see whether it is right, and hence we reject their authority to decide in accordance with our judgement that each individual Christian ought to make up his own mind, and that such authority is not for men but for God to exercise.' And that is just what real sheep do—they flee from a stranger and stay with the voice of their shepherd.

Right here, then, the gospel knocks down all councils and all papal laws, declaring that we should accept nothing without exercising judgement, and affirming that we have the power to judge in this way, and that this judgement persists until the present. But they have taken this sword away from us so that we have not been able to drive off erroneous doctrine, which they have introduced by force. So now, when we take up the sword again, they are horrified. Yet now we must take it up, not as physical force but as the Word, and let go of everything else we own and say: 'I am the sheep of God, whose Word I wish to have and accept, and if you will give me that, I will regard you as a shepherd; but if you set some other doctrine before me and do not give me the unalloyed gospel, I will not regard you as a shepherd and I will not heed your voice, for the limits of the office go no further than the Word says they go.'

IV.2.B *Sola scriptura* was Luther's authority because he held the Bible's message to be quite clear. Read in its simple sense, Scripture spoke plainly about faith in Christ, as Luther insisted to Erasmus in *The Bondage of the Will* (1525). (Latin text in WA 18, 606–609 and 653–655; also available in translations by Packer and Johnston (1957), and together with Erasmus's *The Freedom of the Will* in LCC XVII.)

God and the Scripture of God are two things, just as the Creator and the creature of God are two things. That in God there are many hidden things of which we are ignorant, no one doubts, just as Christ himself says about the last day: 'Of that day knows no one but the Father [Mark 13 : 32]. And in Acts 1 [: 7]: 'It is not for you to know the times and the seasons.' And again: 'I know those whom I have chosen' [John 13 : 18]. And Paul: 'The Lord knows those that are his [2 Tim. 2 :19]; and so on. But that some things are abstruse and not everything in Scripture is accessible is a canard spread by ungodly sophists, whom you are echoing here, Erasmus; but they have never produced, and they cannot produce, a single article to prove this madness of theirs.

Yet with such spectres Satan has frightened men off reading the sacred writings, and has rendered Holy Scripture contemptible, in order to make his own plagues of philosophy dominant in the Church. Of course, I admit that there are many passages in Scripture which are obscure and abstruse, not because of the majesty of the subject-matter, but because of men's ignorance of the vocabulary and grammar; but in no way do they impede our knowledge of all the subject-matter in Scripture. For what more profound questions can the Scriptures still hide now that the seals are broken, the stone rolled away from the tomb, and the greatest mystery of all openly revealed, namely that Christ, the Son of God, became man, that God is three and one, that Christ suffered for us and reigns eternally? Are these things not known and sung even in the crossroads? Take Christ from the Scriptures, and what more will you find in them? Thus the whole subject-matter contained in Scripture has been plainly revealed, even though certain passages remain obscure because the words are unknown. But it is stupid, and ungodly too, knowing that all the content of Scripture has been placed in the clearest light, to claim that because of a few obscure words the subject-matter is obscure. If the words are obscure in one passage, they are clear somewhere else. But the self-same subject-matter, quite manifestly declared to the whole world, is sometimes stated in Scripture with clear words, and sometimes remains hidden in obscure words. Now if the substance stands in the daylight, it does not matter at all if one of its signs remains in the dark, if at the same time many other indications of it remain in the light. Who will say that the public fountain is not in the daylight because those who are in some narrow side street do not see it, whilst all those who are in the square do see it?

. . . Scripture simply declares the trinity of God and the humanity of Christ and the unpardonable sin. There is no obscurity or ambiguity here. But how these things can be, Scripture does not say, as you imagine, nor is there any need to know. This is where the sophists trot out their dreams: accuse and condemn them, and absolve the Scriptures! But if you mean that the very substance of the subject itself has been found obscure, again do not charge the Scriptures with that, but the Arians and those to whom the gospel is a closed book, so that by the operation of their god, Satan, they quite fail to see the clearest testimonies about the triunity of the godhead and the humanity of Christ. And to put it briefly, just as there are these two sorts of obscurity, so Scripture has two sorts of clarity. The first, external clarity is located in the ministry of the Word, the second is situated in the knowledge of the heart. If you are talking about the internal clarity, no one sees a single iota in Scripture except the man who has the Spirit of God. All men have hearts so darkened that even if they can discuss and recite the whole of Scripture from memory, they nevertheless do not experience or really understand any of it. They did not believe God, nor that they are creatures of God, nor anything else, just as Psalm 14 [: 1; Vulg. 13 : 1] says: 'The fool has said in his heart, There is no God.' For the Spirit is required for understanding the whole Scripture and for any part of it. If you are speaking about external clarity, not a single thing is left obscure or ambiguous, but through the Word all has been brought out into the clearest light and everything in Scripture has been openly declared to the whole world.

. . . I do not approve of those who take refuge in boasting of the Spirit. For the past year, I have been, and I am still, waging a pretty fierce battle against those fanatics who subject the Scriptures to the interpretations of their own spirit, on the very same grounds that I previously castigated the pope, in whose realm there is nothing more ordinary or acceptable than the dictum that the Scriptures are obscure and ambiguous, and that accordingly the interpreting spirit must be sought from the apostolic see of Rome. It is not possible to say anything more pernicious, since by this means ungodly men have exalted themselves above the Scriptures and pulled out of their own hats whatever they liked, until the Scriptures were entirely trodden down and we neither believed nor taught anything but the dreams of raving men. In short, that statement is not a human invention, but a virus sent into the world by the incredible malice of the prince of all demons himself!

This is what we say: that spirits are to be investigated and tested with two sorts of judgement. First, they must be tested by an inward judgement, in that, through the Holy Spirit or the special gift of God, the man who has received the light judges with complete certainty in what touches himself and his own individual salvation, and can discern the doctrines and opinions of all men. 1 Cor. 2[: 15] says about this: 'The spiritual man judges all things, and is judged by no one.' This judgement belongs to faith, and is necessary to every Christian, even in private. Above, we called this 'the internal clarity of Holy Scripture'. . . . The second is an external judgement, in which we judge the spirits and doctrines of all men with complete certainty not for our own sakes only, but also for others and for the sake of the salvation of others. This judgement is found in the public ministry of the Word and the external office, and belongs most of all to the leaders and to preachers of the Word; we use it when we strengthen those who are weak in faith and refute adversaries. Above, we called this 'the external clarity of Holy Scripture'. This is our position: all spirits are to be judged in the sight of the Church by the judgement of Scripture. For amongst Christians, this above all must be settled and most firmly held, that the Holy Scriptures are a spiritual light far clearer than the sun itself, especially in those things which pertain to salvation and are indispensable. . . .

In short, if Scripture is obscure or ambiguous, what need was there for it to be divinely handed down to us? Were we not in an obscure and ambiguous enough state already, without heaven adding to us more obscurity and ambiguity and darkness?

IV.2.c For both religious and political motives, Philip of Hesse was anxious to settle the sacramental dispute (see III.3. E) by holding a colloquy. Luther saw no promise in this way of establishing doctrine, and only after months of refusal acceded to Philip's request on June 23, 1529. (German text in Br 5, 101–102: 1438; also translated in full in Smith II, 483.)

To the serene, highborn prince and lord, Lord Philip, Landgrave of Hesse, Count of Katzenelenbogen, Nidda and Ziegenhain, my most gracious lord.

Grace and peace in Christ! Serene, highborn prince, gracious lord! I was glad to receive Your Grace's letter and request, without doubt addressed to me from a gracious Christian motive, and have devoted close attention to it, together with the letter of my gracious lord, Duke John, Elector, etc., in which His Grace also urges me with great diligence to give Your Grace a favourable answer for the good of the cause, that God might give us his grace so that the disagreement amongst us about the sacrament might be removed. Your Grace therefore proposes to me that we foregather at Marburg on St Michael's Day, to engage in a friendly private discussion with the other side. To be sure, I quite believe that Your Grace is completely earnest and genuinely means well. Therefore I, too, am willing and disposed to carry out this Christian undertaking of Your Grace, which I fear will be a wasted, and perhaps for us even dangerous, service. For I too have a hearty desire and love for peace, of which others boast so highly in speaking and writing, but by their actions so dispose themselves that no hope of peace remains. That is all the more reason why in good time I should tell Your Grace bluntly what I think. It seems to me that the opposition is seeking in Your Grace's diligence an opportunity from which no good will come, namely, that afterwards they will be able to boast that no blame rested upon them—'they had prevailed upon such a great prince', and so on— and so in Your Grace's name they will charge us with being intransigent, as if we had no desire for peace and truth, and thus adorn themselves in splendour. I know the devil well; God grant that I am no prophet! For twelve years now I have been taught my lesson soundly by such knavish play-acting, and I have often been badly scorched. For if this were not a false trick, and they were really in earnest about it, they would not need to think up or exploit this grandiose approach, acting through great and mighty princes (who have other things to do). A small stick would work as well, since we are not of such high standing, nor so wild and disorderly, that they might not have informed us and convinced us by letter long since of their great yearning for peace and unity (as they boast).

Accordingly, if Your Grace is willing, I should be very glad, since Your Grace is so involved in the arrangement, if you would inquire of the other side whether they have any inclination to soften their opinion, so that the final outcome will not be an even bitterer dispute. For Your Grace can easily perceive that every colloquy is a waste of time, and every conference in vain, if both sides come with the intention of yielding nothing. For all I have discovered so far is that after they have thoroughly examined our argument they will insist on their own interpretation. And I know perfectly well that I cannot give ground after I in turn have examined their arguments, because I am certain that they are in error. Should we then part from each other still disunited, not only would Your Grace's expense and effort, and our time and labour, be lost, but they would not stop their customary boasting, and this would force us in turn to reply to them anew. In that case it would be better if things had been allowed to remain as they are now. In short, I cannot expect anything good of the devil; he does his worst, however pretty he makes it seem.

However, since Your Grace fears that bloodshed may follow from the present disunity, Your Grace should also know in turn that if this is the outcome (which God forbid), we should be entirely guiltless of it. It is nothing new when turbulent spirits provoke bloodshed. They have demonstrated this already with Franz von Sickingen, Carlstadt and Müntzer, and afterwards by God's grace we were found entirely guiltless. But may Christ our Lord tread Satan under his feet, and under the feet of us all, Amen.
June 23, 1529.

Your Grace's obedient Martin Luther.

IV.2.D   The colloquy held at Marburg in October, 1529, did allay some of Luther's suspicions of Zwingli. After two days of heated debate, they agreed on fourteen points of doctrine drawn up by Luther, but remained split on the vital issue, as *Marburg Article 15* admits. (Latin text in WA 30 III, 169–171; also translated in full, with a text of the colloquy, in Hermann Sasse, *This is My Body* (Minneapolis, 1959), 223 ff.)

The Sacrament of the Body and Blood of Christ:
15. We all believe and hold concerning the Supper of our dear Lord Jesus Christ that one should use both kinds according to the institution of Christ; again, that the mass is not a work by which one obtains grace for someone else, dead or living; again, that the sacrament of the altar is a sacrament of the true body and blood of Jesus Christ and that the

spiritual partaking of the said body and blood is especially necessary for each and every Christian; similarly, that the use of the sacrament, like the Word, is given and ordained by God Almighty, that by it weak consciences may be aroused to faith through the Holy Spirit. And although we have not reached agreement at this time on whether the body and blood of Christ is bodily in the bread and wine, nevertheless each side should give the other Christian love, just as far as good conscience can permit, and both sides should pray fervently to God Almighty that he would confirm us in the right understanding through his Spirit. Amen.

Martin Luther	Johann Oecolampadius
Justus Jonas	Ulrich Zwingli
Philip Melanchthon	Martin Bucer
Andreas Osiander	Caspar Hedio
Stephan Agricola	
Johann Brenz	

IV.2.E The reaction of the participants was mixed. Their impressions soured as time went by, but initially each party felt vindicated. On his way home, Luther sent this account to Agricola on October 12, 1529. (Latin text in Br 5, 160–161: 1479; also translated in full in Smith II, 501.)

To his venerable brother in the Lord, Johann Agricola, the minister of Christ.

Grace and peace in Christ. We have returned from our meeting at Marburg, my Agricola, and while we were in this vicinity wished to describe the outcome to you in a few words. We were received by the Prince of Hesse and magnificently and splendidly entertained. Those present were Oecolampadius, Zwingli, Bucer, Hedio, and three officials, Jacob Sturm of Strasbourg, Ulrich Funk of Zürich, and someone from Basle. They asked for peace with a humbleness beyond measure. We conferred for two days. I replied to both Oecolampadius and Zwingli, and opposed to them the text: 'This is my body.' I confuted all their objections. Nevertheless, we had courteously conferred the previous day in private, I with Oecolampadius, Philip [Melanchthon] with Zwingli. Meanwhile Andreas Osiander, Johann Brenz, and Stephan [Agricola] from Augsburg also arrived. In short, the men are inept and inexperienced in argument. Even when they sensed that their arguments proved nothing, they were still unwilling to yield on the one issue of the presence of the body of Christ, and that, we think, more out of fear and shame than malice; on everything else they gave way, as you will see in the printed report. At the end they asked that we should at least be prepared to acknowledge them as brethren, and the Prince also strongly urged this, but the concession could not be made to them; nevertheless, we gave them the hand of peace and charity, so that for the time being harsh writings and words should stop, and everyone should teach his own opinion without invective, though not without defence and refutation. So we parted. Report these things to our beloved brother, Doctor Caspar Aquila, and pray for us. The grace of Christ be with you, Amen. Jena, October 12, 1529.

Your Martin Luther.

IV.2.F Marburg was a portent that, despite Luther's hopes, doctrinal authority was again to consist of formal dogmatic declarations; and thus academic theology retained an all-important rôle. In 1533, the Wittenberg faculty adopted these new regulations for theological training. (German text in *Urkundenbuch der Universität Wittenberg* I, ed. Walter Friedensburg (Magdeburg, 1926), 154–158: 171.)

Statutes of the collegiate faculty of theology in the University of Wittenberg, drawn up in the year 1533 .

I. On the nature of the doctrine

As in the churches throughout our jurisdiction and in the grammar schools, so in the university the special governance and censorship of doctrine is weaker than it ought to be. We therefore wish that the pure doctrine of the gospel, in agreement with the confession which we presented to the Emperor Charles at Augsburg in 1530, the doctrine which we stated with certainty to be the true and perpetual consensus of the catholic Church of God, should be devoutly and faithfully set forward, preserved, and propagated.

We also most severely forbid, reject and repel the ancient heresies condemned in the synods of Nicea, Constantinople, Ephesus, and Chalcedon; for we consent to the decrees of these synods in expounding the doctrines of God the Father, Son and Holy Spirit, and for the two natures in Christ born of the Virgin Mary, and we judge these things to have been certainly handed down in the apostolic Scriptures. The Augsburg confession makes sufficiently clear what decrees of later synods we approve.

II

There shall be four permanent full-time lecturers, to be subject to the rector of the university, admitted by the judgement of this collegiate faculty, and having the public qualification of the doctor's degree conferred either by this or another university. These four are to be the college of this faculty, and to administer the affairs and actions of this

F

college by common counsel, and above all faithfully to protect concord in doctrine, as it is fitting for those in authority in the Church to do. But if any of them has received his doctor's degree in another university, he shall not be received into this college unless his erudition and experience in public disputation has first been explored. And all who are received, whether they have received their doctor's degree here or elsewhere, are to promise that they will faithfully pursue and demand this consensus of doctrine.

III

Exposition of some book of the Old Testament is always to be offered by one of these, and exposition of a book of the New Testament by another. Expositions of the Epistle of St Paul to the Romans, the Gospel of St John, Psalms, Genesis, and Isaiah are to be repeated most often. For these books are best able to teach students the major points of Christian doctrine. Meanwhile, one of the professors is also to expound the book of Augustine *On the Spirit and the Letter*, so that students may see that the doctrine of our churches also possesses the testimony of learned fathers. And in these expositions the simple truth is to be candidly taught in accordance with God's command, and rightly and properly explained in a clear manner of speech. Professors are not to play with ambiguous conundrums, and are not to reproach or insult their colleagues in any public lectures or disputations; but any who do this are to be punished by the severe judgement of the whole university. . . .

VI

If controversy arises about an ecclesiastical dogma, and one or more people seem to disturb the concord of doctrine, the dean is to refer the matter to the rector and to the council of the whole university. And if the magnitude of the matter so indicates, the university will inform the prince, and the prince and the council of the university will delegate four or five judges to examine the whole controversy diligently, and by their judgement plainly approve true opinions and plainly condemn false. Even if the matter does not seem to merit referring to the prince, the university by its own council will elect suitable judges from several faculties to review the matter diligently and make an adjudication. Propositions which have been condemned are not to be defended, and if anyone does obstinately defend them, he is to be disciplined with such severity that he cannot spread his wrong opinions further.

VII. Concerning promotions

No one is to be admitted to the doctor's degree unless for six years he has heard expositions of the prophetic and apostolic Scriptures by doctors appointed as scholarly lecturers, either here or elsewhere in an academy which has embraced the pure doctrine of the gospel. And if the tranquillity of the time permits various degrees to be conferred at the usual intervals, an arrangement which gives the students useful practice, the customary order is to be preserved.

For the sake of practice, a *biblicus* is to expound the Epistle to the Romans, because this encompasses the sum of Christian doctrine methodically, as it were. . . . The next degree is that of *sententiarius*, so called because he now knows the essential doctrines in order. Once it was the custom to read the Lombard, but because there are some things in his Book III about justification, and many in Book IV about the sacraments, which dissent from the pure doctrine of the gospel professed by our churches, and since the sum of doctrine, as stated above, has been received from Paul, let a *sententiarius* chosen by the judgement of the dean and the senior members of the theological faculty now read some Psalms or something from the prophets. . . .

VIII

There is also to be some selection in admitting those who seek degrees. As Paul teaches that hands are not to be laid indiscriminately on anyone, so not all are to be granted these qualifications, which in fact can be awarded with good conscience only to those suitable. Accordingly, those who are fascinated with distorted opinions which fight against the doctrine of our churches are not to be admitted to a degree. Similarly, no disreputable persons are to be admitted, nor any given to manifest fornication. But let the character of those who are admitted to degrees be modest and chaste, as Paul requires of bishops.

For this reason, we also command that upright married persons who devote themselves to ecclesiastical teaching are to be admitted to all degrees. Permission is also to be granted for upright men who were celibate before graduation afterwards to contract a marriage according to Christian doctrine. Permission is also to be granted for one whose spouse has died to marry again according to Christian doctrine. We do not impose upon anyone the old laws and bonds concerning celibacy, which inflicted weakness on many and in many ordinary men impeded the true invocation of God, since so long as wounds of conscience remain no true invocation can take place. And such wounds are immediately reopened by those unjust laws. Teachers of theology are rather to understand that marriage has been ordained by the marvellous and ineffable counsel of God for the mutual society and assistance of the human race and for preserving the Church. And they are to recognise that this way of life is pleasing to God, and is a school of many virtues for the good.

IV.2.G The pursuit of Protestant unity in the 1530s produced many attempted agreements, none more significant than the *Wittenberg Concord* of 1536, which remained for several years the standard of confessional accord between Upper and Lower Germany. (Latin text in CR III, 75–77; also translated in full in *The Book of Concord*, 265.)

A concord between the teachers of Wittenberg and the teachers of the cities of the Empire in Upper Germany concerning the presence of the body and blood of Christ in the Lord's Supper, drawn up at the command and request of both parties by Philip Melanchthon, in the year of Christ 1536.

We have heard Dr Bucer explaining the opinion which he and the others who have come with him hold concerning the sacrament of the body and blood of Christ, as follows:

I. They confess, according to the words of Irenaeus, that the eucharist consists of two things, an earthly and a heavenly thing. They therefore think and teach that, with the bread and the wine, the body and blood of Christ are truly and substantially present, proffered, and taken.

II. And although they deny that transubstantiation takes place, and do not think that there is any local inclusion in the bread, or any lasting conjunction apart from the use of the sacrament: they nevertheless concede that by sacramental union the bread is the body of Christ, that is, they think that when the bread is offered the body of Christ is at the same time present and truly proffered. For apart from its use, when it is reserved in a pyx or displayed in processions, as the papists do, they do not think that the body of Christ is present.

III. Next, they hold that this institution of the sacrament avails in the Church, and that it does not depend on the worthiness of the minister or the recipient. Accordingly, as Paul says that even the unworthy eat [1 Cor. 11 : 27], so they think that the true body and blood of the Lord is offered even to the unworthy, and that the unworthy receive it, where the words and institution of Christ are preserved. But such people receive it to condemnation, as Paul says, because they abuse the sacrament when they use it without penitence and without faith. For it was instituted in order to testify that those who repent and console themselves by faith in Christ are recipients of the benefit of Christ and become members of Christ.

However, since few of us have come together, and there is a need on both sides to refer this matter to other preachers and supervisors, it is not yet proper for us to finalise the concord until we have referred it to these others. But since they have all professed that they wish to believe and teach in accordance with the [Augsburg] Confession and Apology of the princes, as professing the gospel in all its articles, we desire above all that this concord be sanctioned and established. And it is our hope that if the others on both sides so consent, an enduring concord will result.

> Signed:
> Dr Wolfgang Capito, minister of the church at Strasbourg
> Mr Martin Bucer, minister of the church at Strasbourg
> Licentiate Martin Frecht, minister of the Word of the church at Ulm
> Licentiate Jacob Otther, minister of the church at Esslingen
> Mr Boniface Lycosthenes, minister of the Word of the church at Augsburg
> Wolfgang Musculus, minister of the Word of the church at Augsburg
> Mr Gervase Schuler, pastor of the church at Memmingen
> Mr Johann Bernhardi, minister of the church at Frankfurt
> Martin Germani, minister of the church at Reutlingen
> Johann Schradin, deacon of Reutlingen
> Dr Martin Luther, Wittenberg
> Dr Justus Jonas
> Dr Caspar Cruciger
> Dr Johann Bugenhagen
> Philip Melanchthon
> Justus Menius of Eisenach
> Friedrich Myconius of Gotha
> Dr Urbanus Rhegius, chief superintendent of the church at Lueneburg
> Georg Spalatin, pastor of the church at Altenburg
> Dionysius Melander, minister of the church at Kassel
> and many others.

IV.2.H A general council to restore unity had been postponed too long. By 1537, the Protestant Schmalkaldic League was extremely powerful. It commissioned a definitive statement of doctrine from Luther. He published his *Schmalkald Articles* in 1538 with this preface. (German text in WA 50, 192–196; also translated in full in *The Book of Concord*, 136 f.)

Since the pope, Paul III by name, last year recorded his intention of holding a council at Whitsuntide in Mantua, and then transferred it from Mantua so that no one knows where he will or can hold it; and since we for our part have to anticipate that we shall either be summoned to the council or else condemned unsummoned, I was commanded to draw up and collect the articles of our doctrine in case negotiations arose about where, and how far, we would or could make concessions to the papists, and on what points we determined to persist and persevere to the end.

Accordingly, I have compiled these articles and presented them to our side. They have also been accepted by our side, and unanimously confessed and agreed upon, so that if the Pope and his side should one day become so bold as to hold a genuinely free council, without lying and trickery, earnestly and truthfully as his duty requires, these articles should be presented publicly and set out as the confession of our faith. But the Romish court is horribly afraid of a free council, and shuns the light so shamefully that even its own adherents have been robbed of hope that it will ever again permit a free council, much less hold one itself. (For they are quite properly very distressed at this and have no little ground for complaint, since it leads them to think that the Pope would rather see the whole of Christendom lost and all souls condemned before he would be willing to reform himself or his party a little, and have his tyranny somewhat limited.)

So in the meantime I am publishing these articles anyway in public print, in case I should die before the council takes place (as I quite expect and hope), since these scoundrels who flee the light and shun the day devote so much wretched effort to delaying and hindering the council. By this means those who are alive and remain after me will have my testimony and confession to produce in addition to the confession which I had issued before, by which I have abided so far, and by which I will abide, by God's grace. For what should I say? How can I complain? I am still alive, I still write, preach, and read every day; yet there turn out to be so many venomous people, not only in the opposing camp, but also false brethren who want to be on our side, who presume to quote my writings and teaching directly against me, and let me watch and listen, even though they know perfectly well that I teach otherwise; and they want to embellish their own poison with my labour and lead the poor people astray in my name. What still worse things will keep on happening after my death?

Indeed, am I not right to answer everything while I am still alive? But on the other hand, how can I alone stop all the devil's mouths— especially of those (since they are all poisoned) who are not prepared to listen or take any notice of what we write? Instead, they do all they can to find ways of perverting and corrupting every letter of our words most shamefully. I let the devil answer such people, or at the last God's wrath, as they deserve. I think often of the good Gerson, who doubted if one should write anything good down publicly: if one does not do so, many souls are neglected whom one could save; but if one does, the devil is right there with innumerable venomous, evil tongues which poison and pervert everything, and still the fruit is choked. Yet what they gain by this is as plain as day. For while they have lied so shamefully against us and hoped to gain the people's loyalty with their lies, God has carried on steadily with his own works, and has made their numbers ever smaller and ours greater, he has let them be disgraced by their own lies, and will do so more and more.

I must tell a story: there was a doctor sent here to Wittenberg from France, who said openly before us that his king was sure, and more than sure, that there was no church, no government, no married life amongst us, but we all couple with each other like cattle, and everyone does just what he likes. Now imagine, how will those who in their writings have painted such gross lies to their king and other countries as the pure truth look at us on that day before the judgement seat of Christ? Christ, the Lord and Judge of us all, knows perfectly well that they lie and have lied. They in turn will have to hear his judgement, of that I am sure. May God turn to repentance those who are to be turned—for the others, it means woe and alas, eternally!

To come back to the subject, I would really and truly like to see a genuine council: many matters and many people would be helped by it. Not that we need it, for our churches are now, through God's grace, so illumined and supplied by the pure Word and the right use of the sacrament, with understanding of the various callings and just works, that we on our part ask for no council and on these issues think nothing better can be hoped for or expected from a council. But in bishoprics everywhere we see so many parishes vacant and deserted that one's heart would break. And yet neither the bishops nor the canons inquire how poor people live or die, though Christ died for them, and they are prevented from hearing him speak with them as the true shepherd with his sheep. It makes me quake with anxiety that he may one day send a council of angels upon the land of Germany, to raze us all to the ground like Sodom and Gomorrah, because we so cheerfully mock him with this council.

In addition to such urgent church affairs, there are also countless matters of great importance needing improvement in the secular realm, such as the discord between the princes and the estates; usury and rapacity have burst in like a flood and have become quite lawful, wantonness, lechery, extravagance in dress, gluttony, gambling, exhibitionism, and all kinds of vice and depravity, disobedience on the part of subjects, servants, and labourers, dishonesty in all the crafts and among the peasants—who can reckon it all?—have got so far out of hand that one could not bring them back to rights with ten councils and twenty diets. If a council were to take up these vital matters which oppose God in the spiritual and secular realms, everyone would find their hands so full of things to do that for the time being they could well forget their childish games and tomfoolery like long gowns, great tonsures, wide girdles, bishops' or cardinals' hats or croziers, and all that sort of jugglery. If we had already executed God's order and command in the spiritual and secular realms, we would find time enough to reform food, clothing, tonsures and vestments. But if we too were to swallow such camels and strain at the gnats, or let the beams be while we judge the motes, then we might well acquiesce in their council!

I have therefore drawn up few articles, for quite apart from this we have so many commands from God to perform in the Church, in the government, and in the household, that we could never carry them all out. So what is the point, or how does it help, if we make many decrees and statutes in a council on the subject—especially if we neither observe nor uphold these essential points of God's commands? It is as if he had to honour our juggling act in return for our trampling his solemn commands under foot. But our sins weigh down upon us and force God not to be gracious to us, for we do not repent, but instead want to justify every outrage. Our dear Lord Jesus Christ, hold a council yourself, and deliver your servants by your lordly coming! All is lost with the pope and his crew. They do not want to be yours, so help us poor and wretched people who sigh to you and seek you earnestly, according to the grace which you have given us through your Holy Spirit, who lives and reigns with you and the Father, praised for ever. Amen.

IV.3 REFORMING THE LIFE OF THE FAITHFUL

We can do little more here than to sample Luther's enomously influential and extensive utterances on the life of the faithful in the structures of society. In practice, his most frequent and characteristic vehicle for moral instruction was his preaching, which never failed to make direct, homely, and realistic ethical applications to his hearers' lives. (Nothing makes clearer the proper relation between law and gospel for Luther than his own homiletic practice.) Here, however, we concentrate on two other means by which he delivered specific judgement on pressing moral questions: first, his replies to the ever-widening circle of correspondents, princely, clerical, and lay, who sought his advice; and most directly, the detailed treatises of 1522–24 and 1529–30 in which he expounded his views on law, warfare, usury, education, welfare, marriage and divorce.

IV.3.A   In June, 1524, Elector Frederick requested Luther's judgement on the practical application of evangelical ethics to several pressing legal and economic questions. Luther's reply gave his views of the nature of positive law, taxation, and interest, and identified *Zinskauf* (lump sum 'purchase' of a guaranteed annual dividend) as a form of usury. (German text in Br 3, 306–307: 753; also translated in part in Smith II, 237. See also *On Trade and Usury* (1524) in LW 45, 245 ff.; SW 3, 85 ff.; PE IV, 12 ff.)

Grace and peace in Christ! Serene, highborn Prince, gracious lord! Master Veit [Warbeck] has left some matters here with me on which I am to write to Your Grace.

First, whether one should judge and rule according to the law of Moses or according to the imperial code, since there are some who insist fiercely that to maintain the imperial code is unjust and unchristian. On this point, I have answered previously and I still say: if the imperial code required something which was contrary to God (I know of no such instance), of course one should not abide by it. But since such worldly regulation is an outward thing like eating and drinking, clothing and housing, it has nothing to do with the Christian, who is to be governed by the Spirit of God according to the gospel. Since now it is not Moses' law but the imperial law which is maintained in use in the world, it is not right that we should create a sectarian dissension here by accepting Moses' law and getting rid of the imperial code, any more than we should produce a sectarian dissension over eating and drinking, since faith and love can perfectly well remain alongside and under the imperial code. Indeed, we are duty bound to maintain the imperial code, and not Moses' code, for this reason: love compels us to make ourselves the equal of those among whom we live, when it may be done without endangering faith. At present, of course, we are amongst those who maintain the imperial law and not Moses' law. However, should the Emperor and the princes so direct and introduce Moses' law peaceably, then we too should follow it. Otherwise we should not take up a unique or special position and offend everyone else by it, but we should retain the statement of 1 Corinthians 12 [: 9, 20–21] : 'With the Gentiles I was as a Gentile, with the Jews I was as a Jew.' St Peter means the same thing in 1 Peter 2 [: 13] : 'Be subject to every human ordinance'; and again [v. 17] : 'Honour the king.' Paul says in Romans 13 [: 1] : 'Let every soul be subject to the authorities,' etc. If, now, some such preacher or Moses-promoter becomes emperor and gets the world for his own, let him choose Moses's or Elias's or Adam's law, and maintain that. We are duty bound to observe that law which our government and neighbours observe.

Secondly, whether a prince should permit usurious purchase of interest [*Zinskauf*]. It would be a fine thing if a tenth of all goods were given to the government yearly, after the practice of the ancient world; that would be the godliest kind of interest possible, since the people who paid it would not be oppressed by it. Whether God gave abundance or scarcity of goods, the tenth would vary accordingly. In fact, it would be very desirable and even more tolerable if all other imposts were removed, and a fifth or a sixth were collected from the people as Joseph did in Egypt. But since no such orderly system exists in the world, I must abandon this idea, and say that it is most necessary that the purchase of interest be justly regulated in all regions. On the other hand it is not right to abolish it altogether, for it could readily be made just. But I do not advise Your Grace to give people your protection or prevent them from paying this usurious interest. For this is not a law originating from a prince, but a common plague which everyone has adopted; so it should be borne with, and the mortgagees held to it so that they bear it and do not absolve themselves by finding their own special way out, but make themselves equal to everyone else even to their own detriment, as love demands, until God puts it into the hearts of the princes to change the system peacefully. Meanwhile let the burden rest on the consciences of all those who take unjust interest. I say this, however, of interest that does not yield more than four or five per cent, which is usurious not because of the sum involved, but because it is guaranteed and does not share the risk as it should. But where the yield is more than five per cent, each prince and government should take steps to bring it down to five or four per cent, with some of the amount applied to reducing the capital in proportion to the length of time involved, and the same thing should be done with the produce, so that in this way a start may be made on setting right the whole purchase-of-interest question, and eventually an element of fair risk may be introduced. . . .

IV.3.B   Inevitably, Luther's doctrine of civil obedience and God-given vocations immediately raised the dilemma of Christian participation in war. Luther outlined some principles for both rulers and subjects in his important 1523 treatise *On Temporal Authority*. (German text in WA 11, 276–278; translated in full in LW 45, 81 ff.; SW 2, 271; PE III, 228 ff. See also *Whether Soldiers, Too, Can Be Saved* (1526) in PE V, 34 ff.)

You may ask: 'Should a prince not engage in war? Should his subjects not follow him into battle? Answer: This is a far-reaching question. But to answer briefly: to act in a Christian manner, I say, no prince should make war against his overlord, such as the king, or the emperor, or some other liege lord, but in this case let him who takes, take. For one should not withstand a superior authority by force, but only with confession of the truth; if it is swayed by this, well and good, if it is not, you at least are free from guilt and suffer injustice for God's sake. However, if your opponent is your equal, or inferior to you, or a foreign government, first of all you should offer him justice and peace, as Moses taught the children of Israel. If he refuses, then consider your own best interests and protect yourself with force against force, as Moses has so excellently described in Deuteronomy 20. And in so doing you must pay attention not to what you own and how you may remain lord, but to your subjects to whom you are responsible for protection and aid, in order that such tasks may be done in love. For since your whole land stands in danger you must take this risk, if God will aid you, so that it will not all be lost. Even if you cannot prevent some from being widowed and orphaned, you must still make sure that everything is not trampled under foot with the result that only widows and orphans are left.

In this task subjects are duty bound to obey, staking their life and property upon it. For in this situation one must wager his goods and his own self for the sake of others. In such a war it is both Christian and a work of love courageously to slay, rob, and burn the enemy, and do everything to harm him until he is overthrown by warlike means (except that one must restrain himself from sin, and not violate wives and virgins). Then, when he has been overthrown, mercy and peace should be displayed to those who surrender and humble themselves—this is the way to let the saying, 'God helps the strongest', apply in such a case. This is what Abraham did when he smote the four kings (Gen. 14): he certainly slew many people and did not display much mercy until he had conquered them. For one should regard this situation as sent from God, that thereby he may sweep the land clean all at once and drive out wicked men.

What, then? If the prince is not in the right, is his people still duty bound to follow him? Answer: No. For no one ought to act against the right, but one must obey God (who wants the right to prevail) more than men. What if the subjects do not know whether the prince is in the right or not? Answer: Because they do not know, and cannot find out by any possible effort, they may follow him without risk to their souls. In this case one should use the law of Moses in Exodus 21, where he writes that a murderer who has unknowingly and unintentionally killed someone should be acquitted by flight to a free city and by a judicial decision. Then whichever side is defeated, whether it is in the right or in the wrong, must accept defeat as a punishment from God; but a side which fights and wins in such ignorance should regard its battle as like, say, someone falling off a roof, hitting someone else and killing him, and thus leave the matter in God's hands. For with God it is all the same whether he deprives you of property and life by a just or an unjust lord. You are his creature, and he may do with you as he will, if only your conscience is guiltless.

IV.3.c One of the abiding passions of the Wittenberg reformers was the provision of sound liberal education for the youth of Germany. To replace the inadequacy of monastic schools and to counter popular anti-intellectual sentiment, Luther appealed in 1524 *To the Councilmen of All Cities in German Lands, That They Establish and Maintain Christian Schools*. (German text in WA 15, 45–46; translated in full in LW 45, 347 ff.; PE IV, 103 ff.; SW 3, 39 ff.)

'Well,' you say, 'everyone is perfectly able to teach his daughters and sons himself, or to train them with discipline.' Answer: Yes indeed, it is obvious how such teaching and training work! Even when discipline is applied most rigorously and turns out well, it achieves nothing more than a forced little air of respectability; otherwise they remain just the same utter blockheads who do not know how to distinguish this from that and are unable to give help or advice to anyone. But if they were taught and trained in schools or other places, there would be learned and qualified masters and mistresses, the languages and other arts and history would be taught, they would hear of the doings and sayings of the whole world, what happened to various cities, kingdoms, princes, men and women, and thus in a short time could set before themselves, as in a mirror, the nature, life, advice and values, successes and failures of the whole world from the beginning. From this they could then improve their minds and conduct themselves in the course of their lives in the fear of God, and from the same histories become sensitive and prudent about what to seek and what to avoid in this outward life, and then also advise and direct others. But training undertaken at home without such schools tries to make us wise through our own experience. Before that happens, we shall have died a hundred times, and lived our whole life unreflectively, for 'our own experience' takes a long time.

Since, then, young folk must laugh and jump or have something else to do, and since they take pleasure in these activities which should not be denied them—and it would not be a good thing to deny them everything—why should such schools not be set up and such studies be offered? For by the grace of God things have now changed to the point where children can learn with delight and game-playing, be it languages or other arts or history. And the hell and purgatory of our schools is a thing of the past: schools where we were tormented over cases and tenses, and where we learned nothing, absolutely nothing, through all the whipping, quaking, anguish and misery. Since so much time and effort is devoted to teaching children to play cards, to sing and to dance, why should as much time not be devoted to teaching them reading and other skills while they are young and have leisure and are apt and eager to do so? For myself, I say: If I had children and could do it, I would see to it that they not only studied language and history, but also learned singing and music and the whole of mathematics. For what is all this but sheer child's play? In olden days the Greeks trained their children in these things, and thus became a wonderfully accomplished people, qualified in every respect by these pursuits. To be sure, how sorry I am now that I did not read more poets and historians, and that no one taught me about them. Instead, I had to read that devil's dirt, the philosophers and sophists, at so much cost, effort, and injury that it is all I can do to cleanse myself of it.

IV.3.D   Six years later in 1530, as he waited at the Coburg during the Diet of Augsburg, he appealed again to parents for both temporal and spiritual ends to see to their children's education. (*Sermon on Keeping Children in School*: German text in WA 30 II, 586–588; translated in full in PE IV, 142 ff.; SW 4, 121 ff.)

I hold that it is the duty of the government to compel its subjects to keep their children in school, especially those children of whom I have spoken before. For it is certainly responsible for maintaining the offices and professions I have described, so that the supply of preachers, lawyers, pastors, writers, physicians, schoolmasters and the like may continue, for we cannot do without them. If it can force its subjects who are capable of it to bear pikes and guns, man the walls, and perform the other duties which war demands, how much more it can and should force its subjects to keep their children in school, for here a far more bitter war is involved—with the accursed devil himself, who goes about sucking cities and principalities dry and emptying them of capable persons until he has completely bored out the kernel, leaving an empty husk of utterly useless people with whom he can play and juggle at will. That is really the way to starve out a city or a country: before anyone knows it, it crumbles inwardly without a struggle. The Turk, after all, acts differently. He takes the third child throughout his whole kingdom and trains it for whatever he wishes. How much more should our lords take at least some children for school, since this does not take a child away from his parents, but in their best interests and for the common good trains him for an office in which he will earn enough.

So if you can wake up, wake up to this! Let the government, when it sees a capable boy, have him kept in school. If his father is poor, he should be helped with church property. The rich should make provision for this in their wills, like those who have endowed certain stipends; this is a good way to bequeath your money to the Church.

This way you do not loose departed souls from purgatory; rather, by maintaining the God-given offices you help both the living and those yet to be born to avoid purgatory—indeed, to be released from hell and to make their way towards heaven; and you help the living to enjoy peace and comfort. That would be a praiseworthy Christian will in which God would take delight and pleasure, and he would bless and honour you by granting you delight and joy in him in return. Well, you dear Germans, I have said enough to you, you have heard your prophet! God grant us to follow his Word, to praise and thank our dear Lord for his precious blood so freely poured out for us, and may he protect us from the horrible crime of ingratitude and forgetfulness of his blessing. Amen.

IV.3.E   As a pastor, Luther had grieved at the agony of conscience inflicted by the existing canons and customs regarding marriage. Few of his pastoral teachings had so direct a bearing on the lives of his followers as his several treatises about celibacy, marriage, and divorce. He expounded his view of marriage as an ordained estate in *On Married Life* (1522). (German text in WA 10 II, 294–296; translated in full in LW 45, 17 ff.)

To be married and to understand married life are two completely different things. The man who is married and does not understand married life can never live in marriage without constant distaste, pain, and misery. He is bound to complain and blaspheme like the heathen and unreasoning, blind men. But the man who understands it has uninterrupted delight, love, and joy in it; as Solomon says [Prov. 18 : 22]: 'He who finds a good wife finds a good thing', etc.

Those who understand it are those who firmly believe that God himself instituted marriage, gave the man and wife to each other, and ordained that they should beget children and care for them. They have God's Word for this, and they are certain that he does not lie (Gen. 1 [: 27–28]). They are therefore also certain that the estate of marriage itself pleases him, and so do all its activities, works, sufferings, and everything else in it. Now tell me, how can a heart have a greater good, joy, and delight than it has in God when it is certain that its estate, activity and work please God? See, that is what it means to 'find a wife'. Many men have wives, but few find wives. . . .

Now see, when that clever whore, natural reason (which the heathen have followed, wishing to be as clever as possible) turns her attention to married life, she screws up her nose and says: 'Oh, do I have to rock the baby, wash its napkins, make its bed, smell its stench, stay awake at night, listen to its cries, cure its rashes and pimples, and after that, care for a wife, support her, labour, worry here and worry there, do something now and do something then, suffer this and suffer that and whatever else the estate of marriage teaches of unpleasantness and drudgery? Why should I be caught like that? Oh, you poor, wretched man, have you taken a wife? Shame, shame, on such misery and distress. It is better to remain free and lead a peaceful life, free of worrying. I will become a priest or a nun, and make my children do the same!'

But what does the Christian faith say to this? It opens its eyes and sees all these insignificant, unpleasant, despised tasks in the Spirit, and becomes convinced that they are all adorned with divine good pleasure as with the costliest gold and precious stones. And it says: 'O God, because I am certain that you made me a man and have begotten this child from my body, I am equally certain that it is entirely pleasing to you, and I confess to you that I am not worthy to rock the baby or to wash its napkins, or to look after it or its mother. How is it that, all undeserving, I find myself counted worthy to be certain I am serving your creature and your dearest will? Ah, how gladly I will do it, even if it becomes more insignificant and despised. Now neither frost nor heat, neither misery nor toil will discourage me, because I am sure that in this way you are well pleased.' The wife should also regard her duties in the same way, when she suckles the child, rocks, bathes, and does other things for it, and when she toils at other tasks and obeys her husband. These are all noble works of pure gold.

IV.3.F Whilst retaining the propriety of parental consent, Luther staunchly opposed forcing arranged marriages upon children. He issued a treatise on this subject in 1524, and repeated his views in this 1530 treatise *On Marriage Matters*, where he also expounded his attitude to divorce. (German text in WA 30 III, 236 and 241. See also *That Parents Should Neither Hinder nor Compel Their Children's Marriage, etc.* (1524) in LW 45, 385 ff.)

God has created man and woman in such a way that they should come together gladly with desire and love, willingly and from the heart. And conjugal love, or the desire to marry, is a natural thing implanted and prompted by God. It is for this reason, too, that conjugal love is so highly praised in holy scripture and is often adduced as an image of Christ and his Christendom. Accordingly, parents sin against God and nature when they force their children into marriage or to take a spouse when they have no desire to do so. Thus we read in Genesis 24 [: 57–58] that when Rebecca's family betrothed her, they asked Rebecca herself and inquired from her whether she wished to have Isaac, and they regarded it as right that her own agreement to the match should be obtained. The Holy Spirit does not have this sort of example recorded without purpose: by this means he intends to corroborate the natural right which he has created—that marriage partners should be given to

each other without constraint and without compulsion, but with willingness, desire, and love.

Daily experience also teaches us and makes us perfectly well aware
what sort of a mess results from forced marriage. A marriage that turns
out well, that starts off amicably in accordance with God's blessing and
command, obediently and with desire and love, requires such great grace
against the devil, the flesh, and the world that one dare not undertake it
against God's law in an unwilling, unfriendly way, and thus paint the
devil over the door—he will come soon enough by himself! And it is a
very peculiar thing that a man should wish to take a bride when he
knows that she does not wish or desire to have him; parents too must be
extraordinarily stupid to force their children into endless repugnance
and distaste. The unreasoning beasts would not do it! And if God and
nature had not already forbidden it, so that marriage should be uncon-
strained, surely even fatherly or motherly affection towards the children
should not tolerate its happening without desire and love. . . .

We have noted that death is the only factor which dissolves a marriage. And since in the law of Moses God has commanded that an
adulterer be stoned [Lev. 20 : 10], it is plain that adultery also dissolves marriage, for by it the adulterer is sentenced to death and condemned. Therefore Christ too, in Matthew 19 where he forbids a
married person to gain a divorce, makes an exception of the adulterer
and says [v. 9] : 'He who puts away his wife, except because of immorality, and takes another, commits adultery.' Joseph, too, confirms this
rule in Matthew 2 [1 : 19], where he intends to put Mary away, regarding her as an adulteress, and yet still receives the evangelist's praise
as a godly man. Now he certainly would not have been a godly man in
planning to put Mary away if he did not have the power and right to do
so. I am therefore unable and unwilling to deny that, where a spouse
commits adultery and can be openly shown to have done so, the other
party is free, and may obtain a divorce and contract a marriage with
someone else. Nevertheless, where the wronged party can be reconciled
to the other and they stay together, that is far, far better. But if the
innocent party is not so inclined, he may exercise his rights in the name
of God. Above all, because such a divorce should not take place on one's
own individual authority, but should be pronounced by the advice and
judgement of a pastor or magistrate, it would be good if he preferred
(like Joseph) to have it happen secretly and to leave the country; otherwise, if he wishes to remain, he should execute the divorce openly.

In order to keep such divorces as far as possible to a minimum, the
innocent party should not be permitted to remarry too quickly, but
should wait at the very least a year or six months. Otherwise it gives a
scandalous appearance, as if he was pleased and delighted that his
spouse had committed adultery, and was gleefully seizing the occasion

to be rid of her and to take a fresh, new wife, and thus exercise his wantonness under cover of justice. For such despicable behaviour reveals that it was not from disgust at the adultery, but from envy and hatred against his spouse and an itchy lust for another, that he so readily put away the adulteress and so eagerly sought another.

V

OLD MAN LUTHER

THE MEAGRE GLEANINGS of the formative years have received meticulous biographical attention. The prodigiously rich records of the later years, paradoxically, have hardly been exploited for biographical purposes. Yet the fact is that much of what we know of Luther's personality is drawn from the persistent creativity, the prolific correspondence, and the frank self-disclosure of his later years. (Indeed, much even of our knowledge of his developing youthful identity is reflected—and refracted—by reminiscences from his seniority.) Luther's accomplishment was not complete by Worms, nor yet by Augsburg. These were decades when by personal example, by his ever-widening sphere of influence through students, readers, and correspondents, and by the ever-maturing genius of his biblical insight, he stamped the hall-mark of his intuition and identity upon the movement he had almost inadvertently created. The influence of Luther's own home on the life-style of Protestant churchmen is incalculable. The biblical theology of his last twenty years not only moulded the shape of Lutheranism, but indelibly affected Christian thought and practice everywhere to the present day. His counsel to princes on the nature of Christian government, to pastors on the nature of Christian order, and to laymen on the nature of Christian vocation were ingredients in the cultural formation of modern Europe. Whilst it is true that in his closing years the spotlight shifted to a second generation of reformers, both Catholic and Protestant; whilst it is true that afflicted by ill-health, slander, and disappointment he sometimes, in the obtuse manner of the elderly, refought old battles, and that rather too acrimoniously; yet he did not display any decline in intellectual power, nor ever lose the vital, wise, humane sense of what man's life, in all its suffering and joy, its fear and freedom, is truly like.

V.1 THE PATERFAMILIAS

Though he was far from the first of the rebels to marry—he had already encouraged many others to do so both by his public attack on celibacy and by private exhortation—Luther's own marriage at the age of forty-one to an apostate nun created enormous repercussions, providing decisive embodiment to his convictions and a ready target to his detractors.

Within the joys and sorrows of his marriage, Luther blossomed into the full freedom and creativity of his powers. Here his theology of the home (*oeconomia*) gained substance and exemplary force. Here his relationship to his own father reached moving and positive resolution. Here, too, his pastoral sensitivity grew if possible still keener. (See *Luther: Letters of Spiritual Counsel*, LCC XVIII, for an illuminating selection of his pastoral letters.)

V.1.A Luther's future wife, Katherine von Bora, was one of twelve nuns who made a daring and dangerous escape from Marienthron convent at Nimbschen in Ducal Saxony in 1523. Nine of them were brought to Wittenberg, as Luther described to Spalatin on April 10. (Latin text in Br 3, 54–55: 600.)

Grace and peace! Those nine apostate nuns have come to me. They are a wretched crowd, but they were conducted here by some upright citizens of Torgau, Leonard Koppe and his nephew, Wolf Dommitzsch, so there are no grounds for unjust suspicion. I pity them very much; but most of all I pity the huge number of others everywhere who are perishing from their accursed and unchaste celibacy. Their sex, so extremely weak by itself and linked by nature (or rather by God) to man, perishes when separated by such cruelty. Oh tyrants, oh cruel parents and families in Germany! But you, pope, and you, bishops, who can curse you properly? Who can sufficiently execrate the blindness and fury by which you teach and enforce such things? But this is not the place for that. You ask what I shall do with them? First I shall indicate to their families that they should support them. If they will not, I shall take care that they are looked after elsewhere, for people have promised me some help. I shall also arrange marriage for some of them, where I can. These are their names: Magdalena Staupitz, Elsa von Canitz, Ave Gross, Ave Schonfeld and her sister Margaret Schonfeld, Laneta von Goles, Margaret Zeschau and her sister Katherina Zeschau, and Katherine von Bora. They are the sort of people who genuinely need pity, in whom one may serve Christ. It is extraordinary that they managed to escape. I pray that you too will do a work of charity, and beg from your rich courtiers some money for me to feed them for a week or fortnight, until I can satisfactorily hand them over to their relatives or those who have made me promises. For my Capernaites are making such progress from the extraordinary richness of the daily Word that the other day I myself in person was not able to raise a loan of ten florins for a poor fellow citizen! The poor, who would give gladly, have nothing; those who are richer either say no, or yield with such difficulty that either they must lose the grace of giving in God's sight, or I have to sacrifice my liberty; but this is nothing unusual for the world and its ways. Finally, as far as my annual stipend is concerned, I have only

9 Old Schock, besides which not a single mite comes from the city either to me or to my brothers. But on the other hand I do not make any demands on them, in order to emulate Paul's boast of spoiling the other churches by any means to serve my Corinthians for nothing [2 Cor. 11 : 8]. . . . Farewell, and pray for me! Wittenberg, Easter Friday, 1523.

Mart. Luther.

V.1.B   Most of the girls were successfully provided for, but Katherine von Bora's family was unable to support her, and she remained in Wittenberg. After two abortive efforts to gain her a husband, Luther—who had said in 1521, 'They'll never force a wife on me!'—was convinced by duty and his father's wish that he should marry her. He did so with privacy and dispatch on June 13, 1525. Two weeks later he invited several friends, including Amsdorf, to a feast marking the public announcement. (Latin text in Br 3, 541: 900; also translated in part in Smith II, 329.)

Grace and peace in the Lord! A messenger was just being found for me to bear this letter to you, my Amsdorf, when lo and behold your letter was brought to me. Indeed the story is true that I have suddenly been married to Katherine, before I had to listen to people mouthing tirades against me as usually happens. For I hope that I may stay alive for a short time yet, and I was unwilling to deny to my father, who entreated this last obedience, his hope for descendants, and at the same time to confirm in deed what I have taught in words, since I discover that so many people are timid even in the great light of the gospel. Thus God wished and God acted. For I am not in love, nor do I burn with desire; but I cherish my wife. Next Tuesday therefore I shall give a feast in celebration of my marriage, at which my parents will be present. I wanted you by all means to be present, and so, since I resolved to invite you, I now invite you not to be absent, if it is at all possible for you to come.

The report about the Elector is false, but the people of Meiningen, Mellerstadt, Neustadt, Münnerstadt, and ten other towns have surrendered themselves to the Elector's favour, and he is proceeding there to settle everything peaceably.[1] It is really the case that in Franconia 11,000 peasants in three different locations have fallen, 61 good cannons were captured and the citadel of Wurzburg set free. The Margrave Casimir attacked his peasants fiercely because of two breaches of faith. In the duchy of Württemberg 6,000 have fallen and in various places in Swabia 10,000. It is said that the Duke of Lotharingia has slain 20,000 in Alsatia. Everywhere else the wretched peasants are perishing. Word is presently awaited of what the Bambergers are suffering. None

---

[1] The Peasants' Revolt was at its height: see III.2.

the less they still persist with their seditions in Breisgau and in the county of Tyrol, so that from Innsbruck as far as Trent everything is in commotion. The bishops of Brixen and Trent are ready to flee. Duke George is holding a meeting next Monday in Dessau with the Marquis and the Bishop of Mainz. The rumour is that, inflated by his successes, he will hunt me out in Wittenburg; he believes that I am similar to Müntzer in doctrine! Christ will grant grace. Take care that he does not hunt in Magdeburg! Farewell and pray for me! Wednesday after Corpus Christi, 1525.

V.1.c   If at first Luther cherished, but was not in love with, his gracious and handsome Katie, he very soon discovered deep and lasting affection for her. (*Table Talk*, June, 1532, and January, 1537: German–Latin text in Tr 3, 211: 3178a and 380: 3530.)

The first year of marriage gives one strange sensations. Seated at table, a man thinks: 'Before, I was alone; now there are two of us!' In bed, he wakes up and sees a pair of plaits lying beside him which he had not seen before. Similarly, wives bring to their husbands, however busy they are, a host of useless matters, as when my Katherine used at first to sit with me when I was studying hard and she was spinning, and would ask: 'Lord Doctor, is the Hochmeister the Margrave's brother?'
    The highest grace of God is when love flowers perpetually in marriage. First love is fervent, an intoxicated love which blinds us and leads us on; when we have slept off the intoxication, then in the godly there remains sincere married love, but the ungodly harbour regret.

V.1.d   The new Elector, John the Constant, presented the Black Cloister to the Luthers as a wedding gift. Katherine was an excellent housekeeper, a hardworking, thrifty manager of the Luther farms and gardens, and a devoted mother. Luther came to rely upon her deeply. (*Table Talk*, mid-1531: German–Latin text in Tr 1, 17: 49.)

'I would not exchange my Katie for France or for Venice: first, because God has given her to me and has given me to her; secondly, because I have often discovered that there are more faults in other women than in my Katie (even though she has some too, they are counterbalanced by many great virtues); thirdly, because she preserves the faith of marriage, that is, loyalty and honour. A wife in turn should think this way about her husband.'

V.1.e   The Luther household was daily thronged by crowds of students, friends, and visitors. Meal times became occasions for warm hospitality, for long conversation, for collecting the great man's apophthegms—and sometimes for banter! (*Table Talk*, April, 1532: German–Latin text in Tr 2, 105: 1461.)

On taking a wife: 'The time will come that a man will take more
than one wife.' The doctor's wife replied: 'The devil believe it!' Said
the doctor: 'The reason, Katie, is that a wife can bear only one child a
year, but her husband knows how to beget many.' Katie answered:
'Paul says that everyone should have his own wife.' Then the doctor
replied: ' "His own," yes, but not "only one"; that is not in Paul.' The
doctor jested in this way for a long time, until the doctor's wife declared: 'Before I would put up with that, I'd rather go back into the
monastery and leave you and all your children!'

V.1.F   Luther's home was also a bastion of strength in grief and danger.
         When the plague swept Wittenberg in late 1527, the university
         fled to Jena, but Luther remained behind to expound Scripture
         and to assist Bugenhagen in pastoral care, even though he was
         recuperating from severe illness and Katherine was expecting
         their second child. He wrote as follows to Amsdorf on November
         1. (Latin text in Br 4, 274–275: 1164.)

Grace and peace! As it pleases the Lord, so it transpires, my
Amsdorf, that I who to date have been accustomed to comforting everyone else am now in need of all consolation myself. This one thing I seek
—you seek it with me—that Christ may do with me what He pleases, if
only He will take care that I do not become ungrateful and hostile to
him whom I have preached and worshipped with such zeal and fervour
until now, though certainly not without offending him with many and
grievous sins. Satan is asking to be given someone else as a Job, to sift a
Peter with his brethren, but Christ condescends to say to him: 'Preserve
his soul', and to me: 'I am your salvation', and I hope that he will not
be angry with my sins to the end. I want to reply to the Sacramentarians,
but unless I grow stronger in spirit I am not capable of anything. I shall
keep your copy, but return it in good time.

My home is turning into a hospital. Augustin [Schurf]'s Hanna
suffered the disease internally, but has recovered. Margaretha von
Mochau gave us cause to fear with a suspicious abscess and other signs,
but she too has regained strength. Naturally, I fear for my Katie's
approaching confinement, especially since my little boy has been sick
for three days now and is eating nothing and feeling miserable; they
say it is teething trouble, and both of them are thought to run the risk
of infection. Georg Rörer's wife, herself close to delivery and seized by
the plague, is now concerned about whether her infant can be saved;
may the Lord Jesus be merciful with her.[2] So there are battles without,
quakings within, and adversities aplenty; it is Christ's visitation upon
us. The one consolation is that we are opposing Satan in his fury—at

[2] Rörer's wife, Hanna, died in Luther's home the following day, after giving
birth to a stillborn child.

least, that is, we have the Word of God for preserving the souls of the faithful, even if he devours their bodies. So commend us to the brethren, and to yourself, to pray for us that we may bear the hand of the Lord with fortitude, and conquer the force and guile of Satan whether by death or by life. Amen. Wittenberg, All Saints' Day, tenth anniversary of the trampling down of indulgences, from memory of which we derive double consolation at this hour, 1527.

Your Martin Luther.

V.1.G The Luthers' first child, Hans, was born amid great joy on June 7, 1526. But Elizabeth, born on December 10, 1527, lived less than a year. They had four more children: Magdalena, May 4, 1529; Martin, November 9, 1531; Paul, January 29, 1533; and Margarethe, December 17, 1534. During the Diet of Augsburg in June, 1530, Luther wrote this letter home to his firstborn, Hans. (German text in Br 5, 377–378: 1595; also translated in full in LCC XVIII, 144 f.)

To my dear little son Hans Luther at Wittenberg:
Grace and peace in Christ! My dear son, I am glad to see that you are studying well and praying diligently. Do that, my son, and keep on doing it. When I come home, I will bring with me something beautiful for you from the fair. I know a beautiful, charming, happy garden. Many children go there—they have golden robes on and they gather beautiful apples under the trees, and pears, cherries, yellow plums and purple plums, they sing and jump and are happy. They also have pretty little ponies with golden reins and silver saddles. I asked the man who owned the garden who the children were. He said: 'They are children who like to pray, study, and be good.' And I said: 'Dear Sir, I too have a son. He is called Hans Luther. May he come into the garden too, and eat these beautiful apples and pears and ride such fine ponies and play with these children?' Then the man said: 'If he says his prayers and does his studies happily and is good, he may come into the garden. Lippus and Jost too. And when they all arrive here, they will have fifes and drums and lutes and all sorts of other instruments as well, and they will dance, and shoot with little bows and arrows.' And then he showed me a grand lawn in the garden, all ready for dancing. All over it there were hanging golden fifes and drums and beautiful silver bows and arrows. But it was still so early that the children had not yet eaten, so I could not wait for the dances, and I said to the man: 'Ah, dear Sir, I want to hurry away and write about all this to my little son Hans, so that he will really study hard, pray well, and be good so that he too can come to this garden. But he has an Aunt Lena whom he must bring with him.' The man answered: 'Excellent, go back and write that to him.'
So Hans, my dear little son, study and pray really happily and tell

Lippus and Jost about it too so that they will also study and pray, and so you will all reach the garden together. Herewith I commit you to our dear God. Greet Aunt Lena and give her a kiss from me. Your loving father,

Martin Luther.

V.1.h   His letter to his son, Hans Jr., was written only three weeks after the death of his father, Hans Sr. On February 15, 1530, Luther had written his dying father this letter of consolation and filial devotion. (German text in Br 5, 239–241: 1529; also translated in full in LCC XVIII, 30 ff.)

To my dear father, Hans Luther, burgher in Mansfeld in the Vale, grace and peace in Christ Jesus, our Lord and Saviour. Amen.

Dear Father! My brother Jacob has written to me that you are dangerously ill. Because the atmosphere right now is so foul, and there is danger everywhere else as well as from the season, I am disturbed and anxious about you. For even though God has so far given you a strong, hardy body and kept you vigorous, at these times your age still gives me anxious thoughts. Besides, none of us either is or should be secure for a single hour of our life. On this account, I would have come to you myself in person with the greatest willingness; but my good friends have advised me against this and dissuaded me, and I too am forced to think myself that I should not tempt God by placing myself in danger; for you know how well disposed the princes and lords are to me! But it would be the greatest joy for me (if it were possible) if you would agree to be brought with Mother here to us, as my Kate, and all of us, beg with tears. I hope that we will look after you as well as possible. So I have sent Cyriac[3] to see whether this would be possible in view of your illness. For whatever God's will has in store for you, be it in this life or the life to come, it would give me such heartfelt joy (as indeed it ought) to be with you in person and in accordance with the fourth commandment to show myself thankful to God and to you with filial devotion and service.

Meanwhile, from the bottom of my heart I pray the Father who has made and given you to be my father that he will strengthen you according to his infinite goodness and will enlighten and protect you with his spirit, so that you will confess with joy and thanksgiving the blessed teaching of his son, our Lord Jesus Christ, to which also you have now been called through his grace and have come out of the former awful darkness and error; and I hope that his grace which has given you such knowledge and has thus begun his work in you will guard and perfect it to the end, both in this life and in the joyful future of our Lord Jesus Christ. Amen.

[3] Luther's nephew, Cyriac Kaufmann, had accompanied him to the Coburg.

For he has already sealed such teaching and faith in you, and has confirmed it with characteristic signs, namely that on account of my name you have undergone with all of us so much slander, insult, derision, ridicule, scorn, hatred, enmity and danger. But these are the true hallmarks in which we have to become alike and conformable to our Lord Christ, as St Paul says, so that we may also be sharers in his future glory [Phil. 3 : 8 ff.].

So now in your illness let your heart be alert and confident; for there in the life to come we have before God a sure and faithful helper, Jesus Christ, who has slain sin and death for us, and for us is now seated above, and watches and waits for us with all the angels when we set out, so that we must not be anxious or fear that we shall sink or fall to the ground. For he has such great power over death and sin that they can do nothing to us; and he is so warmly faithful and good that he cannot and will not let us go, if only we will ask without doubting.

For he has declared, promised, and pledged it; he will not and cannot lie or deceive us, there is no doubt of that. 'Ask,' he says, 'and you shall receive, seek and you shall find, knock and it shall be opened to you. [Matt. 7 : 7]. And elsewhere: 'All who call upon the name of the Lord shall be saved' [Joel 2 : 32]. And the whole Psalter is full of such consoling promises, especially Psalm 91 [Vulg. 90], which is particularly good for all who are ill to read.

I wanted to have this talk with you in writing because of my anxiety about your illness (since we do not know the hour) so that in this way I might share in your beliefs, struggles, consolations, and thanks to God for his holy word which he has so richly, powerfully and graciously granted us in this time.

But if it is his godly will that you should postpone that better life even longer, to go on sharing and suffering with us in this wretched and unhappy vale of woe, to see and hear sorrow, and together with all Christians to help endure and overcome it, then he will also give you grace to accept all these burdens willingly and obediently. Yet to be sure, this accursed life is nothing but a real vale of woe—the longer a man lives in it, the more sin, evil, plague, and sorrow he sees and feels, and there is no end or escape from it all until someone carves it out for us with a shovel—there at last it must end and let us sleep peacefully in the repose of Christ, until he comes and awakens us again in joyfulness. Amen.

So I commend you to him who holds you more dear than you hold yourself, has proved this love by taking your sin upon himself and making payment with his own blood, has let you hear about it through the gospel, and enabled you to believe it through his Spirit. Thus he has prepared and sealed everything most surely, so that you ought no longer to be either anxious or fearful for yourself, since you and your heart remain calm and confident in his Word and faith. As this is the situation, let him do the worrying: he will do what is best—yes, he has already done everything for the very best, more than we can imagine. May he, our dear Lord and Saviour, be with and by you, so that (God grant be it here or there) we may joyfully see each other again. For our faith is sure, and we have no doubt that we shall see each other again shortly in Christ's presence, since the journey from this life is much shorter before God than if I travel from you in Mansfeld to here, or if you travel from me in Wittenberg to Mansfeld. It is surely true that it takes only a little hour's sleep, and then it is all different.

So now I hope that your pastor and preacher will do you true service by pointing all these things out to you very richly, so that you will hardly need my prattling. Yet I cannot fail to ask forgiveness for my physical absence, which God knows makes me grieve in my heart.

My Katie, little Hans, little Lena, Aunt Lena, and the whole house greet you, and are praying for you faithfully. Greet my dear mother and all our friends. God's grace and power be and remain with you forever. Amen.

Wittenberg, February 15, 1530.

Your dear son
Martin Luther.

V.1.ɪ   Luther responded with softening emotion to the news of his father's passing in a letter to Melanchthon on June 5, 1530. (Latin text in Br 5, 351: 1584.)

Today Hans Reineicke wrote to me that my dearly beloved father, Hans Luther, Sr., departed this life on Exaudi Sunday[4] at 1 o'clock. This death has cast me into deep mourning as I remember not only his nature but also his sweetest love. For it was from him that my Creator gave me everything I am and have; and although it consoles me, as Hans writes, that he gently fell asleep strong in the faith of Christ, yet compassion and the memory of his sweetest conversation have so rent my inward being that I have scarcely ever despised death so much. But 'the righteous man is taken away from calamity and enters into peace' [Isa. 57 : 1–2]—in other words, we die many times before we die once and for all. I now succeed to the heritage of his name, since I am almost the oldest Luther in my family. To me also now belongs not only the opportunity but the right of following him through death into the kingdom of Christ, a right graciously granted to us all by him for whose sake we are more wretched than all men and the scorn of the whole world. I am too sad to write any more now, since it is meet and right for me filially to mourn such a parent, from whom the Father of mercy

---

[4] May 29, 1530. The Sunday after Ascension, called *Exaudi* Sunday from the first word of the introit for the day, 'Hear, O Lord, when I cry . . .'.

begat me and through his labours nourished and fashioned whatever I
am. Indeed, I rejoice that he lived in these times, so that he beheld the
light of truth. Blessed be God in all his deeds and counsels forever.
Amen. Of other things elsewhere. Greet all our friends. The Day of
Pentecost, 1530.

Martin Luther.

V.1.J   These were by no means the Luthers' last experience of pressing
illness and grief. Luther's mother died on June 30, 1531. Luther
himself suffered persistent ailments, one in 1537 almost fatal.
There were several more outbreaks of plague, and famine struck
in 1539. Then in 1542 Magdalena, now fourteen, died of fever in
her father's arms. (*Table Talk*, September, 1542: German–Latin
text in Tr 5, 187–193: 5491–5499.)

As his daughter's illness grew worse, he said: 'I love her very much.
But if it is your will, dear God, that you will take her from us, I will be
content to know she is with you.' Then he said to his daughter as she
lay in bed: 'Magdalenichen, my little girl, you are happy to stay with
me, your father, and are you also happy to go to your Father in
heaven?' The sick girl answered: 'Yes, dearest father, as God wills.'
Her father said: 'Dear little daughter!'
  ' "The spirit is strong, but the flesh is weak" [cf. Matt. 26 : 41]. I
love her so very much. If this flesh is so strong, what will the spirit be?'
  Amongst other things he said: 'In a thousand years God has not given
any bishop such great gifts as he has me (for it is right to glory in God's
gifts). I am angry with myself that I cannot rejoice from my heart and
thank God—though now and then I do sing a song and thank God a
little. Whether we live or die, we are the Lord's. (Lord's with an
apostrophe, not without!)'
  As his wife became deeply distressed Martin Luther comforted her.
'Think where she is going! It will be good for her to go there. The flesh
is fleshy, but the spirit breathes. Children do not argue. They believe
what people tell them. Everything is simple with children; they die
without anxiety, complaint, or fear of death, with little physical pain,
as if they were going to sleep.'
  When at last his daughter was in the agony of death, he fell on his
knees by the bed, and weeping bitterly prayed that God would be
pleased to set her free. Then she breathed out her life in her father's
arms. Her mother was in the same room, but farther away from the bed
because of her grief. It was past nine o'clock on the Wednesday after
Trinity, 1542.
  After she died, he said: 'I am joyful in spirit, but after the flesh I
grieve deeply. The flesh is so unwilling here. The separation distresses
one beyond all measure. It is extraordinary to know for certain that she

is in peace, that it is good and best for her to be there, and yet to sorrow like this!'...He said to those who came: 'Do not let yourself be sad! I have sent a saint into heaven—indeed, now I have sent two of them there.'

V.2 THE MATURE THEOLOGIAN

To savour the power and eloquence of Luther's mature theology, there is simply no alternative to extensive reading in his voluminous biblical lectures and sermons. These few selections merely sample some central and perennial themes, and sketch the style of his theology. For a few years, Luther tried tentatively to rework the systematic categories of scholastic theology, to see if they could adequately contain his vital, empirical insights—notably in *Against Latomus* (1521), and *The Bondage of the Will* (1525) (a reply to Erasmus' *Discourse on Free Will*). After the mid-twenties, he virtually abandoned the attempt in favour of a mode more fitting 'the living voice of the gospel', a rich rhetoric of address, admonition, and promise, echoing the language of Scripture itself.

V.2.A   Relations between Luther and Erasmus had long been a mixture of tentative respect and suspicion. When Erasmus finally yielded to pressure to write against Luther, the latter swiftly replied in *The Bondage of the Will* (1525), which closes with this summary. (Latin text in WA 18, 785–787; also translated in full in Packer and Johnston, eds., *The Bondage of the Will*, 316 ff.; and LCC XVII: *Luther and Erasmus on Free Will*, 331 ff.)

If the light of the gospel, which avails through the Word and faith alone, is so effective that a problem debated in all ages and never solved [namely, that the innocent suffer] is so easily analysed and resolved, what do you think will happen when the light of the Word and faith has ceased and the reality, the divine majesty, is revealed in itself? Do you not think that the light of glory will then be able to solve with the greatest ease a problem [namely, predestination] which is insoluble by the light of the Word and grace, seeing the light of grace has so easily solved a problem insoluble by the light of nature? Grant me the three lights, the light of nature, the light of grace, and the light of glory, as the common and valuable distinction has it. By the light of nature there is no explanation of the justice of the good man's suffering and the wicked's prospering. But the light of grace dissolves the problem. By the light of grace it is insoluble how God condemns someone who is unable by any of his own powers to do anything but sin and be guilty. Here the light of grace, just as much as the light of nature, declares that the blame lies not with the wretched man but with an unjust God—

they can reach no other conclusion about a God who freely crowns an ungodly man without merits, and does not crown but condemns another who is perhaps less, or at least not more, ungodly. But the light of glory judges otherwise, and one day it will reveal that God, who alone exercises the judgement of incomprehensible justice, is a God of utter and manifest justice, if only in the meantime we believe it, instructed and assured by the example of the light of grace, which performs a similar feat for the light of nature.

I shall end this booklet here, prepared, if need be, to pursue the issue further, although I think that more than enough has been presented here for the godly man and anyone who wishes to believe the truth without obstinacy. For if we believe it to be true that God foreknows and foreordains all things, next that he can be neither mistaken nor hindered in his foreknowledge and predestination, and finally that nothing happens unless he wills it, as even reason is forced to concede: it follows by the testimony of reason itself that there can be no *free* will in man or angel or any creature. Similarly, if we believe that Satan is the prince of this world, constantly plotting and warring against the kingdom of Christ with all his strength, so that he does not let go of captive men unless he is compelled by the divine power of the Spirit, it is again obvious that there can be no *free* will. Similarly, if we believe that original sin has so corrupted us that even in those who are led by the Spirit it demands the most strenuous effort by its struggle against the good, it is clear that in a man devoid of the Spirit there is nothing else which can turn itself towards the good, but only towards evil. Again, if the Jews, who pursued justice with all their strength, instead fell headlong into injustice, and the Gentiles, who pursued ungodliness, attained to justice freely and unexpectedly, it is equally obvious from man's own toil and experience that without grace he can will nothing but evil. But above all, if we believe that Christ has redeemed men with his own blood, we are bound to confess that the whole man was lost, or else we make Christ either superfluous or redeemer of the most insignificant part of us, and that is blasphemy and sacrilege.

Now, my Erasmus, I pray you in Christ's name, please do what you promised. You promised that you were prepared to yield to anyone who taught better things. Put aside respect of persons. I acknowledge that you are a great man, adorned by God with many of the noblest endowments, genius, learning, an almost miraculous eloquence, not to mention your other gifts. I, on the other hand, have and am nothing, except that I may perhaps boast of being a Christian. Then, too, I vigorously praise and acclaim in you the fact that in contrast with all others you alone have attacked the real substance, the supreme issue, and have not wearied me with those extraneous issues about the papacy, purgatory, indulgences, and similar trifles rather than issues, with which virtually everyone has vainly pursued me so far. You, and you alone, perceived the pivotal point and made for the jugular, for which I thank you from my heart; for I can gladly go on dealing with this issue for as long as time and opportunity permit. If those who attacked me earlier had done this, and if those who now boast of new spirits and new revelations would do the same, we would have had less sedition and sects and more peace and concord. But in this way God, through Satan, requites our ingratitude. Even so, if you cannot deal with this issue in any other way than you have managed in this Discourse, may I express my great hope that you, content with your own gift, may cultivate, adorn, and promote literature and languages as you have done so far with great profit and honour. By your learning you have greatly aided me, too, and I confess myself much indebted to you, and I certainly venerate and esteem you in that respect with a sincere heart. That you should be equal to our present issue, God has not yet willed or granted. Please do not think that this remark springs from arrogance. Indeed, I pray that the day is close when the Lord will make you as much my superior in this matter as you are already my superior in all others. It is nothing new for God to enlighten Moses through Jethro, or teach Paul through Ananias. For since you yourself say that 'you have wandered far from the mark, if you do not know Christ', I think that you see yourself what the situation is. For everyone will not make the same mistake, if you or I go wrong. God is he who is declared to be 'wonderful in his saints' [Ps. 68 : 35; Vulg. 67 : 36] so that we may regard as saints those who are very far from saintliness. And since you are human, it would not be difficult for you either not to understand, or not to observe carefully enough, the writings or sayings of the fathers by whose guidance you believe that you have kept the mark. The fact that you write that you 'assert nothing, but have simply made a collection', is a clear enough sign: someone who perceives the issue clearly and understands it correctly does not write like this. In this book, however, I HAVE NOT MADE A COLLECTION, BUT I HAVE ASSERTED AND DO ASSERT, and I do not 'want judgement to rest' with anyone, but I urge all to make their submission. But may the Lord, whose cause this is, enlighten you and make you a vessel of his honour and glory. Amen.

V.2.B   The all-important relation between justification and ethics was the subject of Luther's lecture on 1 John 3 : 11–20, September 30 and October 1, 1527. (Latin and German text in WA 20, 707 and 711–717.)

First we are urged to believe; then we are urged to love—these are the two parts of Christianity. For man is justified by faith in Christ, and then, after the gospel has first been preached, good works and the fulfilment of the law follow through love. . . . Love is not the sort of thing it is possible to hide: you can see it in a man. It is very plainly discernible. It is not as easily hidden as the hatred of self-styled saints. For love speaks well of its neighbour, is warm towards him, and gives him comfort. If I have money in hand and do not give it to my neighbour who is in need, the case is plain: the fact that men do not love their brethren has such manifest and obvious fruit. If I console my brother, pray for him, teach him—if I even have to die 'that the truth of the gospel may be preserved among you' [Gal. 2 : 5]—all these things can be seen. It is not love, as the sophists stupidly prattle, when I merely wish my neighbour well. 'If anyone is a hearer of the Word and not a doer, he is like a man who observes his face in a mirror; he observes himself and goes away and at once forgets what he was like' [James 1 : 23]. Such men do not have their heart in love, which expresses itself in work. 'Love thinks no evil' [Cor. 13 : 5]. Why is this love such a remarkable thing? Because Christ laid down his own soul for us in just this way. Love is therefore not something inherent in the soul, but something which must be elicited. Christ laid down his life— here you hear what love is! This is love carried to its very peak. Christianity is no cold thing! Of course, not every instance is to be counted as an occasion for laying down one's life; but the Word does provide one rather powerful instance—to lay down one's life so that a brother is not deprived of the Word. For example, a deadly plague is upon us here: how can we deprive the city of the Word and the ministry of the sacraments? . . .

I repeat, love is not a hidden thing. If a man should lay down his life for his brother, how much more should he bestow his substance on him. In other words, a man should lay down both his body and his property for his brother. Otherwise 'how can the love of God dwell in him?' [1 John 3 : 17]. I see my brother destitute and hungry, and I have this world's goods, but I do not sustain or support him. Here there is none of that love which feeds the hungry, clothes the naked, and takes in the stranger [cf. Matt. 25 : 35 f.]. . . . In other words, the man who is parsimonious and greedy is not a Christian. And now, in this period when the gospel is being taught once more, there is even more stinginess than before! Satan is doing it. So it is not surprising that this plague has ensued, seeing we have not acted in accordance with the gospel's command. It is fitting that we should undergo disease, hunger, perhaps even the sword, lest God give place to his wrath. Otherwise we should not have had *our* God, but a stupid god. Since God, then, is merciful, he is not idle. He is compassionate and abundant in mercy to the contrite and humble, but the man who sins wantonly he does not acquit. 'The angel of the Lord encamps about those who fear him' [Ps. 34 : 7; Vulg. 33 : 8].

To apply this statement only to cases of extreme or absolute necessity, as some of our people have done, is stupid and ungodly. To be sure,
there are certain gradations of love: your enemy is not to be harmed;
your brother is to be helped; your household is to be provided for. You
are sufficiently familiar with Christ's command to love your enemies.
But you owe more to your brother who returns love for love. There are
several methods of giving him material aid: the first method is to make
an outright gift; the second is to lend him money, or to return a gift;
the third is to help him when we see him lacking the necessities of life.
And if he is deceiving us, what then? He should still be helped. And yet
we often laugh at genuine beggars. You owe most of all, however, to
your own family. 'If anyone does not provide for his relatives and
especially for his own family he has disowned the faith and is worse
than an unbeliever' [1 Tim. 5 : 8]. . . .

Faith itself is confirmed by fruit-bearing, use, and exercise. Otherwise faith is very feeble. Faith must be exercised if it is to be freed
from an evil conscience to serve our brother. Then we may fly to the
mercy of God; then we can comfort and lift up our hearts before him,
and be confident. Our works have no value as righteousness, but they
nevertheless promote faith, they do not impede it. When I am troubled
in conscience because I am unstable and fallible, a freer conscience is
available here, one which will not oppress me with my instability. If this
were not so, then a fierce battle against faith would result, and the soul
would be exceedingly tormented. But God does not leave those who
cannot assure their hearts in this way without consolation. Even though
we fall into some sin, do not give way to doubt. . . . Despair has been
forbidden. In short, our conscience creates havoc, an angry God, and a
cowardly heart in us; but 'God is greater than our heart' [1 John
3 : 20]. Our conscience is less than our God in numberless ways.
Against an evil conscience you may say: 'You are a tiny droplet, and
God is an infinite fire which will swallow you up.' No sin is greater
than faithlessness—'because they do not believe in me' [John 16 : 9].
Only faithlessness has no forgiveness, because it fights against forgiveness of sins, all of which have forgiveness. This is an extraordinary
statement, and the sweetest of promises. Does your wickedness surpass
God's goodness? Do your sins outweigh the graciousness of God? The
honour must be given to God that he is greater in infinite ways.

V.2.c   Justification by faith, for Luther, was not an abstract legal notion.
He thought of it rather as a union between Christ and the faithful,
a perfect sharing where 'the great exchange' of sin and righteousness took place, as he depicted in this sermon on John 1 : 29 of
November 3, 1537. (German text in WA 46, 680–681; also translated in full in LW 22, 158 ff.)

The love of the Son of God is so great towards us that the greater the filth and stench upon us, the more he gives himself to us, cleanses us and takes all our sin and wretchedness, lifts them off our shoulders and lays them on his own back. . . . What does it mean that the Son of God should be my servant, and so utterly debase himself that he should take the burden of my misery and sin—indeed, the whole world's sin and death? He says to me: 'You are no longer a sinner, but I am. I step into your place—you have not sinned, but I have. The whole world is in sin, but you are not in sin—I am. All your sins are to lie on me and not on you.' No one can grasp this: there in the life to come we shall gaze for ever blessed upon this love of God. And who would not gladly die for Christ's sake? The Son of Man does the basest and filthiest work—not just wearing a beggar's tattered coat or old trousers, or washing us like a mother washes a child, but he bears our sin, death, hell, our wretchedness of body and soul. When the devil says: 'You are a sinner', Christ interrupts: 'I will reverse that, I will be the sinner—you shall go free.' Who can be thankful enough to our Lord God for this mercy?

V.2.D   Faith does not justify because it is faith, but because it is faith in Christ. In the same 1537 series, this time on John 1 : 16, Luther gave dramatic expression to his central theological principle: that Christ alone is necessary and sufficient for salvation. (German text in WA 46, 652–653; also translated in full in LW 22, 124 ff.)

If we would glory, then we must glory in this, that we have received from the fullness of the Lord Christ: by him we are enlightened, receive forgiveness of sins, and become God's children. This is the heart of the matter: whoever wishes to be safe from the devil's power—to escape sin and death—must draw from this fountain, Christ, from whom all salvation and bliss flow. This fountain is inexhaustible; it is full of grace and truth before God; it never runs dry, if we draw from it as much as we will. Even if we all keep drawing from it without pause, it cannot be exhausted, but remains an endless source of all grace and truth, an unfathomable fountain and eternal spring. The more we draw from it, the more richly it gives—a water, St John says, that springs up to eternal life. The precious sun is not dimmed or darkened because it gives so much light; yes, it supplies the whole world with its shining, brilliant beams, yet it retains its light quite whole. It loses nothing, it is a measureless light that could light ten more worlds. Or again, you could kindle a hundred thousand lamps from one lamp, and yet that one lamp, which ignited and kindled so many other lamps or tapers, would not lose any of its own brilliance. A learned man, too, can make a thousand others learned without sacrificing any of his own skill— indeed, the more he shares, the more he has. So Christ our Lord, to whom we must flee and from whom we must ask for everything, is an

G

endless well and fountain-head of all grace, truth, righteousness, wisdom and life, without measure, end, or limit.

V.3 THE AGEING PROPHET

Luther's last ten years were in many respects the happiest of his life, bringing joy in his family, the esteem of a vigorous international movement, and the fruition of his expository powers. Yet there is another, sadder aspect of these years. Doctrinal dissension was unrelenting, even among his close associates. He was disillusioned by political scandal and disloyalty, and by the indifference and immorality of German society. He suffered repeated illnesses and bereavements. Like many an ageing leader, he grew hypersensitive to opposition, and wrote polemics more caustic than ever before. Yet his inflexibility in public was tempered always by his private generosity; his public brashness by a deep-seated and unflagging personal humility.

V.3.A   One of the most serious of Luther's repeated illnesses in later life was an almost fatal attack of kidney stone in February, 1537, at Schmalkalden, during a meeting of the Protestant League. (*Table Talk*: German and Latin text in Tr 3, 387–390; 354A; also translated in full in LW 54, 225 ff.)

Some sayings of the reverend father and lord, Dr Martin Luther, as he lay in peril of death at Schmalkalden: When Philip (Melanchthon) looked at him and dissolved in tears, he said: 'As Johann Löser would say, there is no art in drinking good wine, but to be able to drink bad wine—that is an art! So now you think that I must learn to practise this art and be able to be calm even when I despair of life and suffer these pains. If we accept good from the Lord's hand, why do we not tolerate evil? The Lord gives, the Lord takes away, blessed be the name of the Lord [Job 2 : 10 and 1 : 21]. I have played this game against the pope and Satan long enough now, and the Lord has wonderfully preserved and comforted me. Why should I not bear calmly what he does with me now according to his will? Yet our death is nothing beside the death of the Son of God. Anyway, so many very holy men, of whose company we are not worthy, have been buried before us; and if we wish to be with them, as we certainly do, we too must die. In fact, we should seek this with an eager heart, because our Lord, who has us in his hand, is the Lord of life. There is certainly a great change in me: yesterday my mind was alert enough and my body strong; today, as you see, I am miserably broken in strength. How changed I am from the person I was yesterday! Yesterday I was soaring over the trees without a care. But O good God, how we and all that we have are nothing, even at the moment when we are everything! I might well have prayed, or even

importuned, our Lord God to let me die in my prince's territory. But if
that is not to be, at whatever hour and place the Lord calls me, I shall
be ready. I shall be and die an enemy of all the enemies of my Christ,
and if I die under the pope's excommunication, he too will die under
my Christ's excommunication.'

Next day, that is, February 26, when he was vomiting from the sickness, he said: 'Ah, dear Father, take this dear soul in your hands! I
thank you and bless you, and may all your creatures bless you; grant
that I may be swiftly gathered to my fathers!' When the vomiting
stopped, he said: 'Depart, my dear soul, depart in God's name! How
pitiful and wretched we men are! There is almost no strength left in
me, and yet what little strength I have is so wretchedly goaded and
vexed by Satan! My Father, give me then constancy and patience in
your faith, that I may overcome. To you, my Amsdorf, I commend my
wife Katie. I have no doubt that Satan kindles and sharpens these pains.
He sticks little plugs in us to stop the stone and the urine from passing!
But by God's grace, I will be better off after this life. So the fact that I
am now suffering these things from the devil does me no harm at all. I
shall be happy to be torn apart, if only Satan does not triumph in the
Church after my death. It is just this that I fear so much, because contempt and ingratitude for the gospel are so great.' (Here he very bitterly
shed many tears and drew very deep breaths, wringing his hands with
great sobs.) . . . Then he drank some extract of almonds and said: 'Bless
it to me, dear God, either for death or for life! If this illness lasts much
longer, I am sure I shall go mad, but even if that happens, I know that
my God remains wise and prudent. Good God, this very wretched little
body is vulnerable to so many deaths! If it were not for my faith in
Jesus Christ, it would be no surprise if I took my own life with the
sword. The devil hates me, so he aggravates my illness like this—he has
me caught in his claws now. And I have well and truly earned it from
him! But, Christ, avenge yourself on your enemy. I have done him
much harm by wrestling with the pope; now I must withstand him
again in this. If a good result should come of it, it should happen not so
that I may be restored, but so that the power of the devil may be shattered eternally. He gives us grief, but God will not desert us, and he
renders to each according to his works. If only God would take me
away, then, and pay the devil what he has earned. Amen.'

That same day, when the nobleman Ponikau, the Elector's chancellor,
was present, he said: : 'So I am to be "stoned" like Stephen! That will
give the Pope some joy, but I hope that he will not laugh for long. My
epitaph should truly stand: "Living, I was your plague, dying, I shall
be your death, Pope!"' Afterwards he gave God thanks that he had
preserved him in the faith and in the confession of the Word and of his
name. Then he asked Ponikau to commend his children and his wife to

the Prince, and to thank him for his great benevolence. Next day he said the same thing to the Prince in person: first he commended to him the care of the Church, and afterwards the care of his own home. Then the Prince said that he hoped that 'our Lord God would not treat his land and people so grievously'; but if he did die, he would 'protect the Doctor's wife and children as if they were his own.'

V.3.B   Dissensions among Luther's colleagues soured the happiness of these years, especially the 'antinomian' dispute over the status of the law provoked by Johann Agricola, against whom Luther wrote several disputations and a treatise between 1537 and 1540. (*Table Talk*, March 21, 1537: Latin and German text in Tr 3, 405: 3554; also translated in full in LW 54, 233 f.)

A certain scholar showed him statements contending that the law ought not to be preached in the Church because it did not justify. He grew angry and said: 'That already this idea should arise from our own people while we are still alive! That is Agricola's opinion, and he is driven by hatred and ambition. Ah, if only we gave Master Philip [Melanchthon] due credit! He teaches the use of the law so very clearly and eloquently, and I defer to him (although I too have dealt with this issue clearly in my Galatians commentary). Indeed, it will fulfil the prediction that Count Albrecht wrote to me: "There is another Müntzer lurking behind this." For in politics, a person who abolishes the law also abolishes both civil and domestic order; if he abolishes it in the Church, no recognition of sin remains. For the gospel does not expose sin except through the law, which is spiritual and which restrains sin against God's will. Good-bye to the man who says that transgressors do not sin against the law but only dishonour the Son of God! Such speculative theologians are the plague of the churches. Without conscience, without knowledge, without logic they confuse everything with teachings like these: "Love is the fulfilling of the law, and so we need no law." But those wretched people overlook the minor premise: that this fulfilment, namely, love, is weak in our flesh, and that we must wrestle in spirit against the flesh every day, which belongs under the law.'

V.3.C   In 1540, the revelation that Philip of Hesse had married bigamously with Luther's consent was a massive setback to Protestantism both morally and diplomatically. On June 10, Luther wrote to the Elector explaining the origin of the scandal. (German text in Br 9, 133–134: 3493; also translated in full in LCC XVIII, 289 ff.; Smith, *Martin Luther*, 377 ff.)

Most serene, highborn Elector, most gracious Lord! I have heard that Your Grace has unjustly received complaints from the court of Dresden about the business of the Landgrave, and that Your Grace wishes to be in a position to respond to these clever men of Meissen.[5] For both Philip and I have been reluctant to inform Your Grace of what the matter is about, because we regard it as a confessional secret. For in confessional matters it is proper to keep secret both the matter itself and the confessional advice, and if the Landgrave had not revealed the confessional matter and our advice, none of this sickening unpleasantness need have happened.

And I still say: if such a case were brought before me today, I would give no other advice than what I gave. So I am concealing nothing (as will become obvious later). I leave aside the question whether I am as clever as they think they are. The chief features of the situation are as follows:

Martin Bucer brought us a letter and indicated that the Landgrave, because of certain faults in his wife, did not know how to keep himself chaste, and had previously lived in various ways which were not right. He desired to be evangelical, and therefore to be at one with the principal leaders. Accordingly he swore, by all that was highest and dearest to him, before God and his own conscience, that he could not henceforth keep himself clean from such vices unless he was allowed to take another wife. But we were horrified by this tale, especially on account of the vulgar scandal that would follow, and begged His Grace at all costs not to do so. Then we were told again that he could not abandon it; if we were unwilling to permit it, he would do it anyway in spite of us, and obtain permission from the emperor or the pope. To forestall this, however, we humbly begged that if His Grace really intended to do it, or (as he said) in conscience and before God was unable to do otherwise, His Grace would at least keep it secret because such necessity had driven His Grace to it, and it could not be defended before the world and the laws of the realm. We were promised that this would be the case. Accordingly we were prepared, as far as possible, to help cover it before God with examples, such as Abraham and so on. All this was conducted and handled in the manner of a confession, so that no one can accuse us of having acted willingly and gladly or with delight and joy. It was hard enough for us emotionally, but because we could not prevent it, we still thought we should counsel his conscience as much as we could.

Certainly, both under the papacy and later, I have heard in confession and given advice about other matters which, if they were made public like this, I should have to deny, or else announce the confession. Such

[5] Dresden, in the county of Meissen, was capital of Albertine Saxony, which under Duke George had led Catholic opposition to the reformation. On Duke George's death in 1539, the senile Duke Henry (under his wife's influence) had half-heartedly adopted the reform. But opposition remained strong in courtly circles until the accession in 1541 of Duke Maurice, who applied the reform with vigour.

matters do not belong in a secular court, nor should they be published. Here God has a court of his own: he has to counsel souls where no law or skill in the world can help. My preceptor in the cloister, a fine old man, also handled many such matters, and once was forced to say with a sigh: 'Ah, such matters are so deceptive and dubious that no wisdom, law, or reason can give advice here. One must commit them to the divine goodness.' In the light of this sort of experience, I have dealt with this matter, too, according to divine goodness.

But had I known that the Landgrave had already been thoroughly satisfying his 'pressing need' for a very long time, and could satisfy it with others (as I now find out for the first time he has done with the lady of Eschwege), surely no angel would have induced me to give such counsel. My decision was taken on the basis of the inescapable necessity, weakness, and jeopardy of conscience which Bucer had presented to us. Even less would I have advised that there should be a public wedding to which the young lady should come as princess and Landgravine (this too was completely undisclosed), which is surely insufferable and intolerable to the whole realm. Rather I understood and hoped, since he had to travel the common path of the weakness of the flesh with sin and shame, that he would keep some honourable maiden secretly in a house, and meet the urgently pressing need of his conscience in a secret marriage (even if it did not have the appearance of marriage before the world), and ride to and fro, as not infrequently happens with other great lords—just as I have also advised some pastors and bishops under Duke George that they should secretly marry their cooks.

This is the confessional counsel which I should far rather have kept secret, but now that necessity has wrung it from me, I cannot do so. But the people in Dresden talk as if I had taught the self-same thing for thirteen years, whilst they give us to understand what a completely friendly attitude they bear towards us, and what a great desire they have for love and unity, as if amongst them there was no scandal or transgression ten times worse before God than this advice of ours. But after all, the world gladly removes the splinter from its neighbour's eye and forgets the beam in its own! If I now have to defend everything that I have said and done for years, especially at the beginning, I must ask the Pope to do the same. If they try to justify their former course (I overlook the present), they will belong more to the devil than to God.

I am not ashamed of this advice, even if it should come to the whole world's attention, except that from repugnance I should far rather it were, if possible, kept secret.

M. Luther, by his own hand.

V.3.D   Proud of his accomplishment, but utterly weary of opposition and dissent, the ailing Luther often declared himself ready to die.

(Table Talk, Winter 1542/43; Latin and German text in Tr 5, 222: 5537; also translated in full in LW 54, 448, and in part in Smith, *Martin Luther,* 409 f.)

After he had suffered a severe headache for some days, at the evening meal he said: 'Katie, if I do not feel better in the morning, I shall have our Hans sent home from Torgau, because I should like to have him here at my end.' Then she said: 'Look, Sir, that is your imagination!' The Doctor answered: 'No, Katie, it is not imagination! I shall not die suddenly. First I shall be laid low and be ill, but I shall not lie there for long. I have had enough of the world, and it has had enough of me; and that makes me quite happy. The world thinks that it would be grand, if only it could be rid of me; it will find out about that, to be sure! It is, after all, as I have often said: I am ripe dung, and the world is a wide arsehole; and so we do well to part. I thank you, dear God, that you let me stay among your poor flock which suffers persecution for the sake of your Word; for it is certainly not for whoring or usury that they perse-cute me, that I know for sure!'

V.3.E   Near the end, Luther refought old battles against the papacy and the Zwinglians with the most cantankerous polemics of his career. He wrote to his friend Amsdorf (whom he himself had recently consecrated bishop) on April 14, 1545. (Latin text in Br 11, 71–72: 4091; also translated in full in Smith, *Martin Luther,* 404 f.)

To the reverend father and lord in Christ, Lord Nicholas [Amsdorf], bishop of the church at Naumburg, his esteemed in a greater Lord.

Grace and peace in the Lord! Thank you, reverend father in Christ, for your high opinion of my little book *Against the Papacy.* It has not pleased everyone equally. Yet it pleased the Prince so much that he has distributed twenty guldens' worth of copies. But you know my disposi-tion: I usually do not notice what displeases the many, if only it is godly and useful, and pleases a few good men. Not that I think the others are evil, but either they do not understand the substance, quantity, quality, and all the categories, kinds, species, properties, distinctions, and acci-dents—in other words, all the horrendous and horrible monstrosities— of the papal abomination (for no one has eloquence and genius enough to measure or represent them); or else they fear the anger of rulers. The Zürich sacramentarians have written against me in Latin and German, because of my little book, *The Short Confession* [*Concerning the Sacrament*]. I have not yet decided whether I want to reply to them, since I have condemned them so often, both before and now. They are fanatical, proud, but at the same time laggardly men. When the move-ment began, and I sweated alone to bear the fury of the pope, they bravely kept silent and looked on at my success or my danger; later, when the papacy was somewhat shattered and the opportunity for freedom had been created, they then burst forth as glorious victors—they had derived nothing from anyone else, but everything from their own powers! Thus, thus does one labour and another reap the harvest. Finally they turned their attack upon me, by whom they were freed. They are a cowardly swarm of drones, trained to eat honey gathered by another's labour. Their judgement will come upon them. If it seems right to reply, I shall do it briefly and reaffirm my sentence of condemnation. For I have decided to complete the remaining booklet against the papacy while strength permits.

The Emperor in Belgium, the French king in France, rage viciously against the gospel. Ferdinand is acting no more temperately in Hungary and Austria. In just this way Caiaphas advised that the Son of God should be sacrificed lest they lose the country and the people [John 11 : 50]. Thus they cannot conquer the Turk unless they fill their hands with the blood of the martyrs and brothers of Christ. The wrath of God has come upon them at last [1 Thess. 2 : 16]. May the Lord hasten the day of our redemption, Amen. Farewell in him, your reverence. April 14, 1545.

Your Martin Luther.

V.3.F   He was increasingly offended by the loose morals of his students and townsfolk; and in July, 1545, he left Wittenberg in disgust. In a letter to his wife, he suggested making his departure permanent, but was prevailed upon to return. (German text in Br 11, 149–1550: 4139; also translated in full in Smith, *Martin Luther*, 416 f.)

To my dear, beloved housewife, Katherina Luther von Bora, Preacheress, Breweress, Gardeneress, and whatever else she may be.

Grace and peace! Dear Katie, Hans will tell you all about how our journey is going, although I am still not certain whether he should stay with me, in which case Dr Caspar Cruciger and Ferdinand [von Maugis] will still tell you about it. Ernst von Schönfeld received us well at Löbnitz, and Heinz Scherl much better still at Leipzig. I should very much like to arrange things so that I do not have to come back to Wittenberg at all. My heart has gone cold, so I do not want to be there any more. I wish that you would sell the garden and the land, the house and the farm, and I would give the big house back to my gracious lord. It would be better for you to settle at Zulsdorf: while I still live, I could help you with my salary to improve the property. For I hope that my gracious lord will at least let my salary continue for the one last year of my life. After my death, the four elements will not suffer you to live any longer in Wittenberg. So it would be better to do during my lifetime what will have to be done afterwards anyway. The way Wittenberg is going with its government, perhaps it will catch, not St Vitus' dance or St John's dance, but the beggar's dance or Beelzebub's dance, as they have begun to do: the women and girls bare themselves behind and before, and there is no one to punish or prevent it, and so God's Word is mocked. All I can say is—off and away with this Sodom! If that pig-filthy knave and deceiver, our other Rosina, has not yet been jailed, do what you can to help the wretch befoul himself.[6] In the country I have heard more reports than I came across in Wittenberg itself, and so I am sick of that city and do not want to return, if God helps me.

The day after tomorrow I am going to Merseburg, since Prince George has sent me a pressing request to do so; and in this way I shall wander here and there and eat beggar's bread before I will martyr and defile my poor old last days with the inordinate life of Wittenberg, with the loss of my bitter, costly labour. You may, if you wish, let Dr Pomer [Bugenhagen][7] and Master Philip [Melanchthon] know, and ask Dr Pomer if he will therewith bless Wittenberg in my name! For I can no longer bear my anger and disgust at it. God be with you, Amen. 'Garlic Tuesday'[8] [July 28], 1545.

Martin Luther.

V.3.G On February 18, 1546, returning home from mediating a dispute between the Counts of Mansfeld, Luther suffered a fatal stroke in his birthplace of Eisleben. He was buried on February 22 in Wittenberg: this is the official University notice. (Latin text in Friedensburg, *Urkendenbuch der Universität Wittenberg*, I (Magdeburg 1926), no. 276.)

It is beyond question that Dr Martin Luther, a reverend man and our most beloved father and preceptor, was divinely raised up to purify again the ministry of the gospel and to show forth the Son of God, as God in his immense mercy, sending good teachers time after time, has restored the light of the gospel to the Church and dispelled the darkness. This is to be acknowledged as God's blessing; but while we must give the thanks to God, we must at the same time love such ambassadors of heaven. As the Hittites said to Abraham, 'You are truly a prince of God amongst us' [Gen. 23 : 6], so Dr Martin Luther was truly a prince of God amongst us. Let us therefore mourn that he has been called away from fellowship with us here, and let us pray the Son of

---

[6] 'Our other Rosina:' apparently a reference to a dishonest servant in the Luther household, since the maid Rosina had been dismissed earlier for her disgraceful behaviour.

[7] Johann Bugenhagen, or Pomeranus (1485–1558), pastor of Wittenberg and professor of Old Testament, who had introduced the Reformation into Hamburg, Brunswick, Lübeck, Pomerania, Denmark, and Norway, and was now also Lutheran superintendent of Saxony.

[8] Garlic and garlic sausage was eaten on the feast of St Pantaleon, a patron saint of physicians, because garlic was believed to have medicinal qualities.

God, our Lord Jesus Christ, that he will mercifully preserve this Church.

Since his funeral is to take place today, possibly at noon sharp (we are not yet sure of the hour, but a signal for the time of assembling will be given by sounding the small bell), we order that all members of the school gather in the forum, there await the reverend lord pastor of our church, and follow him thence as he casts off the mortal garments which were, and again will be, the tabernacle of the Holy Spirit.

During these funeral solemnities, let the scholars reflect on the blessings granted to the Church through this teacher, and give thanks to God for them. For it is certain that he has faithfully brought to light the doctrine of repentance, the true invocation of God and genuine worship, where previously it had been overwhelmed with sordid abominations and false heathen opinions. This doctrine, even if despised by the great majority, is nevertheless most truly that pearl for which the Son of God orders us to give all our wealth in exchange. And let them offer fervent prayers that God will not allow the light of the gospel to be put out, and that we may order the manner of our life with greater concern, lest God be provoked to loose his anger against us.

General Stilicho often said of Ambrose that when he died, Italy would perish; and this was no empty prophecy, for immediately upon the death of Ambrose the Goths and Vandals laid waste the whole of Italy. So let us reflect that by the death of this our teacher we are forewarned of punishment to come—which may God mitigate!

FINAL COMMENTS

FASHIONS IN LUTHER studies have passed through many stages, to the extent that there is now an expanding literature reviewing Luther historiography. The accuracy with which historians' images of Luther have mirrored their own religious or ideological commitments has been demonstrated for Swedish theology by Edgar M. Carlson, for German Protestantism by Otto Wolff, Horst Stephan, and Heinrich Bornkamm, for Catholicism by Adolf Herte, and for the German nation by Ernst Zeeden. Zeeden comments in *The Legacy of Luther* that 'the changing picture of Luther through the decades and centuries has one constant factor, in that it is a reflex of religious ideas. . . . Light on the successive transformations undergone by Luther and the Reformation, in the minds of successive generations, is bound to show some portion of the road along which the German nation—or a part of it—travelled.'[1] Jaroslav Pelikan also remarks: 'To the gallery of earlier portraits our century has added Luther the Nazi, Luther the Kierkegaardian, and Luther the Barthian, while some American Protestants, in mistaken zeal, have tried to draw a picture of Luther the Jeffersonian.'[2]

Whilst these historiographical reviews have concerned themselves largely with Luther the theologian in the hands of subsequent generations, the same thing is true of Luther the man. Fashions in Luther biography, too, have undergone many changes over the years. The earliest sixteenth-century biographers, including his friends and close associates Melanchthon, Bugenhagen, Mathesius, and Sachs, concentrated on the second half of Luther's life, his years as reformer, both because they knew these years at first-hand and because as members of the new movement they naturally regarded them as all-important. The mere stylised sketches they gave of his first thirty-five years have frustrated our modern inclination to look for explanations for Luther's reforming zeal in his upbringing, training and development. Consequently, in the Luther renaissance of the present century, biographical

[1] Ernst Zeeden, *The Legacy of Luther: Martin Luther and the Reformation in the estimation of the German Lutherans from Luther's death to the beginning of the age of Goethe*, translated by Ruth M. Bethell, London 1954, pp. xi f. Works of the other authors mentioned here may be found in the bibliography.

[2] Jaroslav J. Pelikan, *Luther the Expositor: Introduction to the Reformer's Exegetical Writings*, Companion Volume to LW, St Louis 1959, pp. 33 f.

focus has been on the formative years and the break from Rome, but perhaps at the expense of the older Luther. Luther lived for another quarter century after the Diet of Worms. Most modern biographies are as sketchy about these senior years as were the contemporary accounts about his youth.

The effect is curious. Modern biography has devoted painstaking effort to sifting critically inaccurate scraps and slanted reminiscences to piece together a convincing picture of emerging religious passion and theological genius. Some of this critical work has been masterful, especially the meticulous labours of Otto Scheel and Heinrich Böhmer. As a result we have a reliable idea of what trustworthy information is available about this period of Luther's life. Yet it remains true that Luther's youth is the period of his life about which we know least. So it is curious to observe that most major recent biographies have devoted so much attention to Luther's early life, and so little to his two last crowded decades. Since Julius Köstlin's *Life of Luther*, now ninety years old but still eminently readable,[3] and Preserved Smith's sixty-year-old *Life and Letters of Martin Luther*,[4] there has been scarcely a single fully-rounded treatment. To mention only a few of the most valuable modern biographies: Roland Bainton's graceful, sympathetic, anecdotal *Here I Stand*[5] is surely the most readable biography of Luther ever penned, and it yields invaluable insight into how Luther's passions and moods made their mark on his theology; yet to all intents and purposes the narrative finishes with Luther's marrying and establishing a household. There is no better narrative in any language of Luther's break from Rome than E. Gordon Rupp's *Luther's Progress to the Diet of Worms*,[6] but it undertakes to go no further than 1521. Similarly Heinrich Böhmer in *Der junge Luther* (translated as *Martin Luther: Road to Reformation*)[7] deliberately limits his scope to the period up to 1521. There is more sheer meticulous information in E. G. Schwiebert's monumental *Luther and his Times*[8] than in any other biography. This thoroughly researched work is elegantly and clearly presented, and it contains information available nowhere else about the town and University of Wittenberg and about the rôle of the University in the growing Reformation. For these reasons I believe it is the most valuable

[3] Julius Köstlin, *Life of Luther*, translated from the German edition of 1881, London 1883.

[4] Preserved Smith, *The Life and Letters of Martin Luther*, Boston and New York 1911.

[5] Roland H. Bainton, *Here I Stand: a Life of Martin Luther*, Nashville 1950.

[6] E. Gordon Rupp, *Luther's Progress to the Diet of Worms*, Chicago 1951.

[7] Heinrich Böhmer, *Martin Luther: Road to Reformation*, translated from *Der Junge Luther* (Gotha 1925), Philadelphia 1946.

[8] Ernest G. Schwiebert, *Luther and his Times: the Reformation from a new Perspective*, St Louis 1950.

of the recent biographies; yet it too fails to give a thorough biographical account of Luther in the 1530s and 1540s. There is rich opportunity for further research here. As Professor Rupp said in his opening address at the Third International Congress on Luther Research in Finland in 1966: 'We still wait for a full, learned modern study of the mature and ageing Luther.'[9]

Furthermore, the character of the sources upon which our knowledge of Luther's childhood and youth is based is even more an issue now than it has been before, in view of extremely subtle and brilliant reflections recently offered upon Luther's psychological development. Psychological studies of Luther are not new. Indeed, shortly after Luther's death a former opponent, the Catholic polemicist Johann Cochlaeus, already offered psychological observations about Luther in his short biographical essay *Commentaria de actis et scriptis Martini Lutheri* (Mainz, 1549). Under the impact of Freudianism, this century has seen several new psychological essays, including Preserved Smith's 'Luther's early Development in the Light of Psychoanalysis', the Danish psychiatrist Paul J. Reiter's *Martin Luthers Umwelt, Charakter und Psychose*, and most notable of all, Erik Erikson's widely-read *Young Man Luther: a Study in Psychoanalysis and History*. Erikson's interpretation has received even wider notoriety from the use to which John Osborne put it in his play 'Luther'. In his keynote address to the Third Luther Research Congress, Professor Rupp called Erikson's book 'the most intelligent essay on Luther in English of our time . . . a brilliant but one-sided and entirely unconvincing psychological study.'[10]

Erikson's subject is how a gifted young man evolves psychologically into a great young man. It is not a study in pathology, though there were pathological elements in Luther's make-up; rather, it is an account of how conflicting elements in Luther's youth and adolescence, some pathological and some healthy, some positive and some negative, some retrogressive and some progressive, resolved themselves in an integrative 'identity crisis' with world-changing spiritual, mental, and emotional ramifications. In creating this account, Erikson draws constantly on clinical concepts derived from his own analyses of adolescents undergoing identity crises. He speaks of Luther's conflicts over obedience, and the transference of those conflicts from a stern and sometimes disapproving father to a severely judging and demanding God, to a monolithic and unyielding church. He speaks of a period of moratorium in which a gifted youth remains, as it were, poised between positive and

[9] E. Gordon Rupp, 'Luther: the contemporary Image' in Ivar Asheim, ed., *The Church, Mysticism, Sanctification and the Natural in Luther's Thought: Lectures Presented to the Third International Congress on Luther Research, Järvenpää, Finland, August 11–16, 1966*, Philadelphia 1967, p. 19.

[10] Rupp, 'Luther: the contemporary Image,' p. 9.

negative identity, between allness and nothingness, and he sees the monastic years as providing such a moratorium for Luther. Luther's theological discoveries about Christ and faith and the Word he compares to 'certain steps in psychological maturation which every man must take':[11] internalisation of the father–son relationship, crystallisation of conscience, establishment of identity, and reaffirmation of the basic trust of infancy.

A substantial part of Erikson's description rests upon his picture of the relation between Hans Luther and his son Martin: the reader must form his own judgement whether the primary sources really tell us as much about that relationship as Erikson maintains, but it is my opinion that they do not. Moreover, Erikson feels free to draw upon his wide clinical experience of gifted young men to fill gaps in the documentary evidence about young man Luther: this procedure also poses a nice question in the logic of historical explanation. Most seriously, however, Erikson has simply omitted a wealth of primary material with psychological import. In short, he has brilliantly pointed out a vital field of investigation, but his own essay barely scratches its surface. Much remains to be done.

Even though few men in history have been so frank in revealing themselves and their most private thoughts and actions to the world, an unavoidable obscurity does cloud Luther's earliest years. Luther's later reminiscences about his childhood were usually in the form of illustrations of some theological or conversational point. It is therefore quite possible that his father's family was not as lowly as he suggested, parental discipline not so forbidding, his schooling in Mansfelt, Magdeburg and Eisenach not so oppressive. Given the fragmentary character of the evidence, it is perhaps not even possible to decide for certain whether these memories represent Luther's whole judgement about his boyhood, let alone describe that boyhood adequately. For his undergraduate years, there is next to no detailed evidence. For the monastic years, there is a larger number of later reminiscences, but reminiscences now explicitly coloured by hind-sight. Luther's accounts of his monastic experience are always refracted through his later discovery of forgiveness and his violently negative rejection of monastic spirituality.

When Luther becomes a professor of the Bible, however, we are in a far stronger position. The number of extant letters begins to rise, and they now reveal a Luther who is his own man, no longer torn between a positive and a negative identity. Moreover, we have the first substantial evidences of his theological creativity. Much of the revival of interest in Luther-studies in this century is the fruit of the discovery and exploitation of previously unpublished academic materials from Luther's early teaching career. The catalyst for much of this modern

[11] Erikson, *Young Man Luther*, p. 207.

study was Johann Ficker's rediscovery, in the Royal Library of Berlin in 1905, of Luther's long-lost manuscript of his lectures on Romans from 1515–16. In 1908 (three hundred and ninety-two years after delivery) Luther's lectures were first published. The possession of the Romans' lectures made possible a far deeper investigation of the evolution of Luther's theological concepts, his steady progress towards independence as a biblical expositor, and his detailed relationship to late medieval theology. The excitement of constant new discoveries in these areas is the chief reason for the disproportionate biographical attention paid to the young Luther in this century.

When he resumed his duties as professor of the Bible at Wittenberg in 1513, Luther was still committed to medieval methods of exegesis both in theory and in practice. At first he adopted the interpretative device of the *Quadriga*, or four-fold sense: one literal sense, which was basic; and three figurative senses, an allegorical sense referring to Christ, an anagogical sense referring to the Church or the end-time, and a tropological sense referring to the moral life. He also maintained the traditional practice of providing his students with glosses (marginal and interlinear comments on the language of the text) and scholia (running commentary on the passage). Within this inherited framework, he soon confronted the age-old issue of the relation of the literal sense to the spiritual senses so much more highly valued by tradition. At first, Luther was particularly influenced by his older contemporary, the French humanist, Lefèvre d'Étaples, whose *Quincuplex Psalterium* (Paris, 1509) he used in his earliest lectures. Under Lefèvre's influence, Luther came to identify two sorts of literal sense in the biblical text: a lifeless and purely factual literal-historical sense, and a vital and inspired literal–spiritual sense. Using this distinction to refine the allegorical method, Luther began to seek two senses in every text: a christological and a closely related tropological meaning. That is, at first he believed that careful philological study of the text would yield the faithful reader a literal–spiritual reference to Christ, and since what is true of Christ literally is true of the Christian by faith, also a tropological application to the life of the believer.

This way of finding Christ in the Old Testament text before him soon dissatisfied Luther, however. It required him to read each Psalm in the first instance as either spoken by or literally signifying Christ; and many Psalms read this way of course produced insoluble riddles. So in the midst of his Psalms lectures, he realised that much of the Old Testament, in its simple historical sense, consisted of God's promise of redemption; so an additional spiritual sense was unnecessary for finding the connection to Christ—it was already obvious. This insight into the themes of covenant and promise liberated the Old Testament from shackles which for a thousand years had effectively prevented it from being read by Christians in its own terms.[12] Now Luther turned more and more for insight away from his earlier favourite, Lefèvre, to Nicolas of Lyra, whose historical comments on the Old Testament he had only a year earlier disdained as mere dead literalism. He proceeded to expound Romans, therefore, determined to work out his theology of grace in the light of what he had newly discovered about the Old Testament promises.

However, the intense light cast on Luther's theological evolution has also provoked the most serious continuing dispute in modern Luther studies—the debate over when his crucial discoveries occurred.

After Luther entered the Augustinian monastery at Erfurt in 1505 as a fearful and scrupulous young man clinging to every churchly means of grace as his only hope of salvation, his theological training under Johann Paltz and later under Johann Nathin assured an intimate acquaintance with the teachings of William of Ockham and the theological systems of Ockham's disciples, notably Gabriel Biel (who in turn had been Nathin's teacher).[13] Luther was also introduced to the major competing school of theological thought, the doctrines of Duns Scotus, the *Doctor Subtilis* (like Ockham, a Franciscan trained at Oxford). As one step in his academic progress, Luther lectured on the standard repository of traditional dogmatics, the *Sentences* of Peter Lombard, and he consulted the major scholastic commentaries on the *Sentences* (including Bonaventura, Scotus, Ockham, d'Ailly, and Biel). Yet it is dramatically clear in the very earliest words from Luther's own pen— marginal notes on his copy of the *Sentences*—that he found the turgidities of late medieval scholasticism virtually unbearable from the outset, and in private he turned instead with eagerness and relief to the study of the Bible and St Augustine. Yet at another, deeper level, Luther took the pastoral theology of his day all too seriously.

According to the nominalist theology which Luther was taught, God in his ineluctable divine freedom could exercise his power as he wished: this was the *potentia dei absoluta*. But in dealing with the contingent order of the world, God decreed that he would act in certain chosen ways: this was the *potentia dei ordinata*. According to his absolute power, God was bound by no necessity, and man could have no certainty of his standing before God. According to his ordained power, however, God has committed himself to a conditional necessity, and man may therefore seek acceptance with God on the basis of God's undertaking to accept a morally good act as meritorious (that is, de-

<hr>

[12] See James Samuel Preus, *From Shadow to Promise: Old Testament Interpretation from Augustine to the young Luther*, Harvard: Cambridge, Mass., 1969.
[13] See Heiko Oberman, *The Harvest of Medieval Theology: Gabriel Biel and late Medieval Nominalism*, Harvard: Cambridge, Mass. 1963.

serving reward). A morally good act, the nominalists taught, was possible to man even in the state of sin and unaided by grace, since, if a man did all that lay within his natural power, he could perform an act which was formally good in that it met the literal requirements of the divine or natural law. If one performed an act thus congruous with the letter of the law, God in his generosity had undertaken to regard such an act as having a sort of merit, called *meritum de congruo*. This 'merit for a congruous act' was not yet worthy of salvation, but it did deserve as its reward the infusion of 'first grace'. Aided, now, for the first time, by divine grace, man could produce an act not merely congruous with the letter of the law, but (because it was performed in a state of charity and grace) actually meeting the standard of divine justice and meriting acceptance before God. This was called *meritum de condigno*.

Patently, this teaching was Augustinian in theory and Pelagian in practice. That is, by protecting God's freedom in ordaining this means of grace and in attributing *meritum de congruo* to God's liberality, it theoretically protected the initiative of God and the helplessness of man in achieving salvation. But since in practice the first step was always 'to do what lay within one' (*facere quod in se est*), the practical implication was that one earned one's own salvation. This key phrase—*facere quod in se est*—was subject to the same ambiguity as our English phrase 'Do your best!', which can mean, depending on its inflexion, 'Do your very utmost' or 'Do as much as you can manage.' In their dogmatic writings, it is plain that Ockham and Biel insisted on the former, strict sense: only an act which was indeed formally good would suffice. But in the manuals of pastoral care for dealing with scrupulous consciences, the latter, more permissive attitude prevailed. In a sense it could be claimed that Brother Martin, Augustinian monk, was plunged into an agony of conscience because he tried with utter seriousness to apply what others had preached but not practised.

See how the nominalist schema of salvation works when applied to the sacrament of penance, the crux of Luther's turmoil. The penitent comes, in a state of sin and unaided by grace, to make confession of his sins and thus display his love towards God. In order to attain that infusion of first grace which makes the supernatural love of God possible, the act of contrition must be formally perfect. He makes his confession, but no sooner has he done so than he remembers some act of commission, omission, or disposition which has passed unrepented or unconfessed. His penitential act was thus not formally complete, and so failed to attain even *meritum de congru* or the aid of first grace. Instead of expressing his love towards God, then, he finds himself fearing and finally hating God for placing his grace so far beyond the grasp of one who knows himself to be a sinner through and through.

Luther at first remained unresponsive to the wise, sympathetic counsel of his godly and learned superior, Johann von Staupitz. Indeed, he was caught in the meshes of a doctrinal system which became more and more hopeless the more seriously it was taken. Staupitz urged further academic attainment upon a reluctant Luther as a distraction from his scrupulous turmoil. At length—it seems to have been after Luther received his doctorate, and just as he took up his teaching duties— Staupitz apparently broke through the web of emotional upheaval and doctrinal confusion and pointed Luther with such clarity and simplicity to God's promises in Scripture that he knew at last his sins were forgiven 'in the sweet wounds of Christ our Saviour'. Luther's dislike of scholastic dogmatics grew from mere intellectual antipathy into disgust at a teaching which had systematically withheld the joy of the gospel from him.

His earliest lectures, then, are the work of a man who knows himself to be the recipient of God's mercy, is bold and vital in that knowledge, and is actively seeking new ways of expressing and transmitting to others the heartfelt joy of the knowledge of Christ. But as he said of these years as he looked back from the end of his long life, he did not learn his theology all at once; and it was ten years or more before he was entirely confident in the new theological style which was to break like the dawn across western Christendom.

The intense examination of Luther's earliest lectures has brightly illuminated some of the stages along that way: his growing Christocentrism; his abandonment of the notion of an active, punishing justice of God for what he called 'the passive justice of God', namely that God justifies man when a man first justifies God by acknowledging the justice of God's condemnation of him; his consequent description of faith's progress as passing from self-disgust and self-accusation, through true humility and abasement, to trust in God; the imputation of Christ's righteousness as the basis of that trust; and accordingly, an insistence of the spontaneous character of Christian repentance and the joyful character of Christian obedience.[14] During these years, his theology still had much in common with what he had learnt from Gerson and Staupitz. He delightedly identified what he had discovered with the position of Augustine in *On the Spirit and the Letter*, and with the simple German mystical piety of Johann Tauler and the *Theologia Deutsch*. He as yet saw no reason to question the power of the pope, or to reject the doctrine of the treasury of merits, purgatory, and the intercession of the saints, or to rethink the theology of the sacraments. These developments had to wait on the tumultuous pressures of the church struggle.

Whether the fresh and vivid theology of the years immediately preceding the church struggle already contains the fundamental elements of

[14] These developments are excellently reviewed in Rupp, *The Righteousness of God*, pp. 81 ff.

Luther's mature doctrine remains the subject of the most deep-seated disagreement amongst contemporary Luther scholars. A vocal but persuasive minority of Luther scholars has argued that the fundamental theological break with Catholicism took place after, rather than before, the indulgence controversy. For many years there had been a muted discussion about the dating of Luther's 'tower discovery' of justification by faith. Various scholars had assigned dates ranging between 1508 and 1519, but the majority opinion was most clearly argued by Erich Vogelsang in his *Die Anfänge von Luthers Christologie*,[15] where he dated the tower discovery in 1514 and found Luther's mature doctrine already present in the later lectures on the Psalms and the lectures on Romans. The striking implications of the debate were given fresh prominence in the 1950s by Uuras Saarnivaara's *Luther Discovers the Gospel*,[16] which pointed out how widely Luther scholars had differed, and argued on theological grounds that the decisive shift did not take place until late in 1518. Subsequently, the case for a late date has received its most thorough and sophisticated exposition from Professor Ernst Bizer, whose treatise *Fides ex auditu* has already passed through three editions within a decade and has been greatly admired even by those who remain unconvinced.[17] Attempts at two Luther Research Congresses to resolve the issue have proved unsuccessful, and the case for an early dating has been restated against Bizer by Professor Rupp in England and by Heinrich Bornkamm in Germany.[18] The issue is indeed crucial for the interpretation of Luther.

Professor Rupp declares: 'It is clear, in all essentials, his theology was in existence before the opening of the church struggle of 1517.'[19] But F. Edward Cranz insists: 'The differences between the early and the mature works are so great that only confusion results from the assumption that we are dealing with a single, unified position.'[20] Depending on one's choice between these options, one joins the dominant German school of Luther interpretation in integrating the viewpoints of the young Luther with materials from his maturity; or else one rigorously distinguishes his early emphases from mature positions and refuses

[15] Erich Vogelsang, *Die Anfänge von Luthers Christologie*, Berlin 1933.

[16] Uuras Saarnivaara, *Luther Discovers the Gospel*, St Louis 1951.

[17] Ernst Bizer, *Fides ex auditu: Eine Untersuchung über die Entdeckung der Gerechtigkeit Gottes durch Martin Luther*, 3rd edition enlarged, Neukirchen 1966 (1st edition, 1958).

[18] See Rupp's review of Bizer in *Zeitschrift für Kirchengeschichte* 71 (1960), pp. 351 ff.; Heinrich Bornkamm, 'Zur Frage der Iustitia Dei beim jungen Luther,' in *Archiv für Reformationsgeschichte* 52 (1961), pp. 16 ff. and 53 (1962), pp. 1 ff.

[19] Rupp, *Luther's Progress to the Diet of Worms*, p. 7.

[20] F. Edward Cranz, *An Essay on the Development of Luther's Thought on Justice, Law, and Society*, Harvard Theological Studies XIX, Cambridge, Mass. 1959, p. xiv.

them an all-important place in Reformation theology. The two results
are very different. In the first instance the existential 'theology of the
cross' of his early writings becomes the characteristic spirituality of all
Luther's doctrine. Faith is the humility and courage to trust God in the
face of his apparent contradiction. Every Word of God may be taken as
law or as gospel depending on man's trust or lack of it, since faith is that
inner transformation of the soul in which a man discovers God's 'Yes!'
hidden beneath his 'No!' In the opposing view, however, Luther moves
beyond this position to a doctrine of 'alien' justification: righteousness
is alien to us—outside us—because Christ achieved it in historical
occurrences quite apart from us; and God's 'No!' is no longer transformed into his 'Yes!' by a movement of faith, but the law and the
gospel are two clearly distinguishable forms of speech, one a demand
and the other a promise.

We should do well to heed Professor James Samuel Preus's warning
that at this point in Luther's career new ideas 'roll in upon one another
like waves, so that it is difficult to tell which belong to the incoming tide
of the Reformation, and which to the ebb tide of the Middle Ages.'[21] My
own judgement is this: in retrospect, Luther was embarrassed by what
he had written before 1519, and warned his readers against its defective
theology. Yet it is undeniable that the 'passive' sense of God's justice is
already present in the lectures of 1514–16 on the Psalms and Romans.
It is quite consistent with Luther's warning to suppose that the tower
discovery which 'opened the gates of paradise' took place early in the
decade, and nevertheless that he underwent such decisive later developments, after the church struggle had begun, that he felt obliged to
repudiate the 'crude and inchoate muddle' of his pre-1519 writings (and,
from his mature standpoint, was right to do so). Moreover, the process
of working out these decisive later insights took several years more, and
awaited the intense biblical labours of the mid-twenties to attain final
consistency.

In the confidence of these new insights, Luther mounted his shattering critique of the entire churchly fabric, and became the ideological
leader of a burgeoning new community of Christians. Yet by the time
Protestantism became a formidable political force in Germany, practical
leadership of the Reformation had really passed from Luther's hands.
As the stormy decade of the 1520s progressed, Luther withdrew from
the national arena both from necessity and choice. He knew, he declared
later, that at Worms he could have grasped a heroic rôle of national
leadership. Instead he chose deliberately to lay that rôle aside, and to
persist in the rôle (no less heroic to him) of pastor, teacher, and prophet.
Indeed, so far from remaining its noblest commendation, Luther's
activities brought inadvertent discredit upon the infant evangelical

[21] Preus, *From Shadow to Promise*, p. 146.

cause. He gravely disappointed his impetuous knightly supporters by his withdrawal from the public stage. He alienated potential radical support by his fiercely negative reaction to spiritualist religion. He alienated the Swiss reformers, whom he identified (understandably but incorrectly) with the radicals, by his high-handed dismissal of their sacramental views. He alienated sympathetic Catholic humanist opinion by his devastating and sometimes supercilious demolition of Erasmus' *Discourse on Free Will*. He gained a reputation for arrogance by his scornful barbs at such highborn opponents as Henry VIII, and for ferocity by his immoderate reaction to the renewed outbreaks of peasant insurgency. His successful attacks on monastic foundations, clerical celibacy, and cultic practices cut to the heart of what many held fervently to be most sacred; many more were scandalised by his marriage in 1525 to a former nun. Enrolments at the University of Wittenberg plummeted to their lowest level in 1526. Sometimes, oppressed by ill-health and the bitterness and disappointment of controversy, Luther verged on despair at the parlous state of the cause he had championed.

Yet in another sense, the real impress of Luther's life and thought was stamped upon Protestantism in these later, maturer years. By the sheer force of his moral authority and theological genius, he determined by precept and example what Lutherans would believe and what institutions they would create. From Wittenberg he sent out generation after generation of Lutheran pastors and theologians. He maintained a prodigious correspondence with leaders in church and state throughout Europe. He issued practical proposals for the organisation of the personnel and property of the churches. He instructed the people of Germany in the nature of the Christian's civic and domestic calling and the character of the moral life. His German translation of the Bible, a milestone in the history of the German language, made Scripture immediately accessible to the lay people. His sermons and biblical lectures were edited by his colleagues, published far and wide, and assiduously read and copied. He found this ideological leadership both personally congenial and fitting for one called to be a Doctor of the Bible. He appealed constantly to his duty as a teacher of the Word as the basis of his authority to be heard.

This sort of leadership was thrust upon him by the very success of his appeal for rejection of current ecclesiastical structures. When congregations severed their ties with the hierarchy, new structures of authority were needed. Luther's successful onslaught on monasticism and celibacy created a sudden vacuum in the areas of health and welfare, education, and missions, since the religious orders had been the Church's shock troops on these battle-lines. Luther's proposals for dealing with these urgent social needs were highly successful in education, less so in the provision of welfare services, and Protestantism lacked effective agencies of missionary outreach for many decades. In place of the monastic life, however, Luther's teaching and example gave rise to a new phenomenon—the Protestant manse, whose influence on the image of godly family life was to be incalculable.

Luther's doctrine, which Protestants have held in veneration from that day to this, and which is currently the object of intense new Catholic scrutiny, was elaborated in the heat of controversy during these years. Luther's opponents played a highly significant rôle in the development of his thought, and they were legion! He debated with Catholic opponents: curial upholders of the churchly system of authority, learned university champions of the scholastic doctrine of grace, and humanistic proponents of a liberal Catholicism. He waged a far fiercer battle against enthusiasm and spiritualism in the radical wing of the religious revolt, defending the authentic means of grace handed down by tradition against the subjectivising appeal to pure spirit. He opposed Sacramentarians who wanted to make the eucharist a symbolic memorial meal, and Anabaptists who wanted to make the efficacy of baptism depend on the believer's faith. He condemned those of any party who would take recourse to anarchy or violence in pursuit of either personal justice or religious truth. While Luther's polemics are sometimes immoderately expressed, they are never indiscriminate: he knew clearly what he opposed and why, and his reasons were consistently non-partisan and genuinely theological.

These polemics were so constant and so multi-faceted that they may easily be misconstrued as Luther's major preoccupation. This is anything but the case. Both in bulk and in importance, Luther's polemical writings are eclipsed by his uninterrupted labours as a biblical expositor. If one asks what Luther did during the remaining quarter-century of his professional life after the Reformation began, the answer is that he was a professor of the Bible, and produced in the lecture hall and the pulpit, and even in his home, an unending stream of biblical commentaries. It is to these expository works that one must turn to find the real genius of Luther both as theologian and stylist. They are works of unsurpassed distinction in the tradition of Christian thought.

Some of his greatest works were the fruit of those years of maturity which recent biographers have most ignored. A rich mine of investigation awaits those who address their curiosity to these years: did Luther achieve new insights even as an elderly man? In what respects did the course of public events affect his views; and how much, in turn, did he continue to influence public events as ideological figure-head of the reform movement? Can it be demonstrated whether his persistent illnesses affected his powers significantly? How much personal responsibility must he bear for the intra-Lutheran dissensions which so swiftly followed his death? There is yet much to be learnt from close study of

Luther's domestic, academic and ecclesiastical rôles in later life: to read in chronological order his correspondence, table conversation, biblical lectures, sermons and utterances on public policy is to discover the deep workings of a mind and personality still of extraordinary vigour, neither deceived nor retiring, rough-hewn, but humane and sensitive, penetrating the profound issues of life and death in a startling and moving way. The material cries out for skilful description. We may hope that the elderly Luther soon receives the biographical treatment he deserves.

This, then, was Martin Luther, a man of manifest greatness, undisguisedly stamped with our common humanity; an unusually complex man with a child-like love of simplicity; sensitive to the very edge of normalcy, yet unswerving in the face of enmity and mortal fear; in the presence of need warm-hearted to the point of gullibility, but fierce to the point of abusiveness in the defence of truth. He was by turns (and sometimes at once) gentle and bawdy, witty and compassionate, clownish and sublime. Of brilliant mind and passionate soul, he feared his own mildness and native courtesy more than his outspoken reproof of error, yet castigated himself in secret for causing his antagonists pain. A master of language, he found his own creations a burden and hoped they would be forgotten. A zealot in defence of the authority of his office, he vehemently repudiated any authority in Luther the man. Like all heroic accomplishments, his path to greatness had to surmount huge obstacles. He was so nearly trapped by pathological self-doubt; he might have settled cheaply for a soothing local *succès d'estime*. Two equally realistic self-assessments struggled within him: the image of a worthless, beaten sinner, and the image of a richly endowed champion of Christ. He became the Reformer because he was able in faith to hold both images in true perspective. This salutary tension, the mark of hard-won but deep-seated wholeness, allowed him to transmit to a whole culture an ideal of Christian manhood which, in all its fallibility and fear, knew that it stood whole at last in the light of divine acceptance.

BIBLIOGRAPHY

ABBREVIATIONS

ARG   *Archiv für Reformationsgeschichte*

ATR   *Anglican Theological Review*

CH   *Church History*

CTM   *Concordia Theological Monthly*

FS   *Franziskanische Studien*

HTR   *Harvard Theological Review*

JMH   *Journal of Modern History*

LQ   *Lutheran Quarterly*

LW   *Lutheran World*

SHPF   *Bulletin, Société de l'Histoire du Protestantisme français*

TLZ   *Theologische Literaturzeitung*

ZKG   *Zeitschift für Kirchengeschichte*

BIBLIOGRAPHICAL AIDS

Books

ALAND, KURT. *Hilfsbuch zum Lutherstudium.* 2nd edn Gütersloh 1957. An essential index and guidebook to the German editions of Luther's works.

COMMISSION INTERNATIONALE D'HISTOIRE ECCLESIASTIQUE COMPARÉE au sein du COMITÉ INTERNATIONAL DES SCIENCES HISTORIQUES. *Bibliographie de la Réforme: Ouvrages parus de 1940 à 1955. I: Allemagne – Pays Bas.* 3rd edn Leiden 1964. II: *Belgique – Suède – Norvège – Danemark – Irlande – Etats-Unis d'Amerique.* Leiden 1960. III: *Italie – Espagne – Portugal.* Leiden 1961. IV: *France – Angleterre – Suisse.* Leiden 1963. V: *Pologne – Hongrie – Tchéco-*

slovaquie – Finland. Leiden 1965. VI: *Autriche (ouvrages parus 1940–1960).* Leiden 1967. A thorough listing, by countries, of recent materials.

Luther-Jahrbuch. Jahrbuch der Luther-Gesellschaft. Munich, Hamburg, Amsterdam 1919 ff. Each annual edition contains a bibliography of newly published works.

SCHOTTENLOHER, KARL. *Bibliographie zur deutschen Geschichte im Zeitalter der Glaubensspaltung 1517–1586.* 7 vols. 2nd edn Stuttgart 1956–62. A monumental bibliography of materials published up to 1960.

WOLF, G. *Quellenkunde der deutschen Reformationsgeschichte.* 2 vols. Gotha 1915–22.

Articles

DILLENBERGER, JOHN. 'Major Volumes and Selected Periodical Literature in Luther Studies, 1950–1955'. *CH,* 25 (1956), pp. 160 ff.

— 'Major Volumes and Selected Periodical Literature in Luther Studies, 1956–1959'. *CH,* 30 (1961), pp. 61 ff.

FORELL, GEORGE W. 'Lutherforschung in den USA'. *TLZ,* 81 (1956), pp. 757 ff.

GRIMM, HAROLD J. 'Luther Research since 1920'. *JMH,* 32 (1960), pp. 105 ff.

KANTZENBACH, F. W., PRENTER, R., HAIKOLA, L., LINBERG, C., and PESCHE, O. 'Luther Research since 1945'. *LW,* 143 (1966), pp. 257 ff.

LOEWENICH, WALTHER VON. 'Die Lutherforschung in Deutschland seit dem zweiten Weltkrieg'. *TLZ,* 81 (1956), pp. 750 ff.

PAUCK, WILHELM. 'The Historiography of the German Reformation during the Past Twenty Years'. *CH,* 9 (1940), pp. 305 ff.

RUPP, E. GORDON. 'Die Lutherforschung in England, 1945–1956'.*TLZ,* 81 (1956), pp. 753 ff.

SUESS, THEODORE. 'Die Lutherforschung in Frankreich', *TLZ,* 81 (1956) pp. 759 ff.

VINAY, VALDO. 'Die Lutherforschung in Italien'. *TLZ,* 81 (1956), pp. 762 ff.

PRIMARY SOURCES

Luther's Works

Dr Martin Luthers sämtliche Schriften. Ed. JOH. GEORG WALCH. 23 vols in 25. St Louis 1880–1910.

Erasmus–Luther: Discourse on Free Will. Trans. ERNST F. WINTER. New York 1961.

First Principles of the Reformation or the Ninety-Five Theses and the Three Primary Works of Martin Luther. Ed. HENRY WACE and C. A. BUCHHEIM. London 1883.

LUTHER: *Lectures on Romans.* Ed. WILHELM PAUCK. The Library of Christian Classics 15. London 1961. Excellent translation and masterful introduction.

Luther: Early Theological Works. Ed. JAMES ATKINSON. The Library of Christian Classics 16. London 1962. Translations not always reliable.

Luther and Erasmus on Free Will. Ed. E. GORDON RUPP. The Library of Christian Classics 17. London 1969. A most useful edition.

Luther: Letters of Spiritual Counsel. Ed. THEODORE G. TAPPERT. The Library of Christian Classics 18. London 1955. A moving and representative selection; occasionally copies Preserved Smith's fanciful translations.

Luther's Correspondence and other Contemporary Letters. Vol. I. Ed. PRESERVED SMITH. Philadelphia 1913. Vol. II. Ed. PRESERVED SMITH and CHARLES M. JACOBS. Philadelphia 1918. The widest selection of important letters up to 1530; translation occasionally more imaginative than accurate.

Luthers Werke in Auswahl. Ed. OTTO CLEMEN, ERICH VOGELSANG, HANS RUCKERT, EMANUEL HIRSCH. 8 vols. Berlin, numerous edns. A distinguished German student edition.

Luthers Werks, Kritische Gesamtausgabe. Weimar 1883 ff. The standard critical edition, approaching completion in nearly ninety volumes.

Luther's Works (American Edition). Ed. HELMUT LEHMANN and JAROSLAV J. PELIKAN. St Louis and Philadelphia 1955 ff. The most comprehensive and useful edition in English; nearing completion.

Martin Luther on The Bondage of the Will. Trans. J. I. PACKER and O. R. JOHNSTON. London 1957. A felicitous translation.

Martin Luther. Selection from his Writings. Ed. JOHN DILLENBERGER. Chicago 1961. A good introductory collection.

Reformation Writings of Martin Luther. Ed. BERTRAM LEE WOOLF. 2 vols. New York 1953–56.

Selected Writings of Martin Luther. Ed. THEODORE G. TAPPERT. 4 vols. Philadelphia 1967. The most useful edition for student purchase.

Standard Edition of Luther's Works. Ed. J. N. LENKER. 11 vols. Minneapolis 1903–09. Uncritical, but contains material not available in English elsewhere.

Three Treatises. Philadelphia 1943. The three masterworks of 1520, from the Philadelphia Edition (see next entry).

Works of Martin Luther (Philadelphia Edition). 6 vols. Philadelphia 1943. The only English source of several important treatises.

Other Contemporary Sources

Concordia or Book of Concord: the Symbols of the Evangelical Lutheran Church. St Louis 1957. Includes Augsburg Confession, Schmalkald Articles, and Luther's two Catechisms.

Corpus Reformatorum. Vols. 1–28. *Melanchthonis Opera*. Halle 1834 ff. Vols. 29–87. *Calvini Opera*. Braunschweig 1863 ff. Vols. 88–101. *Zwinglis Werke*. Leipzig 1905 ff.

Deutsche Reichstagsakten unter Kaiser Karl V. Ed. A. KLUCKHOLM and A. WREDE. 5 vols. incomplete. Gotha 1893–1935.

Epistolae Obscurorum Virorum (*'Letters of Obscure Men'*). Ed. and trans. F. G. STOKES. London 1909.

ERASMUS, DESIDERIUS. *Erasmi Epistolae.* Ed. P. S. ALLEN and H. M. ALLEN. 12 vols. Oxford 1906–58.

— *The Praise of Folly.* Trans. H. H. HUDSON. Princeton 1941.

MORE, THOMAS. *Responsio ad Lutherum.* The Yale Edition of the Complete Works of St Thomas More, Vol. 5. Ed. JOHN M. HEADLEY. 2 parts. New Haven and London 1970.

— *Utopia.* The Yale Edition of the Complete Works of St Thomas More, Vol. 4. Ed. E. SURTZ and JACK H. HEXTER. New Haven and London 1965.

MÜNTZER, THOMAS. *Schriften und Briefe. Kritische Gesamtausgabe.* Ed. GUNTHER FRANZ and PAUL KIRN. Gütersloh 1968.

OBERMAN, HEIKO A., ed *Forerunners of the Reformation: the Shape of late Medieval Thought illustrated by Key Documents.* Translations by PAUL L. NYHUS. New York 1966. A very valuable collection of works from the eve of the Reformation, including Biel, Staupitz, Höen.

THOMAS A KEMPIS. *The Imitation of Christ.* Ed. ALBERT HYMA. New York 1927. Also trans. LEO SHERLEY-PRICE. Harmondsworth 1952.

Wittemberger Heiligthumsbuch, illustriert von Lucas Cranach d. Alt. Wittenberg 1509. Facsimile edn Munich 1884. The catalogue of Frederick the Wise's relic collection.

ZIEGLER, DONALD J. *Great Debates of the Reformation.* New York 1969. An invaluable collection.

Collections of Selected Sources

ALAND, KURT, ed. *Martin Luther's 95 Theses.* Trans. from the German edn (Hamburg 1965). St Louis and London 1967. The Theses and supporting documents, with a good short introduction and excellent notes.

BAINTON, ROLAND H., ed. *The Age of the Reformation.* Anvil Book 13. Princeton and Toronto 1956. Brief extracts, with a good introductory essay.

FOSDICK, HARRY EMERSON, ed. *Great Voices of the Reformation.* New York 1952.

HILLERBRAND, HANS J., ed. *The Reformation in its own Words.* London 1964. A rich, well-executed selection, with good bibliographical aids; some important omissions.

KIDD, B. J., ed. *Documents illustrative of the Continental Reformation.* Oxford 1911. The fullest one-volume selection of documents; German sources are translated, Latin and Greek are not.

KÖHLER, WALTHER, ed. *Dokumente zum Ablasstreit von 1517.* Tübingen and Leipzig 1902.

RUPP, E. GORDON and DREWERY, BENJAMIN, eds. *Martin Luther.* London 1970.

194

LUTHER

SCHEEL, OTTO, ed. *Dokumente zu Luthers Entwicklung (bis 1519)*. Tübingen 1911. The basic collection on the young Luther.
SPITZ, LEWIS W., ed. *The Protestant Reformation*. Englewood Cliffs, New Jersey 1966. Brief selections illustrate the high points of the Reformation.

REFORMATION HISTORIES

The Cambridge Modern History. Vol. II: *The Reformation*. Ed. A. W. WARD, G. W. PROTHERO, and STANLEY LEATHES. Cambridge 1903 and reprints. Now dated, it makes a fascinating exercise in historiography to compare this with its newer counterpart, which is the next entry.
The New Cambridge Modern History. Vol. II: *The Reformation 1520–1559*. Ed. G. R. ELTON. Cambridge 1958. A first-rate history.
Propyläen Weltgeschichte. Vol. V. *Das Zeitalter der religiösen Umwälzungen*. Berlin 1930. New edn Berlin 1940. The outstanding German compendium.
BAINTON, ROLAND H. *The Reformation of the Sixteenth Century*. London 1953. Deceptively brief, this is easily the best short introduction to the period.
— *Studies in the Reformation*. Boston 1963, London 1964. Collected papers on various topics.
BRANDI, KARL. *Deutsche Geschichte im Zeitalter der Reformation und Gegenreformation*. 3rd edn Munich 1960. First published in 1927, it is still a basic work.
— *The Emperor Charles V*. Trans. C. V. WEDGWOOD from *Kaiser Karl V*. Vol. I (Munich 1937). London 1939. The standard work.
CHADWICK, OWEN. *The Reformation*. The Pelican History of the Church 3. Harmondsworth 1964. Eminently readable short survey.
DANIEL-ROPS, HENRI. *The Protestant Reformation*. Trans. AUDREY BUTLER from the 1st French edn (Paris 1958). London and New York 1961. Mildly pro-Catholic and occasionally inaccurate.
DICKENS, A. G. *Martin Luther and the Reformation*. New York 1969. A sound short treatment.
— *Reformation and Society in Sixteenth-Century Europe*. London 1966. Brief and rather superficial; well illustrated.
ELTON, G. R. *Reformation Europe, 1517–1555*. A fine survey by the doyen of British Reformation historians.
FISCHER-GALATI, STEPHEN A. *Ottoman Imperialism and German Protestantism 1521–1555*. Harvard Historical Monographs XLIII. Cambridge, Mass. 1959. The effects of the Turkish threat lucidly described.
GREEN, VIVIAN H. H. *Luther and the Reformation*. London 1964. Reliable, and with useful helps.
— *Renaissance and Reformation: a survey of European History between 1450 and 1660*. London 1952.
GRIMM, HAROLD J. *The Reformation Era 1550–1650*. New York 1954. 2nd edn 1965. Extremely useful general survey.

HARBISON, E. HARRIS. *The Age of Reformation*. Ithaca, New York 1955 and reprintings. Brief and general.

HASSINGER, ERICH. *Das Werden des neuzeitlichen Europas, 1300–1600*. Braunschweig 1959.

HERMELINCK, HEINRICH. *Reformation und Gegenreformation*. Tübingen 1931.

HILLERBRAND, HANS J. *Landgrave Philipp of Hesse 1504–1567: Religion and Politics in the Reformation*. Foundation for Reformation Research: Reformation Essays and Studies 1. St Louis 1967. Summarises much of the earlier literature.

HOLBORN, HAJO. *A History of Modern Germany: the Reformation*. New York 1959, London 1965. Masterful; the Reformation from the national standpoint.

HOLL, KARL. *The Cultural Significance of the Reformation*. Trans. KARL and BARBARA HERTZ and JOHN H. LICHTBAU from *Gesammelte Aufsätze zur Kirchengeschichte*. Vol. I. Luther (Tübingen 1948). New York 1959. A justly famous interpretative essay on the cultural effects of the Reformation.

HUIZINGA, JOHAN. *The Waning of the Middle Ages*. 1st edn London 1924. Harmondsworth 1955. A brilliantly readable account of the spirit of the pre-Reformation period.

JEDIN, HUBERT and DOLAN, JOHN, eds. *Handbook of Church History*. Vol. 4. Ed. ERWIN ISERLOH, JOSEF GLAZIK, and HUBERT JEDIN. Trans. from *Handbuch der Kirchengeschichte*. Vol. IV (Freiburg 1967). New York 1969. The best modern Catholic scholarship; excellent bibliographies.

JEDIN, HUBERT. *A History of the Council of Trent*. Vol. 1. Trans. ERNEST GRAF, O.S.B., from *Geschichte des Konzils von Trient*. Vol. I (Freiburg 1949). Edinburgh 1957. The definitive account of the conciliar situation in the late fifteenth and early sixteenth centuries.

JCACHIMSEN, PAUL. Die *Reformation als Epoche der deutschen Geschichte*. Berlin 1951. A separate edition of his brilliant essay in *Neue Propyläen Weltgeschichte* (1940).

LINDSAY, THOMAS M. *A History of the Reformation*. Vol. I. *In Germany*. Vol. II. *In Lands beyond Germany*. 2nd edn Edinburgh 1907, often reprinted. Old and dry, but still profitable.

LORTZ, JOSEPH. *The Reformation in Germany*. Trans. RONALD WALLS from *Die Reformation in Deutschland* (3rd edn Freiburg 1949). 2 vols. London 1968. A classic of modern Catholic scholarship; first-rate.

PAUCK, WILHELM. *The Heritage of the Reformation*. Revised edn Glencoe 1961; Oxford 1968. A scholarly interpretation of the effects of Luther's Reformation.

PLUMMER, ALFRED. *The Continental Reformation*. London 1912. Old-fashioned and rather sketchy.

RANKE, LEOPOLD VON. *History of the Reformation in Germany*. Trans. SARAH AUSTIN from Vols. I–III of *Deutsche Geschichte im Zeitalter der Reformation* (5 vols. Berlin 1839–47). 3 vols. London 1845–47. A master work of the father of modern historiography.

H

RITTER, GERHARD. *Die Neugestaltung Europas im 16. Jahrhundert*. Berlin 1950. A separate edition of his excellent contribution to *Propyläen Weltgeschichte*. Vol. V, for which see earlier in this section.

SKALWEIT, STEPHAN. *Reich und Reformation*. Berlin 1967. A thorough modern treatment of the political aspects of the Reformation; excellent bibliography.

SMITH, PRESERVED. *The Age of the Reformation*. New York 1920. Suggestive and readable, though dated; strong on social and economic aspects.

WEBER, MAX. *The Protestant Ethic and the Spirit of Capitalism*. Trans. TALCOTT PARSONS from *Gesammelte Aufsätze zur Religionssoziologie* (1920). London 1930. This important but suspect thesis contains a notable chapter on Luther's view of 'calling'.

WILLIAMS, GEORGE H. *The Radical Reformation*. Philadelphia 1962. The best modern treatment of the left-wing Reformers; full of detail.

LUTHER HISTORIOGRAPHY

BORNKAMM, HEINRICH. *Luther im Spiegel der deutschen Geistesgeschichte*. Heidelberg 1955.

CARLSON, EDGAR M. *The Reinterpretation of Luther*. Philadelphia 1948. A review of Scandinavian Luther research.

HERTE, ADOLF. *Das katholische Luther-Bild im Banne der Lutherkommentare des Cochläus*. 3 vols. Münster 1943. The baneful influence of Cochlaeus's polemic on later Catholic accounts of Luther.

INTERNATIONAL CONGRESS ON LUTHER RESEARCH. 1st., Aarhus, Denmark, 1956: *Lutherforschung Heute*. Ed. VILMOS VAJTA. Berlin 1958. 2nd., Münster, Germany, 1960: *Luther and Melanchthon*. Ed. VILMOS VAJTA. Philadelphia and Göttingen 1961. 3rd., Järvenpää, Finland, 1966: *The Church, Mysticism, Sanctification and the Natural in Luther's Thought*. Ed. IVAR ASHEIM. Philadelphia and Göttingen 1967. Reports of the best current work in progress.

STEPHAN, HORST. *Luther in den Wandlungen seiner Kirche*. 2nd edn Berlin 1951. The Lutherans' Luther.

WOLFF, OTTO. *Die Haupttypen der neueren Lutherdeutung*. Stuttgart 1938. The modern reworking of Luther's image.

ZEEDEN, ERNST W. *The Legacy of Luther: Martin Luther and the Reformation in the estimation of the German Lutherans from Luther's death to the beginning of the age of Goethe*. Trans. RUTH M. BETHELL from *Martin Luther und die Reformation im Urteil des deutschen Luthertums*. Bd. I. *Darstellung* (Freiburg 1950). London 1954. An excellent account of Luther's fate in German intellectual history.

BIOGRAPHIES OF LUTHER

Books

ATKINSON, JAMES. *Martin Luther and the Birth of Protestantism*. Harmondsworth 1968. A readable but partisan account, weighted to the early years.

BAINTON, ROLAND H. *Here I Stand: a Life of Martin Luther*. Nashville 1950. Deft and anecdotal, the most delightful English biography; weighted to the early years.

BOHMER, HEINRICH. *Martin Luther: Road to Reformation*. Trans. JOHN W. DOBERSTEIN and THEODORE G. TAPPERT from *Der junge Luther* (Gotha 1925). Philadelphia 1946. Excellent narrative of Luther's formative years.

DENIFLE, HEINRICH. *Luther und Luthertum in der ersten Entwicklung*. Mainz 1906. Virulent anti-Lutheran polemic, but brilliant and informative for all its outmoded bias.

ERIKSON, ERIK H. *Young Man Luther: a Study in Psychoanalysis and History*. London 1959. Brilliant, ground-breaking, and unconvincing because factually inadequate.

FEBVRE, LUCIEN. *Martin Luther*. Trans. ROBERTS TAPLEY from *Un Destin: Martin Luther* (Paris 1927). New York 1928. A fetching, intuitive portrait.

FIFE, ROBERT H. *The Revolt of Martin Luther*. New York 1957. Fine, well-documented biography of Luther to 1521.

GRISAR, HARTMANN. *Luther*. Trans. E. M. LAMOND, ed. LUIGI CAPPADELTA from the 1st German edn (3 vols. Freiburg 1911–12). 6 vols. London 1913–17. A Catholic historian's learned but extremely negative critique of Luther.

— *Martin Luther: his Life and Work*. Trans. FRANK J. EBBLE, ed. ARTHUR PREUSS from the 2nd German edn. London 1930, often reprinted. A distillate of the above.

HOLL, KARL. *Gesammelte Aufsätze zur Kirchengeschichte*. Vol. I: *Luther*. 7th edn. Tübingen 1948. Collected papers of the doyen of twentieth-century Luther scholars.

ISERLOH, ERWIN. *Luthers Thesenanschlag, Tatsache oder Legende?* Wiesbaden 1962. Calls in question whether Luther really nailed his Theses to the church door.

— *The Theses were not posted*. Trans. from *Luther zwischen Reform und Reformation* (Münster 1966). Boston 1968. A fuller presentation of the case, and an examination of Luther's theology in transition.

KOOIMAN, WILLEM JAN. *By Faith alone*. London 1954. A readable, popular, short biography.

KOSTLIN, JULIUS. *Life of Luther*. Trans. from the 1st German edn (1881). 1st edn London 1883, 2nd edn 1895, reprinted 1898. One of the most balanced biographies of Luther ever written. The 5th German edn, ed. G. KAWERAU (2 vols. [1902–]1903), is even better.

LAU, FRANZ. *Luther*. Trans. ROBERT H. FISCHER from the German edn (Berlin 1959). Philadelphia 1963. Brief but full of insight.

MACKINNON, JAMES. *Luther and the Reformation*. 4 vols. London 1925–30. Substantial and informative.

MCGIFFERT, A. C. *Martin Luther: the Man and his Work*. New York 1911. Liberal Protestant popular biography; now somewhat dated.

Martin Luther Lectures. I: *Luther Today*. II. *More About Luther*. III:

The Mature Luther. IV: *Luther and Culture.* V: *Luther in the Twentieth Century.* Decorah 1957–61. Lectures of variable quality, but note those by Rupp, Prenter, and Brunner.

RITTER, GERHARD. *Martin Luther: his Life and Work.* Trans. JOHN RICHES from *Luther, Gestalt und Tat* (Munich 1949). London and New York 1963. An authoritative summary.

RUPP, E. GORDON. *Luther's Progress to the Diet of Worms.* London 1951. The best account of Luther's break from Rome.

SCHEEL, OTTO. *Martin Luther. Vom Katholizismus zur Reformation.* 2 vols. Tübingen 1917. A meticulously detailed, if reverential, account of Luther's early development.

SCHWIEBERT, ERNEST G. *Luther and his Times: the Reformation from a new Perspective.* St Louis 1950. For sheer volume of contextual information, the most valuable biography in English.

SIMON, EDITH. *Luther alive: Martin Luther and the making of the Reformation.* New York 1968. Novelistic, derivative, and not well balanced.

SMITH, PRESERVED. *The Life and Letters of Martin Luther.* Boston and New York 1911. A liberal Protestant classic; quotes Luther's correspondence copiously.

THIEL, RUDOLF. *Luther.* Trans. G. K. WIENKE from the 2nd German edn (2 vols. Berlin 1952). Philadelphia 1955. Colourful, panoramic, sensitive portrait constantly reflecting Luther's own words.

TODD, JOHN M. *Martin Luther.* London 1964. A highly favourable Catholic account, somewhat derivative.

VOLZ, HANS. *Martin Luthers Thesenanschlag und dessen Vorgeschichte.* Weimar 1959. A monograph on the preparation and dissemination of the 95 Theses.

Articles

ALAND, KURT. 'Luthers Thesenanschlag, Tatsache oder Legende?' *Deutsches Pfarrerblatt*, 62 (1962), pp. 241 ff. A sceptical response to Iserloh's hypothesis that the 95 Theses were not nailed up.

BAINTON, ROLAND H. 'Road to Reformation'. *CH*, 16 (1947), pp. 167 ff.
— 'Luther's Struggle for Faith'. *CH*, 17 (1948), pp. 193 ff.

HOLL, KARL. 'Martin Luther on Luther'. Trans. H. C. ERIK MITELFORT from 'Luthers Urteile über sich selbst' (1903), *Gesammelte Aufsätze zur Kirchengeschichte.* Vol. I: *Luther* (7th edn Tübingen 1948), pp. 381 ff. in *Interpreters of Luther*, ed. JAROSLAV J. PELIKAN (Philadelphia 1968), pp. 9 ff. The outstanding essay on Luther's personality; essential reading.

STAUFFER, RICHARD. 'L'Affichage des 95 Thèses. Réalité ou Légende?' *SHPF*, 113 (1967), pp. 332 ff. A review of the controversy.

LUTHER AND HIS CONTEMPORARIES

Books

BAINTON, ROLAND H. *Erasmus of Christendom.* New York 1969. An extremely sympathetic and readable life.

— *Women of the Reformation*. New York forthcoming. Admirable narratives of the sometimes decisive distaff influence.

BOISSET, JEAN. *Erasme et Luther*. Paris 1962.

GRITSCH, ERIC W. *Reformer without a Church: the Life and Thought of Thomas Muentzer 1488(?)–1525*. Philadelphia 1967. Sympathetic study of the radical leader.

HINRICHS, CARL. *Luther und Müntzer; ihre Auseinandersetzung über Obrigkeit und Widerstandsrecht*. Berlin 1952.

HOLBORN, HAJO. *Ulrich von Hutten and the German Reformation*. Trans. ROLAND H. BAINTON from the German edn (1929). New Haven and London 1937. The standard modern study.

KÖHLER, WALTHER. *Zwingli und Luther: Ihr Streit über das Abendmahl nach seinen politischen und religiosen Beziehungen*. Vol. I. Leipzig 1924. Vol. II. Gütersloh 1953. Monumental account of the first sacramental controversy in minute detail.

MANSCHRECK, CLYDE. *Melanchthon, the quiet Reformer*. New York 1958. Readable but not profound.

MURRAY, ROBERT H. *Erasmus and Luther: their Attitude to Toleration*. London 1920.

OYER, JOHN S. *Lutheran Reformers against the Anabapists: Luther, Melanchthon and Menius and the Anabaptists of Central Germany*. The Hague 1964. Especially good on Rinck.

Reformers in Profile. Ed. BRIAN GERRISH. Philadelphia 1967. Portraits of the leading figures of the Reformation movement.

RUPP, E. GORDON. *Patterns of Reformation*. London 1969. Deft, excellent essays on the reforming styles of Oecolampadius, Carlstadt, and Müntzer.

STUPPERICH, ROBERT. *Melanchthon*. Trans. ROBERT H. FISCHER from the German edn (Berlin 1960). Philadelphia 1965. A popular account from the leading authority on Melanchthon.

TILLMANS, WALTER C. *The World and Men around Luther*. Minneapolis 1959. Sketchy biographical notes about Luther's associates.

Articles

GRIMM, HAROLD J. 'The Relations of Luther and Melanchthon with the Townsmen'. *Luther and Melanchthon*. Ed. VILMOS VAJTA (Philadelphia and Göttingen 1961) pp. 32 ff. Valuable on some social features of Luther's approach.

PAUCK, WILHELM. 'Luther and Melanchthon'. *Luther and Melanchthon*. Ed. VILMOS VAJTA (Philadelphia and Göttingen 1961) pp. 13 ff. Illuminating and entertaining.

LUTHER'S THOUGHT

Books

Accents in Luther's Theology. Ed. HEINO O. KADAI. St Louis 1967. A collection of uneven essays; note contributions by Sasse and Pelikan.

ALTHAUS, PAUL. *The Theology of Martin Luther*. Trans. ROBERT C. SCHULTZ from *Die Theologie Martin Luthers* (2nd edn Gütersloh 1962). Philadelphia 1966. Detailed, substantial, and often profound.

AULÉN, GUSTAV. *Christus Victor: an historical Study of the three main Types of the Idea of the Atonement*. Trans. A. GABRIEL HERBERT from the Swedish (1930). London 1931 and reprintings. Proposes that Luther's view of the atonement is the 'classic' victory view; provocative and only half right.

BIZER, ERNST. *Fides ex auditu: eine Untersuchung über die Entdeckung der Gerechtigkeit Gottes durch Martin Luther*. 3rd enlarged edn Neukirchen 1966. The most cogent argument in favour of a late date for Luther's discovery of justification; highly controversial since its first publication in 1958.

BLUHM, HEINZ. *Martin Luther, creative Translator*. St Louis 1965. Based on extensive philological scrutiny.

BORNKAMM, HEINRICH. *Luther and the Old Testament*. Trans. ERIC W. and RUTH C. GRITSCH from *Luther und das Alte Testament* (Tübingen 1948). Philadelphia 1969. An outstanding work on Luther's exegesis.

— *Luther's World of Thought*. Trans. MARTIN H. BERTRAM from *Luthers geistige Welt* (Gütersloh 1947). St Louis 1958. Interesting interpretative background.

BRUCE, G. M. *Luther as an Educator*. Minneapolis 1928.

CRANZ, F. EDWARD. *An Essay on the Development of Luther's Thought on Justice, Law, and Society*. Harvard Theological Studies, XIX. Cambridge, Mass. 1959. Valuable and original study of the development of Luther's outlook.

EBELING, GERHARD. *Evangelische Evangelienauslegung*. 2nd edn Darmstadt 1962. Masterful pioneering investigation of Luther's early exegesis.

— *Luther: an Introduction to his Thought*. Trans. R. A. WILSON from *Luther: Einführung in sein Denken* (Tübingen 1964). Philadelphia 1970. A brilliant introduction, somewhat weighted by the author's own theology.

ELERT, WERNER. *The Structure of Lutheranism*. Trans. WALTER A. HANSEN from *Morphologie des Luthertums* (Munich 1931). St Louis 1962. A detailed, scholarly treatment of the development of Luther's theology into Lutheran dogma.

FORELL, GEORGE W. *Faith active in Love*. New York 1954. A good account of Luther's ethics.

GERRISH, BRIAN. *Grace and Reason*. Oxford 1962. An excellent study of the relation of faith to reason in Luther's Galatians.

HÄGGLUND, BENGT. *Theologie und Philosophie bei Luther und in der occamistischen Tradition*. Lund 1955.

HARNACK, THEODOSIUS. *Luthers Theologie, mit besonderer Beziehung auf seine Versöhnungs- und Erlösungslehre*. 2 vols. New edn Munich 1927. The classic nineteenth-century study.

HEADLEY, JOHN M. *Luther's View of Church History*. Yale Publications in

Religion 6. New Haven and London 1963. Good, competent monograph on a neglected topic.

KOOIMAN, WILLEM JAN. *Luther and the Bible*. Philadelphia 1961. A superficial but readable introduction.

KÖSTLIN, JULIUS. *The Theology of Luther in its historical Development and inner Harmony*. Trans. CHARLES E. HAY from the 2nd German edn. 2 vols. Philadelphia 1897. Very good, despite its age.

LOEWENICH, WALTHER VON. *Luthers Theologia Crucis*. 4th edn Munich 1964. An important monograph on Luther's developing spirituality, first published in 1929.

LOHSE, BERNHARD. *Ratio und Fides. eine Untersuchung über die Ratio in der Theologie Luthers*. Göttingen 1958. Scholarly, impressive.

MCDONOUGH, THOMAS. *The Law and the Gospel in Luther*. London 1963. A Catholic theologian sets Luther's early theology against the background of nominalist teaching.

MCSORLEY, HARRY J. *Luther: Right or Wrong?* New York and Minneapolis 1969. Extremely detailed scholastic analysis of the Erasmus–Luther debate by a Catholic scholar sympathetic to Luther.

OZMENT, STEVEN E. *Homo Spiritualis: a comparative Study of the Anthropology of Johannnes Tauler, Jean Gerson, and Martin Luther (1509–16) in the Context of their Theological Thought*. Leiden 1969. Highly technical comparison of the young Luther with his theological predecessors.

PELIKAN, JAROSLAV JAN. *Luther the Expositor*. Companion volume to *Luther's Works* (American Edition). St Louis 1959. Essays on Luther's style of interpretation, with a case study of the words of institution.

— *Obedient Rebels*. New York and London 1964. The balance of continuity and dissent in Luther's struggle with Rome.

— *Spirit versus Structure: Luther and the Institutions of the Church*. New York 1968. Valuable chapters on Luther's efforts to replace rejected church structures by evangelical means.

PFÜRTNER, STEPHEN. *Luther and Aquinas: a Conversation*. Trans. EDWARD QUINN from *Luther und Thomas im Gesprach* (Heidelberg 1961). London 1964. A learned contribution to ecumenical theology.

PINOMAA, LENNART. *Faith Victorious: an Introduction to Luther's Theology*. Trans. WALTER J. KUKKONEN from the Finnish. Philadelphia 1963. An attractive introduction to Luther's doctrine and to Luther research.

PRENTER, REGIN. *Spiritus Creator*. Trans. JOHN M. JENSEN from the 2nd Danish edn (Copenhagen 1946). Philadelphia 1953. The major work on Luther's doctrine of the Spirit.

PREUS, JAMES S. *From Shadow to Promise: Old Testament Interpretation from Augustine to the young Luther*. Cambridge, Mass. 1969. A specialised monograph on interpretative theory in the Middle Ages and Luther's first lectures.

REU, M. *Luther's German Bible*. Columbus, Ohio 1934. Appendix contains selections from Luther's early lectures.

RUPP, E. GORDON. *The Righteousness of God: Luther Studies.* London 1953. Excellent on Luther's theological development.

SAARNIVAARA, UURAS. *Luther Discovers the Gospel.* St Louis 1951. A somewhat simplistic but fervent doctrinal case for a late date of the 'tower experience' of justification.

SASSE, HERMANN. *This is my Body: Luther's Contention for the Real Presence in the Sacrament of the Altar.* Minneapolis 1959. Combines a good account of the sacramental dispute, an apologetic for Luther's view, and a valuable reconstruction of the Marburg Colloquy debate.

SCHWARTZ, WERNER. *Principles and Problems of Biblical Translation.* Cambridge 1955. Good chapters on the hermeneutics of Valla, Erasmus and Luther.

SEEBERG, ERICH. *Luthers Theologie.* Vol. I. *Die Gottesanschaung bei Luther.* Göttingen 1929. Vol. II. *Christus Wirklichkeit und Urbild.* Stuttgart 1937. One of the major products of German Luther research.

— *Luthers Theologie in ihren Grundzügen.* Stuttgart 1950. A condensation of the foregoing work.

SIGGINS, IAN D. KINGSTON. *Martin Luther's Doctrine of Christ.* Yale Publications in Religion 14. New Haven and London 1970. A comprehensive study of Luther's central theme, and an introduction to his style.

SIIRALA, AARNE. *Divine Humanness.* Trans. T. A. KANTONEN from *Jumalallinen inhimillisyys* (Helsinki 1968). Philadelphia 1970. The central chapter of this theological work is a sophisticated reinterpretation of the Erasmus–Luther debate.

VAJTA, VILMOS. *Luther on Worship.* Philadelphia 1958. A theological rather than liturgical approach.

VOGELSANG, ERICH. *Die Anfänge von Luthers Christologie.* Berlin 1933. An essential work in the modern study of Luther's development.

WATSON, PHILIP S. *Let God be God! an Interpretation of the Theology of Luther.* London 1947, reprinted London 1958. The most comprehensive introduction to Luther's theology in English.

WICKS, JARED. *Man yearning for Grace: Luther's early Spiritual Teaching.* Washington and Cleveland 1968. A Jesuit theologian's sensitive study of Luther's early theology, finding a peak of excellence just before the indulgence controversy.

WINGREN, GUSTAF. *The Christian's Calling: Luther on Vocation.* Trans. CARL C. RASMUSSEN from *Luthers lära om kallelsen* (Lund 1942) Edinburgh 1958. A first-rate study of a theme with both doctrinal and ethical implications.

Articles

BAINTON, ROLAND H. 'The Development and Consistency of Luther's Attitude to Religious Liberty'. *HTR,* 22 (1929), pp. 107 ff.

— 'Luther and the Via Media at the Marburg Colloquy'. *LQ,* 1 (1949), pp. 394 ff.

BLUHM, HEINZ S. 'Luther's View of Man in his first published Work'. *HTR*, 41 (1948), pp. 103 ff.

BORNKAMM, HEINRICH. 'Faith and Reason in the Thought of Erasmus and Luther'. In *Religion and Culture: Essays in Honour of Paul Tillich*, ed. WALTER LEIBRECHT (London 1958, New York 1959), pp. 133 ff.

— 'Zur Frage der Iustitia Dei beim jungen Luther'. *ARG*, 52 (1961), pp. 16 ff. and 53 (1962), pp. 1 ff. A rebuttal of Bizer's *Fides ex auditu*.

CLEBSCH, WILLIAM A. 'Luther's Conception of God'. *ATR*, 37 (1955), pp. 25 ff.

FORELL, GEORGE W. 'Luther and the War against the Turks'. *CH*, 14 (1945), pp. 256 ff.

GARRISON, A. E. 'Luther and the Doctrine of the Holy Spirit'. *LQ*, 11 (1959), pp. 135 ff.

GRIMM, HAROLD J. 'Luther's Conception of Territorial and National Loyalty'. *CH*, 17 (1948), pp. 79 ff.

HÄGGLUND, BENGT. 'Was Luther a Nominalist?' *CTM*, 28 (1957), pp. 441 ff.

MCNEILL, J. T. 'Natural Law in the Thought of Luther'. *CH*, 10 (1941), pp. 211 ff.

RUPP, E. GORDON. Review: 'Ernst Bizer: *Fides ex auditu*'. *ZKG*, 71 (1960), pp. 351 ff.

SIIRALA, AARNE. 'Luther and the Jews'. *LW*, 11 (1964), pp. 337 ff.

VIGNAUX, PAUL. 'Sur Luther et Occam'. *FS*, 32 (1950), pp. 21 ff.

INDEX

Compiled by Ilse Shaw